Tuna
the Wonder Dog

Raymond A. Guadagni

Ideas into Books® WESTVIEW
Kingston Springs, Tennessee

Ideas into Books®
W E S T V I E W
P.O. Box 605
Kingston Springs, TN 37082
www.publishedbywestview.com

ISBN 978-1-62880-148-4

First edition, May 2018

Mr. Bojangles quotation on page 328 is used by permission of:

Mr. Bojangles
Words and Music by Jerry Jeff Walker
Copyright © 1968 Mijac Music and Cotillion Music, Inc.
Copyright Renewed
All Rights on behalf of Mijac Music Administered by Sony/ATV Music Publishing LLC, 424 Church Street, Suite 1200, Nashville, TN 37219
All Rights on behalf of Cotillion Music, Inc. Administered by Warner-Tamerlane Publishing Corp.
International Copyright Secured All Rights Reserved
Reprinted by Permission of Hal Leonard LLC

MR. BOJANGLES
Words and Music by JERRY JEFF WALKER
© 1968 (Renewed) COTILLION MUSIC, INC. and MIJAC MUSIC
All Rights Reserved
Used by Permission of Alfred Publishing, LLC

Printed in the United States of America on acid free paper

Acknowledgments

I have received valuable help from several people and would like to thank here those who generously gave me their time and suggestions or who supplied me with photographs or other material.

First and foremost, I want to thank my wife, Ann. She has helped, fully supported, and worked on this endeavor in every imaginable way. She is clearly the rock of our family but still graciously gave of her time because she knew it was important to me. This book could not have been written without her.

I also want to thank Randy Snowden who is a dear friend, member of our writer's club and one of the most intelligent and talented people I know. He was generous with his time, kindness, and brilliant suggestions.

My thanks to Mary Butler, a dear friend, who though a busy person as the Chief Probation Officer of Napa County and interim chief of Health and Human Services, made the time to review and make suggestions in the writing of this book. Many of her suggestions were quite helpful and implemented.

To my friends, Pat and Denise Riddle, my thanks for supplying some of the pictures used in the book.

To Val Flax, the widow of my law partner, Joe Flax, and a friend of mine before Tuna was born, I thank her for going to her garage and locating among many boxes entitled ""mementos" the original telegram sent to Charles Finley when we made an ill-fated attempt to purchase the Oakland Athletics.

To all of you, thank you, thank you, and thank you.

CHAPTER ONE

Only the Lonely

"M om, why is that lady sitting alone? Is she okay?"
"Oh, Raymond, don't worry. I'm sure she isn't lonely. She might be waiting for a friend to arrive. Or maybe her husband is out of town and she's just grabbing a bite to eat," Mom reassured me.

From childhood, I worried about people who were alone. I wouldn't call it people-watching, at least not the way I define it. People-watching is seeing how people act, dress, and behave, akin to bird watching. For me, however, I watched people who were by themselves, and wondered if they were lonely. It was the aspect of solitude and loneliness that caught my attention, and my curiosity was limited to that question. So, I did not watch every person I saw who was alone. It was the combination of the surrounding circumstances and the contextual situation that captured my mind and launched me into a state of doubt mingled with curiosity. I do not know why I had this sensitivity to people who were alone, but I noticed them everywhere – in a movie theater or restaurant, standing on a corner, or sitting on a park bench. It distressed me they might be feeling lonely.

Mom tried to assuage my concerns. She would answer all of my inquiries, assuring me there were many reasonable possibilities to explain why a person was alone and yet not lonely at all. Poor Mom had to repeat these reassurances so often she developed a litany of answers from my prior interrogation sessions concerning solitude

1

and sadness, as if somehow, they would always apply, regardless of the person's circumstances. It became almost ritualistic. I kept asking the same questions to hear these same answers, even though I knew what she was going to say. I knew all of her responses by heart but hearing them from my mom somehow validated them. It was only then I could believe the particular person in question wasn't lonely or sad after all.

As I reflect back on my early years, I realize the reason I was sensitive to lonely people was because I was lonely myself. And it is now clear to me that my loneliness was rooted in my family life.

I'll start with my dad. I called my father "Big Al," not because he was tall but because he was very stocky. He was short in stature, standing only 5 feet 6 inches tall. However, he was strong as a bull and weighed around 210 pounds. He had a broad Italian face with curly black hair, olive complexion, and a rugged, lined face that made him look older than his years. His disposition was overbearing, self-centered, and loud-mouthed. He had a very scary Italian Mafioso look. He was like a cross between an Italian and a pit bull. There was never any doubt when Big Al had walked into a room, with his domineering personality and physical looks.

He always bragged about himself, which I later realized was his unconscious way of compensating for low self-esteem. He was a damaged person with little or no insight. He didn't know how to be a good dad. He never offered praise to his children, believing that praise would make them weak.

Throughout my childhood, my dad constantly undermined my self-confidence. I never felt I could do anything right. Even when doing a chore as menial as washing and drying dishes for my mom, my dad would come along and tell me to do them again because I didn't get them clean enough. He did it so often that I switched and started drying dishes, gladly letting my brother wash. I figured, how could anyone mess up drying the dishes so long as they weren't wet, right? Wrong. My dad inspected a completely dry spoon and declared I wasn't drying correctly. I was leaving water spots on the silverware. I didn't even know what he was talking about. At first, I asked clarifying questions, but these talks with Dad did not go smoothly. In fact, these discussions went as smoothly as Lee Harvey Oswald's prison transfer. Not just clumsy but utter chaos, with hollering and lecturing about how any fool could see the water spots I had left. I should open my eyes and not be so lazy and careless. I quickly gave up on the clarifying questions. Dad's message was loud, clear, and received: I couldn't even dry dishes.

His comments on my hygienic incompetence regarding eating utensils weren't that bad because he was only screaming them in front of my mom, brother, me, and our immediate next-door neighbor, Josephine Pittore, who listened in, whether she wanted to or not, through the open kitchen windows. I now understand why she was always so sweet to me, telling me I could come over to her house to play whenever I wanted.

It was when we were in public that his comments were excruciatingly embarrassing. Like when I would be at bat at a baseball game and he would stand directly behind the backstop (only a few feet from me) and say in his booming voice, "Are you afraid to swing? You're just trying to get a walk, you're not even trying to hit the ball!" I could hear his anger, and I knew other parents and kids could hear it too. I couldn't bear to look at any of my teammates or the other parents, who by now would be sitting quietly in the stands carefully ignoring my father.

Trying to get a walk? You bet I was trying to get a walk! I had the shortest strike zone in the Fly League (Napa's version of the Little League). Getting walks WAS my strength. Now, per Big Al, it was a bad thing. Believe me, I would have rather gotten batting tips from a Ugandan dictator than from my father.

My feelings of loneliness were exacerbated when my parents divorced. I was 13 when Dad left us for another woman. Adding insult to injury, right after this my 17-year-old brother (and only sibling) ran away from home. This left a family consisting of me and my grieving, husbandless mother. She and I continued to live in the family home, which suddenly seemed empty. The very old house had never felt like it belonged to us, and now I knew it never would.

We didn't own the house. We rented. It was an old home in poor shape, with no backyard. I happened to know we rented on a month-to-month basis and could be kicked out on thirty days' notice. It's not that my parents tried to scare me by telling me such things – it was just something I had picked up over the years, listening to my parents' not-so-quiet discussions about money and what was at stake if the bills weren't paid.

Mom was wonderful and very loving, but when Dad left she was consumed with despair. She was socially isolated, had no work skills, and no high school diploma. She was completely at the mercy of my father for support, and he was not one you could count on to pay the bills on a timely basis.

In my own selfish way, I felt sorry for myself. I didn't have many belongings. Not many games or toys. Suddenly I didn't have a family except for Mom. I felt alone.

On top of the hopeless financial situation, my dad's paramour started calling Mom on the phone to gloat, telling her she should have kept a closer eye on her husband. Then she would laugh at Mom. Mom didn't intend to tell me about these phone calls, but I got it out of her one evening when I heard her crying in her bedroom after we'd gone to bed. I sat on my mom's bed trying to comfort her until she cried herself to sleep. I was in the eighth grade.

I was deeply upset. The woman who had pulled our family apart was calling my mother to rub it in. It seemed cruel, over-the-top, and unnecessary. I developed intensely angry feelings toward this woman, whom I never met or saw. I spent hours thinking about sneaking around and locating her car and letting the air out of her tires or breaking all the windows. But on reflection it was clear that would not be enough. So, I went to the most powerful person I could think of.

One night, alone in my room, I knelt by my bed (prayers of this magnitude were not to be said IN bed), and I begin to pray. I started by acknowledging that I was aware killing a human being was a mortal sin. But then I began to explore with God whether, under these egregious circumstances, the Almighty might carve out an exception for this woman's cruel and unusual treatment of my mom. I remember telling God, if it is really not permissible to wish anyone dead, then I wouldn't. But if it was okay, then in such event, she was the one I wished to die. I left it to

His best judgment to decide how to proceed. He made no immediate response.

Many, many years later, long after my mom's death, this person was killed in a gruesome car accident wherein her automobile flipped over, throwing her from the vehicle (she was not wearing a seat belt) and landing on top of her, killing her instantly. I strongly doubt there was any cause and effect relationship between the prayers of one lonely thirteen-year-old boy and her death. Much more likely, it was an entirely coincidental correlation between doing bad things, not following the rules, and then getting your just desserts. Perhaps if I once again prayed to God for someone's death, I could be absolutely sure, but I am pleased to report I have never been tempted to do so.

Dad left during the summer after my 8th grade year and was for the most part gone for the next three years – as I'll explain, he returned in the summer before my senior year of high school. That was how long it took for the flame to go out of Dad's relationship with the other woman.

Eighth to twelfth grades are weighty years for a kid and my father's abrupt departure certainly didn't make them easier. During those years I saw him exactly four times, and each is burned into my memory.

My dad left us on a Thursday. He returned on Saturday to pack up his belongings. It was mid-morning, and Mom and I stood at the edge of the dining room as my dad filed back and forth from the bedroom to his Ford Ranchero parked out at the curb, carrying armloads of shirts, canvas work pants, toiletries, and his favorite kitchen utensils. When he was finished, my mother went into the bedroom to see if he had overlooked anything. Returning from his last trip to the car, he was following her into the bedroom when he suddenly turned and looked at me. I was standing across the dining room at the door to the kitchen, quietly crying. Turning away, he said to Mom with a smirk, "You won't get any help from that one. He's just a cry-baby."

That turned out to be an important moment in my life. It was the moment I decided I had to help my mother as much as I could. Her happiness would need to be my priority. I was heading into high school, which is never easy for parents, but my situation was now different. If I ever got into trouble, I was going to make sure my mom never heard about it. I was going to have to grow up faster and protect her. It was that simple.

The second time I encountered my father during his years away was about six months later. It probably wasn't a coincidence that my brother, who had been living with friends across town had decided to move back home, a couple of months after Dad left. One evening, my brother, my mom and I were returning home from a dinner with some neighbors. The landlady had allowed Mom to change the locks after Dad left, so it was a shock when she let us in the house, flipped on the lights and there was Dad, in the living room, sitting in the big chair with his legs crossed and a victorious smile on his face. He was proud that he surprised us.

Unbeknownst to any of us, Josephine Pittore, our sweet neighbor, had witnessed Dad break into our house. Mrs. Pittore knew my parents were separated and knew what was going on between them because of those open kitchen windows. She didn't need to hear it from Mom. When she saw us arrive at home and heard Dad starting in on one of his bullying rants, she called the police. The police arrived, but Dad took over and told them everything was fine. The police never came in the house.

Standing on the front porch, one of the officers asked Mom if she was okay. Looking at the officer over my father's shoulder, she said yes.

I was upset with her for not telling the police to kick him out. I was upset with myself because I was silent.

When the police left, Dad made it clear that Mom couldn't keep him away if he wanted to be there.

"I pay the bills, so this house is mine. Changing the locks ain't gonna keep me away." He carried on in this vein for another five or ten minutes. Then, casting a malevolent eye over the three of us, he picked up his jacket and left, slamming the front door behind him.

Mom was upset and depressed. I was angry.

Another year elapsed before I saw my father the third time. Mom had arranged for me to visit Dad at his wrecking yard.

"Raymond, you don't have to love your father. You don't even have to like him. But a young man needs to, at least, know his dad."

I did not want to go. Being around him was rarely pleasant. But Mom insisted, so I went.

When I got to the wrecking yard, Dad met us in the front. Mom asked him how long the visit would take, and where and when she should pick me up. He said, "Pick him up in an hour in front of the wrecking yard."

The moment Mom left, Dad started talking about himself and what he had been doing in the year since I had last seen him. It seemed to me Dad had not changed. He was still self-involved and self-centered. He didn't ask me what grade I was in or if I was going to play baseball this summer. He never asked me anything, but when there was a break in his monologue, I told him anyway. I said I had just been elected student body president of Silverado

Junior High School. He responded that he already knew because it had been in the paper.

Without taking a breath, he asked his first question: Was I going to play football in my junior year at Napa High? I told him I was not.

"Why not, are you chicken?"

"No, I played for two years at Silverado Junior High and practiced every day. I only got in four plays in the entire two years. In two of those plays, I made the tackle on the ball carrier. But four plays in two years weren't worth all the time I had put in."

"So, you're a quitter. That's the difference between you and me. I was never a quitter in my life."

My final encounter with my father occurred after the flame went out on Dad's relationship with his girlfriend. It was about seven in the morning on a Saturday when he barged into my room where I was still fast asleep in bed.

He shook me awake. "I'm moving back in."

I was groggy, but managed to say, "Does Mom know this?"

He said he was working on getting her to agree. Personally, I didn't want Mom to take him back. I did not trust him, and I did not like him.

Later I learned that Dad had started calling Mom and was on his best behavior, cajoling and pleading to let him move back in with the family. Mom was resistant for quite some time, because she knew what kind of man he was. But more than anything else she was a forgiving person who longed to have her family together again. Dad kept promising he had changed and things would be different. After months of pleading (and some bullying), Mom decided to give it another chance – on one condition. She had to own the house we would all live in.

My mother's lifelong dream had been to own a home. For her entire life, from childhood to this moment, she had lived in rentals, with all of the uncertainty and inconvenience that go along with not owning your own home. She didn't want to jump back into a marriage she couldn't be certain of and live in a house she could also lose in the blink of an eye.

Of course, Dad agreed to this condition, and for the first time that I could recall, he said he had always known the value in owning your own home. Up to that moment he had frequently argued that renting was better.

"If anything goes wrong with the house, it's the landlord's problem." But in an instant, he did a 180-degree switch, and revised history to say he had always been a believer in owning real estate.

Dad had figured out this would be his ticket home but had one major problem. He had no money. He did not own their home, he did not own the land where the wrecking yard was located, he had no savings, and his checking account was seriously overdrawn most of the time. As the saying goes, he didn't have a pot to piss in.

My father's frequent attempts to reconcile with my mother were now occurring in the summer before my junior year of high school. By that time, I had been working summer jobs for three years and had been able to put some money aside – I thought for college.

But then I realized Mom was about to cave in on her only shot at having her own house. My dad would never be able to do it (and if he had been able to, he would have made himself the sole owner). I couldn't stand it if she gave up.

One Saturday afternoon I found her sitting at the kitchen table. "Mom," I said. "You've done everything for me. You've always had to make the best of impossible circumstances. I've saved enough money from my summer jobs for a down payment. I want you to have it. I want you to have your house."

A long and emotional conversation ensued.

"It's out of the question! I will not accept charity from my son!"

It was almost two weeks later that she came to me and said she would accept my money, but only if she repaid it in monthly installments. It would not be a gift, but a business transaction. I agreed. True to her word, Mom went out and purchased a record book, so she could keep track of her payments. For the rest of her life she did the best she could in making payments.

The $3,000 that my mom "borrowed" allowed her to purchase a three-bedroom, one bath, 900 square foot home in northwest Napa for $16,700.

Despite a profound lack of confidence, I had always been well liked in school. My kindergarten report card said, "Raymond is very popular with his classmates." I didn't know what popular meant, but my mom said it was a good thing. I hated the hollering and arguing around our house, so I went to great lengths to keep the peace with my friends. I figured it was better to make them laugh than have them mad at me. My friends were a much easier audience than my dad. If I messed up around them, I could inject a joke, which let me believe they were laughing with me, not at me. My class clown persona brought me lots of friends, although I sometimes wondered, if they really knew me, would they like me as much?

After grade school, I continued to be popular in junior high and high school. I easily won class offices. I was elected freshman class president, junior class president, and three times, student body president in junior high and high school. I won the senior superlative popularity contest as a senior. The jocks liked me because some of my best friends were jocks and had known me since kindergarten. The guys that took shop class liked me because I was in shop classes with them. The hoods liked me because there was no one better at sucking up. Besides, pounding a little guy would not improve their reputation so they left me alone. Regular guys liked me because that's what I was – I was regular, albeit on the short side of regular.

Girls also liked me. Not the way I wanted them to, but they liked me in their own way. I wanted to be the guy who caught the winning touchdown pass and was carried off the field by my adoring teammates with all the cheerleaders screaming for me. That did not happen. Instead, girls wanted me to be like a brother to them. They wanted me to intercede on their behalf. They wanted me to find out if Johnny liked her or if Tommy had a girlfriend. It was not the role I wanted, but it was the one I got, so I played it to the hilt. I became pretty good at delivering bad news. Stuff like, "Johnny says he really likes you and if he was going to go steady it would be with you, but Johnny wants to play the field and not be tied down."

Embracing this role as intermediary, I decided there was often a classier and kinder way to turn a girl down. It beat what sometimes was the complete truth: "Johnny would rather poke his eyes out than be seen with you."

However, this type of diplomacy had its risks too. When Johnny suddenly started going steady with another girl the very next week, my credibility suffered. This is when I threw Johnny under the bus. "I am so sorry, Darlene. That is what Johnny told me. He is such a jerk. You deserve better than him."

Unfortunately, being like a brother to all the girls is in many ways the death knell for a guy. I was their "friend." It added to my feelings of loneliness. Despite the laughs and popularity, despite all of the class offices and outside trappings that should have made me feel confident, for some reason I always felt I was on the outside looking in.

CHAPTER TWO

Love and Loss

During my junior year in high school, I developed a desire to become a lawyer. I was weary of Dad telling me I was wrong about everything. I knew that even a blind pig finds an acorn now and then. I had to be right about something. If I became a lawyer I would know the law, I would know my rights, and I would know the truth.

When I met with my school counselor to discuss my academic future, I told him I wanted to be a lawyer. He paused and then looked down at my school records in his hand. With a frown, he straightened up, leaned back in his office chair, and, looking over my shoulder at the bare wall behind me, softly said that I should think about a different career. He didn't think I could become a lawyer.

There was a long silence. I began to feel a pit developing in my stomach. He must have looked at my grades and maybe even my I.Q., and knew my choice was not in the cards. I left deflated.

I decided to earn money to at least try to attend college. I spent most of my spare time during junior year playing the accordion for union wages, and working at the Napa Grocery Center, also for union wages, earning as much money as I could.

My mind kept going back to the meeting with the counselor. Maybe it wasn't in my future to be a lawyer. I knew I wasn't the smartest guy around. However, what began as depressed acceptance of my counselor's assessment gradually changed to quiet anger and a rejection of his pronouncement of my abilities. I decided I would go to law school and see for myself if I could make it. I knew I had to first make it to – and through – college. I would do it in baby steps. But I wasn't going to fail without even giving it a try. I didn't want to let any other person make that determination for me.

At the beginning of my senior year, I woke up to the fact that a lot of my friends had done a better job planning and implementing their academic lives. Paul Vallerga had been awarded an athletic scholarship to UCSB. Len Casanega and Dick Abbey were also going to UCSB. Don McConnell and Craig Holliday would be attending San Jose State. Dave Johnson would be enrolling at San Francisco State, Andy Lyerla and Ed Hubbard would enroll at UC Berkeley, and Tom Brown would be attending USF. The rest of us were going to the Napa Junior College, which was located across the lawn from the high school. The Junior College seemed like a step down, especially made for people like me who either didn't have the grades or the money to go away. It felt like I was being left behind as so many of my friends proceeded on with their lives.

One Friday night during a school dance early in my senior year, I noticed a girl I didn't really know well. JoAnn Garcia was one of the cutest and smartest girls in school. I asked her to dance a slow dance with me, and she accepted. I really enjoyed the dance. I asked her to dance again. To my surprise, she accepted. I didn't ask her for any of the fast songs because I was too self-conscious to dance them in public. But we ended up dancing all of the slow songs together. At the end of the evening when the last slow dance ended, I thanked her and started to walk away. She didn't let go of my hand. Transfixed, I stood there holding her hand for what seemed like several minutes. It was long enough for my friends and JoAnn's friends to take notice. Some of them were grinning at us. Finally, stepping into the unknown, I told her I hoped I'd see her on Monday.

I went with my friends to A&W after the dance and we talked about the evening. I remember telling Mike Kerns I hadn't seen the two girls we had taken to the drive-in movies two weeks before. Mike didn't let me get away with that.

He said, "What do you care, Guadagni? You did all right for yourself tonight."

I tried to suppress an ear-to-ear grin. He was right, I didn't care at all about those other girls. I was elated.

The next morning when I woke up, I felt happy. For some reason, I didn't immediately connect my sense of wellbeing to the dance. I just slowly woke up feeling better than I had in a very long time. Mom noticed right away.

"Good morning, Sunshine," she said. "What is it with you this morning? You're cheerful before you've had your breakfast?"

I didn't know what to say, because I still hadn't put it together. But Mom was not the kind of person to let it go when it came to one of her boys.

"Well," she said, "something good must have happened. I don't think I have seen you so chipper in a very long time."

Mom was right. Suddenly, the obvious flooded over me: the reason I was so happy was that JoAnn Garcia had come into my life. But I didn't tell my mom that. I didn't want a cross examination, however well-intended. I just said I'd had a good time at the dance with my friends.

Back in my room after breakfast, I replayed the moment when JoAnn held on to my hand after the last dance ended. I was suddenly swept with a wave of misgivings – was I remembering the moment accurately? Had JoAnn voluntarily clung to my hand, or had I just not let hers go? I was sure there hadn't been a residue of Dixie Peach on my hands that might have glued hers in place. And, I admitted to myself, I didn't have the balls of steel it would have required to make the move. That only left one possibility: yes, she had voluntarily held on.

It was Saturday morning and, for the first time I could remember, I wanted the weekend to be over. After restlessly pacing my room for several minutes, I decided to take a spin in my '55 Chevy, with its brand new sparkling *Crown Sapphire Blue* paint job. I drove to town, parked, and plugged the meter with a dime that allowed me plenty of time to roam about. I walked to Adamo Music Center on Coombs Street, where for a whopping 98 cents I purchased the 45-rpm record of the song that had been my first dance with JoAnn: "So Much In Love" by The Tymes. It had been released by Parkway Records with "Roscoe James McClain" on the B-side. The playing time was only two minutes and 8 seconds, but I spent most of that weekend listening to it.

At last Monday morning arrived. I wasted no time happening to run into JoAnn. It was around 11:00 a.m., on the first floor, near the Indian Head Mascot, right next to the ticket booth where Friday's football tickets were on sale. I planted myself near the auditorium entrance with a direct view of both sides of the hallway, front entrance, and the ticket booth. Before long I saw her walking down the hall with several other girls, approaching the ticket booth. Biting back a rising sense of terror, I took a step forward and asked if she would go with me to the Napa High football game in Santa Rosa on Friday night. For the briefest moment, the world stood still. Her brown eyes

17

glanced at the girls around her. Then she looked back to me.

"Sure…I'd like that."

We bought our tickets. Actually, she tried to pay for hers, but I insisted, and she reluctantly agreed.

I had a date!

The bus ride over and back from Santa Rosa was the real highlight of the game for me. It gave us a chance to begin getting to know each other. It was like a dream. She actually seemed to like me. We were both 16 years old, although she was born the year after me. I learned she was in my grade because she had skipped a year.

We hadn't been on the bus more than a few minutes before I had reached the realization that JoAnn was really, really smart. She talked about her love of reading and before long was running through her favorite authors, some of whom I had never heard of. I barely read anything. Most of my reading involved comic books, Mad Magazine or, if I had an English Literature assignment, Classic Comic Books, which served as a substitute for reading the actual novel. I also had access to my brother's collection of Playboy magazines but that wasn't for the prose. We talked about our classes. Hers were all college prep classes and not the bonehead classes I took. We both were in student government, but she actually cared about working with the student council for the betterment of our school. I was involved in student government but for a completely different reason. It was strictly a popularity contest for me. Elected office gave me the chance to get out of class and hang out with friends preparing for rallies or school activities.

None of this seemed like a problem. A lot of my friends were smart, and we got along well. But most of them had known me since we were little and naturally cut me quite a bit of slack about a lot of things. Among other things I got away with a lot of BS. Early on the bus ride home I learned I would not be able to BS JoAnn.

We were sitting toward the back, it was dark outside, and JoAnn hugged me. I laughed with pleasure and called her the first thing that came into my head: I told her she was "an impetuous little monster." She wasn't offended, but immediately asked me what the word "impetuous" meant. After the briefest hesitation, I told her she should look it up. The truth was, it was a phrase I'd heard Bill Forsythe say to a make-out queen after she had left lipstick all over him. I didn't have a clue what impetuous meant – I prayed I had used it correctly. For a moment, it occurred to me that her intellect and my...more pragmatic approach...might eventually lead to difficulties. But I was so happy to be in her company, I pushed the thought away.

After that football game we started hanging around each other all the time. We couldn't talk on the phone because JoAnn's family didn't have one, so we just got together during school and on the weekends. It wasn't long before we settled into a routine. At school, we would meet for lunch. Then, when afternoon classes began, she would go off to one of her college prep classes and I would depart for auto shop or choir. Fridays were special because we allowed ourselves to purchase food from actual food establishments. We would go to Vern's Foster Freeze for cherry Cokes and then to Bud's Burgers for the wonderful French fries that Bud made from real potatoes drenched in cooking oil.

I was with JoAnn when we learned President Kennedy had been shot. It was Friday, November 23, 1963, and we were at Vern's Foster Freeze for our usual cherry Cokes when three kids in line ahead of us, who had been listening to the radio suddenly cried out, "President Kennedy has been shot!" At the time we didn't know if he had been killed. JoAnn and I were speechless. We prayed he would survive. Deeply upset, we stumbled out of Foster Freeze and began to make our way back to school. But something was different. For all the horror, it was the first time I realized I was sharing my fears and sadness with another person.

JoAnn was five feet three inches tall. She couldn't have weighed more than 100 pounds soaking wet, but her figure was shapely. She wore her shiny, dark brunette hair in the short style of the times. Her lovely complexion was on the light side of olive, and her rich brown eyes radiated kindness and intelligence. More important than her beauty, however, she was very personable and full of energy, with a passion for things important to her. Even though she was scary smart, she was in no way condescending. She continually melted me with her cuteness. After every Friday night football game, she would be hoarse from hollering for our Napa Indians. I loved talking to her the day after a game because her voice was irresistibly raspy.

When she ate popcorn, she would nibble off the brown husk and then any places where the piece of popcorn stuck out, leaving just the little ball in the middle. She would collect those in a dish until it was full of nothing but little puffy balls of corn. Then she would sit back and enjoy the entire bowl. I started doing it too. It wasn't wasted work because the stuff I chewed off initially, I ate as well. That was like the first course. Then the main course was the delicious balls of soft popped corn.

There was a morning at school when I arrived unannounced at her chemistry class to walk her to her next class. She looked so embarrassed. She was wearing a dress with thin vertical stripes of navy blue and white and a shining patent leather black belt that accentuated her tiny waist. She told me that a few minutes earlier she had been standing up at the lab table when she sneezed three times in a row. Her belt popped off in front of everyone. She giggled but was still flushed with embarrassment. She was simply adorable.

It was four months after our first dance, during Christmas break of our senior year, when I told JoAnn I loved her. She responded that she loved me too.

I had never been as happy in my life.

Toward the end of our senior year, some problems began to arise in our relationship. I had started to occasionally catch myself wondering if I was good enough for her. If we were to have a future together, which I wanted more than ever, I knew I would have to be the breadwinner. That was simply the cultural norm. But I was constantly being reminded she was so much more capable. Right now, it was clearly showing itself in academics, but I knew it would be carrying her forward in a successful career, as well.

JoAnn was never one to flaunt her superiority. To the contrary, she tried to talk me out of my growing insecurity. She made excuses for the disparity, like she had so much time to study because she was stuck without a phone in a remote part of the county with no friends nearby. She had nothing to do but study so of course she got good results. I tried to make that rationale work, but the truth was, you could have given me 24/7 to study and I wouldn't have come close to being on a par with her. She took classes like chemistry and trigonometry, and I took classes like drama and metal shop. She got mostly A's. I made a large dagger in metal shop. Her grades in her difficult classes were superior to my grades in my easier subjects.

None of this should have mattered, but it did to me.

My concern continued to grow. I was disconcerted to discover I was developing an anger problem. This surprised me. For years I had been made to feel stupid at home, but now I was feeling that way in my first relationship out in the real world. I couldn't stand it. JoAnn tried and tried, but I couldn't cope with the certainty that I was so inferior to her. I knew she would break up with me sooner or later once she realized the truth about my incompetence in everything. I was not a scholar and I couldn't work with my hands. What was there for her to like? I decided it would be better to break up with her before she saw through me. One day after school, I told her I thought we should stop seeing each other. She told me she didn't want to break up, but I was adamant. We were apart for a few days. But the thing was, I wanted her in my life, so I went back to her and proposed that we try again. She took me back – over and over.

We got through our senior year and started junior college together, but things only grew worse. My confusion, insecurity, anger, and misgivings ruined our relationship. The trust was missing and so was the friendship. I was always upset and unhappy. As a result, so was JoAnn.

As things progressed, I realized JoAnn was gradually withdrawing – and rightly so. It was no fun to be together anymore. I had made us both miserable. Finally, one day she went to a pay phone and called me at my house. She said it was too difficult being together. She gave and gave and gave but could not give anymore. That was it.

Breaking up with JoAnn left me with a desolate sense of emptiness. Falling in love with her had made me happier than I had ever been. But looking back, I realized that from the moment of that first dance, my biggest fear had been losing her. And I made it come true. I had managed to damage, beyond repair, the best thing that ever happened to me.

I was miserable and lonely as I embarked on my second year of college in Napa. My friends did their best to console me, but I was stuck. Everything was the opposite of how it had been. The mornings were gone when I woke up so happy and energized. I woke up every day feeling lousy. The realization kept washing over me that JoAnn was not in my life. I had no reason to be happy or press on with my day. Suddenly the radio in my '55 Chevy only seemed to play songs about loneliness and breakups.

I kept to myself and went right home after my college classes. It wasn't long before I saw JoAnn around campus walking with a big, muscular, handsome football player. These sightings became a frequent reminder that I'd had a real chance with her and I'd blown it. I tried to open up to my friends, but I never told them what an idiot I'd been to her. They didn't seem to care anyway. They knew she was done with me and thought I was just being stupid to still be thinking about her. One friend asked me if I minded if he asked her out. "Go ahead," I said. "We're done." But I felt as though he had gutted me like a fish.

On more than one occasion over the next few months, a friend would notice I wasn't listening to them and would say, "What's wrong, Ray? Are you thinking about JoAnn again?"

I would admit it and they usually responded I was crazy to still be carrying a torch for her. I couldn't help it. I was grieving the breakup and the thing that made it so hard to accept was it had been totally my fault.

I graduated from Napa College in June 1966, without attending the ceremony. This was a far cry from two years earlier when I had celebrated high school graduation with JoAnn and her family and my mom all together and happy.

My feelings of loneliness grew more intense. My friends who were still at the junior college were moving on to four-year institutions. A lot of them were going to Chico State, famous as a party school. Steve Ceriani, Frank Davidson, Fred Teeters, Jerry Davis, and Doug Murray all were transferring there. Others were leaving for other universities or state colleges. I found myself thinking with dread about losing the familiar surroundings of Napa Junior College and the friends I had there. My other friends who had left for college directly after high school were still away. Some were even getting married. They were moving on with their lives. I was going backward. I knew I was never going to meet another girl like JoAnn. My life was over. I was 18.

Toward the end of my second year at the junior college the fog of depression lifted enough for me to figure out that my best chance to be happy was to get out of town.

I managed to pull myself together and submit college applications to Sacramento State College and the University of California at Berkeley. I figured I would get in to Sacramento State College because it had easier entrance requirements. Berkeley was another matter. It was one of the top universities in the world and far more difficult to get into. However, I decided to apply because there was a preference for junior college transfers, and with all the time I had on my hands during my second year at the junior college, I had managed to pull A's in several classes and raise my grades considerably. I even made the Dean's List, which gave me the hope I might be accepted. To my surprise, I was.

That summer I was lucky enough to get a job at the Kaiser Steel Fabrication plant. It was one of Napa's biggest employers. The pay was great, especially if you worked the graveyard shift, which was midnight to 7 a.m. I worked graveyard and made over $7.00 per hour when the minimum wage was $1.25. I earned enough money to pay for a full year's worth of tuition, room, and board. On top of the great pay, many of my friends were working graveyard with me.

I saved every cent, and come September, moved to Oakland with Mike Kerns. I thought this arrangement would be good because I would be with a close and dear friend. However, it didn't work out well. Mike wasn't going to college at that point. He had a job at a bank in Oakland and was training for a boxing career the rest of the time. When he wasn't training, he wanted to party.

I was taking a full academic load. All I did was attend classes, study, attend the Catholic Church in Berkeley (praying that God would send JoAnn back to me), and I started receiving therapy for my newly recognized anger issues. I also enrolled in ROTC so that I could get a deferment to attend law school instead of going off to Viet Nam after graduation. That was a full schedule for me. I once heard Mike tell his mom on the phone that I was no fun because I was always studying. It was true. I had adopted a Spartan life, and when I didn't have my nose in a book I was moping around like Eeyore. Hardly a party animal. After my first year at Cal, Mike said he was not interested in rooming together again, not because he didn't care about me as a good friend, but because we had nothing in common at this time in our lives. I took the end of this arrangement well. It was best for both of us to go our separate ways.

Besides, living in Oakland in an apartment was not an ideal way to assimilate into the campus life of Berkeley. It was almost like being a day student, living away from the city, let alone the University campus. I wanted to be a real college student.

CHAPTER THREE

The Little Ball of Fur

So here I was, in the fall of 1967, a senior business administration major at the University of California at Berkeley, California. From Mike's apartment in Oakland it had taken all of one car trip to move my few belongings into a male-only cooperative on the north side of the campus. At all of the cooperatives, the students worked in exchange for reduced costs for room and board. I drove the lunch truck and worked in the kitchen. I made meatloaf once a week for the hundreds of students who lived in the collective of cooperatives on both sides of campus. The rest of the time I washed dishes or delivered lunch to the other cooperatives.

My cooperative was an old hotel divided into two-bedroom units and three-bedroom suites. I was assigned to a three-bedroom suite. I was also assigned, potluck style, to two roommates. Fortunately, for me, both were nice guys, though they never became close friends. One of my roommates was a freshman. He looked like a surfer with long blond hair and a muscular swimmer's body, and he had a bright personality. His blond girlfriend from high school was also attending Cal, living in a dormitory, but she always seemed to be hanging around our suite. She was quite attractive and effervescent. They were two lovebirds, and very physical with each other even in my presence. My other roommate was a sophomore. He was tall but slightly built, and personable and congenial. He also had a girlfriend who attended San Francisco State

College. I didn't have to see them together, but it was unmistakable when they talked on the phone. They seemed to be in love.

I was aware of the contrast between the love life of my roommates and my lack of a love life. Seeing and living with younger people in love made the job of rebuilding my emotional life more difficult.

There had been plenty of things worrying me while I was growing up in Napa, but I was blessed that not having friends wasn't one of them. Sure, I wished I'd been cooler, maybe taller and more handsome (make that a God-like beauty), but the fact was, from my earliest years, I had enjoyed the companionship of a legion of neighborhood kids and, later, high school classmates.

Berkeley, I quickly discovered, was different. Besides my besotted roommates, I didn't know anyone. And, for whatever reason, I found it difficult to meet people. Every day I moved amongst multitudes of people, walking to their respective classes, many in groups and talking to each other as friends normally do. I didn't know any of them and no one appeared to notice me at all. I was like a plate glass window. Everybody just looked right through me. Being so alone in these throngs of people was not just unpleasant. It exponentially increased my feelings of loneliness.

It didn't help that the late 60's were turbulent times. There was growing distrust of government, and it was evidenced on my campus. There were constant protests by bearded, beaded, and long-haired twenty-somethings passionately yelling about the government taking away our rights. You heard slogans like "shut it down," "protest," "rebel," "don't trust anyone over 30 years old," "don't trust the government." Revolution was in the air – "The people's revolution." I didn't know why everyone was so furious. I didn't even know if these protestors were Berkeley students. I felt isolated. I didn't understand them, I didn't fit in, and I didn't look like them.

The war in Vietnam was raging and was very unpopular – especially, I discovered, in Berkeley, California. Soldiers came home from Vietnam with a Purple Heart but were spit on if they showed their faces in Berkeley.

Martin Luther King, Jr. and Robert Kennedy would soon be assassinated.

Birth control was suddenly widely available, which seemed to be leading to a loosening of sexual standards and frequent mention of "free love." Women's attitudes, in particular, were becoming more liberal compared to the conservative standards in Napa in the late 1950's and early 1960's. As a lonely young adult, I was riveted by the notion that you could meet someone and have sex the same evening. But this was also a new source of anxiety, both on the many evenings I was spending alone and on the occasional nights I managed to get dates with girls I met around the cooperative. As far as I could tell, the love wasn't free.

I spent my first month at the co-op engaged in futile efforts to get some social traction in what felt like a huge, self-obsessed, impersonal university culture with no room for a blue collar Italian kid from the country – and no interest in making any.

I went to some sorority parties based on ads I saw on the co-op bulletin board. The girls were only interested in guys from certain fraternities. I used to attend pledge dinners at fraternities, but that mainly was to get the good food they served. Unfortunately, due to my gluttonous habits, I did it too often at one of the fraternities. As a result, one night a dining room full of guys locked the door and announced, with a heartfelt invitation, that I was fraternity material. They wanted me to be their brother. I didn't know any of them by name, but I guess I was their kind of guy.

Back in my room at the coop later that evening, I reached the conclusion the fraternity/sorority route was just not for me. If they were out, then I needed a different strategy to score free food and try to meet people. Next, I tried the hippies. They were around in the parks and at parties in homes below the campus. At night I would just walk into a house where it looked like a party was going on. This attempt to meet people also failed. The marijuana smoke was pungent, and the sandalwood incense was so strong that it made my tongue swell. The girls I met developed an instant dislike for me. I had no beard, sideburns, or mustache, and the hair on my head was short. Also, some of them smelled because of body odor from lack of bathing and/or not using deodorant. We also spoke different languages. They were laid back and used terms like "far-out" "right-on," or "peace, brother." That is another thing – everyone seemed related because everyone was calling everyone else brother or sister. Things just weren't working out.

One evening I was sitting by myself in my one-third of our co-op suite, pondering my situation, when it occurred to me, maybe I should shift my energies from things I really couldn't control to something I could.

During my early years in Napa, we had had a fox terrier named Trixie. Everybody in the family had loved Trixie in their own way. Even my father, usually after first frightening her, would eventually calm down, pet her, and praise her. Sitting in my room, in the dim light of my desk lamp, it crossed my mind that maybe I should get a dog. A dog of my own. I had figured out I was a small baitfish in the ocean that was UC Berkeley, but if it was the right dog, I thought, he won't care.

It was less than two weeks later when I saw the ad on the cooperative message board advertising free puppies just a few blocks away. I decided to go take a look.

The ad led to a place on the south side of the campus. It was an older wooden shingled two-story house divided into two flats. The lower flat was where the puppies were. As I stood at the front door waiting for someone to answer my knock, spying a large, colorful Native American pot in which a vaguely familiar-looking lacy, brilliant green plant grew, I found myself thinking about what a crazy world we were living in and wondering if I could find a friend who would go through these times with me.

A man answered the door dressed in a brightly colored tie-dyed t-shirt and an old ragged jacket. His pants were baggy cotton trousers and he wore well-worn sandals and beaded jewelry. I had a difficult time telling his age because he had hair everywhere. He had a full beard that was reddish-auburn and a head full of shoulder length black hair. The over-all effect was of a whole lot of hair, to the point I couldn't see enough of him in there to tell how old he was. I told him I thought his beard was a cool looking red.

He must have heard this before because he was ready with a quick response. "Yeah, man, a red beard is a sign of virility, don't you know."

I said, "You learn something every day. Is this the place where the puppies are?"

He confirmed I was at the right place. He invited me in, and I was instantly hit with a waft of scented incense and the distinct smell of patchouli oil, which was used by hippies to cover up the odor of marijuana. A young woman with long sandy brown hair came through a doorway that was adorned with a beaded curtain. She was very attractive and wearing lots of jewelry. Not fancy diamond jewelry, but the kind of stuff little girls seemed to like when they played dress-up. She had jewelry everywhere including anklets and bracelets and necklaces and long dangling earrings. She wore a long, flowing, floor-length dress of bright multi colors. I don't know if they were poor or if they were just embracing the counter culture of the hippie era with its aversion to mainstream, commercial clothing stores. Though their clothes didn't appear to be handmade (other than the tie-dye t-shirt), they did look like they might have come from a flea market or a second-hand store.

I stood in their living room looking at walls adorned with psychedelic rock posters. This is where they spent their Saturday evenings exploring altered states of consciousness? Maybe their Sunday through Friday evenings, too? I clung to studied nonchalance because I was way out of my depth.

When I asked to see the puppies, they led me through the beaded curtain to a large kitchen and dining room. In the furthest corner of the room was a large basket where a dog was lying down. She looked like a sawed-off collie and was introduced as Supercharger. She was the mother of the litter, and as I approached, I saw she was busy nursing six of the cutest little puppies. Half of the litter looked like miniature collies and the other half looked a lot like Labradors.

"They are so cute!" I exclaimed, my nonchalance totally blown.

Sitting at her kitchen table covered by a brightly colored tablecloth, with a vase full of flowers in the center, the woman said, "Right on!"

I asked which ones were available and to my surprise she said they all were. I had the pick of the litter. Gazing into the basket, one in particular drew my attention, and without hesitation I picked up this very special Berkeley-born puppy. I just wanted to squeeze him. That little puppy would have melted anyone's heart.

He was a little black ball of beautiful, fluffy, soft, shiny fur. He was so small, his skin so saggy and loose, he just couldn't fill it up. I sat down on the floor and set the puppy down facing me. When he tried to walk toward me he was uncoordinated and clumsy, but he seemed so lively, wagging his tail a million times a minute even though the tail was just a small stub. When I petted him he instantly started to play, chewing on my index finger with a soft mouth, which could only be described as a restrained bite. I can only speak for myself, but for me, it was love at first sight.

The litter was already old enough, so I was able to bring the puppy home that day. As I walked from the hippies' house back to my co-op, all I focused on was this adorable puppy snuggling in my arms. Already I felt intuitively that this dog would change my life. I introduced him to his new digs at the co-op, where he quickly settled in and our lives together began.

Initially I named the puppy Kingfish. It probably wasn't a great name for a dog, but Kingfish had been my favorite character in the 1950's TV show *Amos and Andy*. Tim Moore, a comedic genius, played the Kingfish, who was the lodge leader of the "Mystic Knights of the Sea." I had been using his catchphrase, "Holy Mackerel!" since the day we got a television. I had affectionately named my mom Sapphire, which was the name of Kingfish's wife. Even my friends called her Sapphire or Saph for short. She carried this name from the early 60's to the day she died.

Kingfish was always trying to lure the amiable but naïve Andy into hilarious get-rich-quick schemes. Most of the episodes involved Andy getting duped initially, only to have Kingfish get his just desserts when the scheme would inevitably backfire on him. Even if the name didn't quite fit the dog, naming him after a comedian did, because it turned out this dog was destined to bring laughter to me, my friends, and my family throughout his life.

Notwithstanding this beginning, eventually Kingfish became known as Tuna. The particular circumstances surrounding his name change, as well as the specific moment in which a renaming was required, will be revealed at the proper time in this book. However, because he lived most of his life under the name of Tuna I am going to call him that from here on.

CHAPTER FOUR

Tuna's Tricks

Tuna's new home was my co-op – as I've explained, it was an old hotel that had been converted to a cooperative housing project for UC Berkeley students. It was located on the north side of the campus and had a sizeable back yard for Tuna to roam. There was also plenty of lawn in the front yard, which was appealing to a young puppy. Tuna lived in our three-bedroom suite with me and my two roommates, neither of whom had dogs, only girlfriends. Tuna quickly became the master of the suite, establishing himself as the dominant dog in the all-male pack in which he had suddenly found himself.

To say he was a Lab was something of a misnomer. On our first visit to the vet, I explained I had been told Tuna was part Labrador and part springer spaniel but was puzzled because his mother looked like a short collie. The vet said it was possible for a litter to have two fathers. I decided the vet's opinion might have some validity, because Tuna could jump to the ceiling like a springer spaniel, but he would point at his prey like a

Labrador. In fact, Tuna pointed at everything. Not just birds or ducks. I mean everything. On more than one occasion, I observed Tuna pointing at a grasshopper (or some kind of insect) before charging after it. When you followed the line of his point it would lead straight to the head, thorax, and abdomen of some small creature. It was sometimes difficult to detect, but you could spot it if you had the patience and took the time to look. Tuna also loved to chase birds. He would just take off upon spotting one of them. I figured he would make a fine retriever.

From the morning after his arrival, Tuna and I went everywhere together. I even took him to some of my classes on campus. We both took great pleasure in walking on campus together. One morning not long after he moved in, Tuna walked with me to one of my business administration classes, where I tied him to a metal bannister pole directly outside the classroom door. I told him to be good, I would see him very soon. The look on his face, when he realized I was going to leave him tied outside, melted me. I felt bad, but I knew I would return, even if Tuna didn't. On a campus where protest was common and acceptable, Tuna began to bark the moment I disappeared through the door. He continued to do so for the entire hour and a half of the class. It was less than halfway through the class when the professor and some of the students started complaining. For a split second I thought about confessing the little puppy was mine, but the growing frustration of my professor and fellow students compelled me to give in to the temptation to shift blame to a thoughtless owner who was both anonymous and fictitious. I joined others, rather loudly, to say how inconsiderate it was for someone to take a little puppy to the campus and allow him to disturb the peace of the entire class.

When class was finally over, I skulked around waiting for the professor and all of my classmates to leave. I kept an eye on Tuna to make sure no one untied him and took him away. The moment everyone was gone I went to him – his delight was so unrestrained I worried he might choke himself on his leash. I picked him up, and the joy he was experiencing as he lavished me with kisses, made the reunion almost worth my large error in judgment. I sheepishly untied Tuna and we walked home. I resolved not to try that again.

As Tuna and I settled in to life together, I learned he loved to play, chew, and excavate. I learned there was no fence so well grounded he could not dig under it to freedom. It melted me to see him take his chew toy and shake it until he conquered it completely. He would retrieve the sticks and his rubber toys that I threw, fetching them from the far corner of the yard and bringing them back to me with great pride. When I settled down to homework or television, he would suddenly be lying next to me, always with some part of his body touching mine. I often caught myself just staring at him. His ability to rest peacefully filled me with a calmness that helped me relax. I would listen to his steady breathing while he slept, with occasional little noises fluttering from his lips. I took comfort knowing he was dreaming the dreams of a happy dog.

Even as a young dog, Tuna began to reveal the character traits I would come to know so well in the coming years. Smaller than a fully-grown Labrador retriever, Tuna was a medium size dog, weighing 30-40 pounds. Besides his great vertical leap, he had fine speed. As to personality or disposition, Tuna usually was friendly unless he spotted other dogs. Then he turned quickly into a macho Alpha dog who believed he was a skilled martial arts expert. Except for those occasional encounters with other dogs, Tuna greeted everyone with tail wagging. I am sure if we had ever been burglarized, Tuna would have assisted the burglar if he could.

Despite Tuna's macho façade when confronted with other dogs, he was not a fighter – at least not a very successful one. He got in many scrapes with other dogs; his record was 2-14, or worse. The modus operandi of his fights consisted of Tuna growling and charging his opponent and ending up on his back within seconds of the commencement of the skirmish. What was so deceptive about his fighting style was that he looked as though he had an unfaltering determination to destroy his foe. When he spotted another dog, his eyes filled with unbridled anger and off he would charge. But the vast majority of his fights ended up with Tuna quickly on his back lying in abject, humiliated surrender. He was like an immature toddler who became frustrated with his father and flailed out. It was completely ineffective. That was Tuna's offense – all bark and no bite.

It became increasingly apparent as Tuna's puppyhood moved to adolescence that he was smart. Nowhere was this more clearly illustrated than when I tried to teach him his first tricks. He was a quick learner and soon mastered all of them. I would like to be able to say I always used my powers as his master to teach him good tricks that bettered humanity and dog-hood. But I was still just a college student, so I have to admit my priority was often tricks that entertained my friends and myself. Unfortunately for Tuna, and ultimately for me, they were not helpful in the sense of improving the human condition.

Tuna's first tricks were command/obey activities such as sitting-up, rolling over, and standing on his hind legs.

He learned these so easily, we quickly moved on to a more sophisticated trick. After some intense training, Tuna could jump into my arms with a running start. I loved this trick, because the moment he was safely in my arms, he would commence licking me repeatedly on my face. These doggie kisses delighted me.

"Looking for airplanes" was a trick that occurred to me when I realized whenever I scratched Tuna, he would move his head from side to side as he looked up toward the heavens. He made a rhythmic, Stevie Wonder-like figure eight movement with his head. He was simply in ecstasy when I scratched him – especially his lower back, immediately sinking into a pleasurable trance-like state. When I realized he did this every time, I knew we had another trick to add to his repertoire. All I had to do was hide my scratching hand from the audience and command

Tuna to "look for airplanes." He performed the trick perfectly every time. Reinforced by my consistent and enthusiastic praise, Tuna was pleased to learn just about anything I asked of him.

My friend Mike Low invented another trick for Tuna. Mike came from my hometown of Napa and later attended law school with me at Hastings. When Mike hung out at my apartment, Tuna would approach him, sit down, and just stare up into his face. Mike, a philosophy major in college, grew tired of the stare but, instead of telling Tuna to go away, he looked him straight in the eye and started explaining the theory of existence. This quickly became known as the "Theory of Existence" trick. It went something like this: we would sit Tuna down in front of Mike. Mike would have a protracted discussion about his theories with Tuna who, after several minutes of nonstop talking from Mike, would slowly drop from a sitting position, to lying down with eyes open, but with his attention still locked on Mike. Then Tuna's eyelids would flutter, and he would drift off to sleep – all the while, Mike continually expounding on his theory. It was the height of rudeness to the speaker, but anyone watching empathized with Tuna, who had clearly endured it as long as he could. After he couldn't stand the tortuous boredom any longer, he would just go to sleep. It was a thing of simple beauty and won over audiences of all ages.

It was several years later when Tuna mastered his most sophisticated trick. "Clear the Table Tuna" was an act we developed when we moved to Stockton, California. We lived in a beautiful Victorian house that had come fully furnished. Among other things, there was a huge beautiful, antique dining room table which was finished in a very shiny black veneer, and covered with an elegant, embroidered, white tablecloth. These became the center stage props for the performance of "Clear the Table Tuna."

Tuna and I discovered the trick quite by chance. One morning, I was sitting at the table sipping my coffee and reading the newspaper. Normally, Tuna would spend this time sprawled on the floor by my feet, but on this occasion, I noticed he wasn't there. Looking around the large room, I spotted Tuna pacing back and forth along the far wall by the doorway to the staircase leading to the front door. Wondering if he needed a potty break or some exercise time, I called out. However, by chance I did not just call out in a regular voice, but rather in a loud and excited tone, calling him over, at the same time banging my hand forcefully on the tabletop. I wasn't angry, I was actually being playful – but it came out as a very assertive playful.

Tuna turned out to be in a very playful mood himself. His head snapped around and he was suddenly coming at me like a charging bull. Possessed with a vertical leap as good as any dog I have ever seen (perhaps it could even be described as a super power), Tuna was in mid-air before I realized what was happening. There was nothing I could do. Time was frozen. Whatever was going to happen, was going to happen.

Tuna easily cleared the leading edge of the table and landed about a quarter of the way onto the tabletop. The lovely, white, embroidered tablecloth acted like a sled on snow, carrying Tuna across the table, who was now suddenly fighting the slide, scrambling in vain to stop himself, right up until he shot completely off the other side, landing in my lap and carrying us crashing backwards. I was flung up against the wall with Tuna pressed hard against my chest. My newspaper flew into the air and coffee went splattering everywhere, especially on Tuna and me. Tuna's most famous trick was born.

Initially, I was so bowled over I didn't consider letting him attempt such a high-intensity trick again. When I eventually did think about it, I figured he would never voluntarily go along. However, I gradually found myself wondering whether with just the right amount of excited coaxing, Tuna might be induced to high jump the table. I figured as long as the sleek tablecloth happened to be on the table, the completion of the trick would be a foregone conclusion.

It was perhaps a month later when I decided to attempt to replicate the trick. I rearranged the table to ensure there were no obstacles that could injure Tuna. Then I called his name enthusiastically and slapped my palm on the middle of the table. To my surprise, it was instantly apparent Tuna welcomed the invitation. He gladly high jumped the table and, with the magic tablecloth, found himself gliding blissfully across the expansive table before the wondering admiration of his master.

Of all of Tuna's maneuvers and performances comprising his bag of tricks (speaking, sitting, sitting up, standing on hind legs, rolling over, jumping in my arms, looking for airplanes), Clear the Table Tuna was, by far, the most entertaining and athletically challenging feat in the riveting arsenal.

Tuna's tricks were offered up as entertainment for my friends and to show off his abilities, so it was natural that I eventually started giving an introduction prior to his performances. Once our audience was seated, I would introduce Tuna who was waiting offstage in the bedroom.

"Ladies and Gentlemen, may I have your attention, please. Management is proud to present, as our main attraction, the internationally renowned canine, Tuna. Tuna will be performing many amazing tricks including the difficult and highly dangerous feat known as Clear the Table Tuna, in which there are no safety nets. What you will see is real. The degree of difficulty is immeasurable. So, without further ado, here is the dog who is known by the Spanish as 'El Fabuloso;' by the French as 'Le Magnifique;' and in America, he bears the moniker 'Tuna the Wonder Dog!'"

At this point I would let Tuna into the living room while the audience clapped wildly. We would start with the easiest tricks (sitting, sitting up, rolling over, etc.) and build up to the thrilling, extraordinary Clear the Table Tuna finale. My impressed friends would often request encores.

Sometimes I felt vaguely guilty using Tuna in this way, but it didn't stop me from showing him off for entertainment purposes. The only dangerous trick was Clear the Table Tuna, but I rationalized it was not a danger to him because I always made sure the room was set up so that when he went off the other end of the table there was nothing around that could cause an injury to him. Also, I would put cushions on the ground to soften his landing. I still have a little guilt when I think back on his performances, but I have to admit they still crack me up.

CHAPTER FIVE

Tuna the Hunter

The flip side of being alone was that I had plenty of time to earn good grades. I had achieved decent grades in my last year at the junior college, which continued during my first year at Berkeley when I was socially alone. In my senior year, Tuna was my social life. Not being close to my co-op assigned roommates and not being involved in a fraternity or other convenient social connection, I had plenty of time to study. My grades continued to rise. After receiving A's and B's in the first quarter of my senior year, I decided I could reasonably consider law school opportunities.

Thinking back, I realize there were several things contributing to my decision to apply to attend law school. First, I wanted to prove that I could become a lawyer, despite the contrary indications from Dad, who said I wouldn't amount to anything, and from my high school counselor, who told me to think of another career. I also liked the idea of helping people resolve disputes and, even more, I liked the notion that I could remedy wrongs.

And then there was Vietnam. It turned out a person could still obtain a post college deferment if he went to graduate school. Law school qualified as graduate school. That was motivation enough for lots of students – a large percentage of my freshman class in law school were there for the deferment. I was no exception. I had joined ROTC at Cal Berkeley when I was a senior, which assured that I qualify for a graduate deferment, as long as I could actually get into graduate school. The other reason I joined ROTC was that, if I did need to serve, I wanted to go in as an officer rather than a draftee or entry-level enlistee. I figured being an officer would be safer than front line duty as a draftee or enlistee. Besides, as an officer and a lawyer, I might be able to join the Army's judge advocate corps and not actually have to fight in battle. Many people were dying in that war and I was terrified at the possibility of ending up on the front lines. If that happened, I was pretty sure I would not come back.

If I'm being honest, my real hope was that by the time I finished my three years of law school and then further training in the Army stateside, the Vietnam War would be over.

These thoughts regarding the war had gradually evolved. When I left Napa, I still believed the United States government did not and would not intentionally lie to its citizens. During my undergraduate years at Berkeley I certainly heard different points of view on this, but I still tended to ascribe to the Domino Theory. I understood the Domino Theory to mean that if we didn't stop the Communists in Vietnam, they would eventually take over all of Asia, then South America, and then the United States itself.

On the one hand, I honestly figured our government knew best. Yet I was part of a new generation that was rebelling against government and authority in general. I began to take note of the many casualties of the war. Every time I listened to the news or read a newspaper, I heard that many Americans and many more Vietnamese and Cambodians had been killed. Even more soldiers were being seriously wounded, physically or mentally. My perspective began to swing, and I eventually came to the conclusion that our government should not have us involved in this war. I no longer believed the conflict was even legal, as there had not been a declaration of war. A strip of rice paddies and jungle in Southeast Asia could not be worth thousands upon thousands of American deaths. This was not like World War II. We had not been attacked. It had stopped making sense. The Domino Theory was just that – a theory. It was outweighed by the human cost of the war.

Of course, hindsight is 20-20. It is clear now that 58,000 dead Americans, millions of dead Vietnamese and Cambodians, and tens of thousands of wounded survivors, made the war a disaster. And, though we had no idea the USSR and Communism would fall 16 years after Vietnam, when they did, it reinforced the notion the war had been needless.

But it took several years for my perspective on the war to develop. As an undergraduate, I remained in ROTC to obtain a deferment and put off military service. It was a great plan as long as I could get into graduate school.

It happened that during my time in Berkeley, I had developed a close relationship with my Business Administration professor. His interest and encouragement provided the support I needed. He wrote a strong letter of reference which accompanied my applications to several law schools where I believed I had a chance of being admitted. To my delight and relief, I was accepted by the Hastings College of the Law in San Francisco.

A few weeks before law school started, when I was still at home in Napa with my parents and dog, an unexpected excursion took place. My friend from high school, Bill Imrie, was also going to attend Hastings Law School, and, in fact, would be my roommate. Bill was also living at home in Napa when he called one bright morning and asked if I would like to go hunting with him at his family's ranch. Originally a homestead, the ranch had been in the Imrie family for generations. It now belonged in equal shares to the Imrie children, Bill's father, and several aunts and uncles. The extended family enjoyed it and maintained it together.

The property was sprawling and contained plenty of land for hunting. In accepting the invitation, I asked if it would be okay to bring Tuna. After all, Tuna was part Labrador retriever and a hunter at heart. I had observed Tuna point at grasshoppers and was sure this must be indicative of his abilities to go after larger prey. Bill had no problem with my request and even said he would loan me a spare shotgun. No hunting license was needed on their private property. Besides, we were just going to shoot birds.

The idea of this adventure was exciting to me because I had never been hunting. But I didn't consider myself completely inexperienced. I had shot an M-14 rifle in ROTC in target practice. Before that, I had shot my BB gun. In fact, when I was 10 years old, I killed a single bird with my BB gun. It made me feel horrible, but I convinced myself it was an important little boy's experience. Now I was a mature adult who would love the hunt. I was pumped up for the excursion.

Tuna and I arrived at the ranch ready for the outdoors, which meant Tuna had on his chain collar and I was wearing my Levis, T-shirt, windbreaker, tennis shoes, and a baseball cap. Bill met us at the main house in full hunter's regalia: chamois cloth shirt, hunting vest, field shooting boots, and brimmed hat. He handed me a 20-gauge pheasant hunting shotgun. Bill said it was a Winchester 101, which was perfect for the hunting we would be doing that morning. I didn't understand Bill's explanation as to why it was such a proper gun for the excursion nor all of the special things the gun had been fitted with. What caught my eye was the beautiful checkerboard walnut stock. Assuming I had some idea of what we were doing, Bill gave me a ten-second lesson on using the gun and off we went on the hunting expedition.

I knew Labradors love to romp and play, particularly with their trusted owners close by. I knew it was an energetic breed designed for flushing birds and swimming after fallen ducks in the water. All of this fit my Tuna. He had energy to spare. He loved chasing birds and practically anything else that moved fast. I also knew from our veterinarian that Labradors needed lots of outlets for their abundant energy. I figured a bird hunt would be the perfect opportunity for Tuna to get a real workout. In my fantasy, I would shoot a bird in the sky from a great distance. Tuna would tear off in hot pursuit of the flapping duck, wounded pigeon, or other fallen bird. Gathering it up in the gentle grasp of the retriever, he would then proudly trot back to me with his prize hanging from his salivating mouth – just like you see in the myriad paintings hanging in the plush offices of so many corporate executives – all of which seem to be labeled "The Hunt." My fantasy even led me to think this adventure might develop into a sport I would pursue and enjoy with Tuna for years to come. Our new hobby offered so many benefits, including exercise and adventure for both of us.

What I did not know was that training a Labrador retriever to hunt requires a dedicated owner, who will instill in his dog not only basic, unwavering obedience (such as sit, stay, come, etc.) but also the many lofty pursuits of hunting and retrieving their owners' prey. Tuna had been mildly trained in the former and not at all in the latter.

Labradors are smart. You can keep them from jumping on visitors, but it will only happen if the dog is trained by his owner not to jump on visitors. It is very similar to instructing a child. There must be discipline, ground rules, and guidance for children. The same applies for Labradors. They must receive enough training to make them capable of self-control and amenable to obeying commands and minding their owner's wishes.

In short, the owner controls what kind of dog his Labrador becomes.

In Tuna's case, he had not been trained, guided, or encouraged to become a hunting dog. No matter what his breeding or genes might have allowed, he was not a hunting dog, and no one was to blame for this but me. I was laboring under the wholly unfounded assumption that Labs had been bred in such a way that they would not be shocked or frightened when they heard a gunshot, even for the first time. I was about to learn no one had mentioned this to Tuna.

Bill and I had not been hunting for more than ten minutes when a large flock of birds came overhead. Bill and I had fanned out, and he was about 100 yards away beyond some oak trees. Tuna and I were making our way through some scattered brush when the birds filled the sky. Like a scene out of Hitchcock's movie *The Birds*, the sky was full of them. I was all over this opportunity. Throwing up my shotgun, I fired in the general direction of the flying birds. At first, I stared into the sky to see if I had hit anything. I had not. Then I looked down to see how my hunting dog Tuna had reacted. He had been standing alertly by my side, ready to charge after the fallen prey. At least, that is what I thought. But when I looked down, he was nowhere in sight. Good, I thought. Even though I missed the shot, Tuna must have instantly registered the report of the gun and, anticipating the fallen bird, taken off in hot pursuit of the prey. Thank goodness one of us knew what he was doing.

When Tuna did not respond to my calls, I shouted out to Bill to inquire if Tuna had ventured over to where he was perched. Bill responded that he didn't see him either. I called out to Tuna again and again, but there was no response at all. None. Tuna had vanished into thin air. I began to wonder whether Tuna had disappeared in the grove of slender, swaying eucalyptus trees or the old, but majestic, oak trees that were spread out over the acreage. I continued to call, expecting him to come bounding out of the brush at any moment. Nothing.

Finally, I told Bill I needed to stop hunting to look for Tuna. I finally realized that Tuna must have been really frightened by the loud shotgun blast. It was completely new to him, and he had been very close to the source of the noise, right by my feet when I shot the rifle. Bill sensed my distress, and being the good guy he was, offered to help me search. We spread out calling Tuna's name. After an hour of intensive searching, I could only think of the worst possible scenarios. Tuna had had a heart attack or a stroke. Tuna fell in a well. Tuna was caught in a fence. Tuna made it to the road and was hit by a car.

We searched for another hour. By now it was early afternoon and Bill and I were hot, dusty, tired, and hoarse from yelling. Discouragement had set in and we were finally considering whether to continue the search, when our eyes were caught by a flicker of motion at the edge of a distant stand of live oak trees. Tuna emerged from the foliage and, responding to our calls, took a tentative step toward where we were standing some 300 yards away. Then he broke into a slow unsure trot. We met half way and I knelt to the ground and began petting him and repeating his name softly. He was trembling – his fear had not dissipated more than two hours after the discharge. I continued to stroke his coat and comfort him for several more minutes before we finally rose and began to make our way back to the ranch house where the cars were parked.

This was the entire collective hunting career of Tuna and myself, consisting of one hasty, errant shot at a large flock of birds that was impressive only in missing all of them, followed by hours spent searching for my "hunting" dog. The moment we found Tuna, the hunting outing was over. I had no interest in hazarding another shot. No, that was it. Hunting trip over. Hunting career over. There would be no safari in our future.

CHAPTER SIX

A Diversion to Napa

Hastings College of the Law was only across the bay from Berkeley, but it may as well have been a million miles as far as Tuna was concerned, because I could not find an apartment that would allow pets. As a result, Tuna and I experienced our first (although not last) separation. Tuna learned he would not be moving with me at the conclusion of what must have appeared to him a routine trip to my parents' home in Napa, California.

My hometown of Napa is a relatively small city, about 40 miles north of Berkeley. The heart of the Napa Valley is lovely wine country with rich vineyards surrounded by a forest terrain in the west and rolling hills to the east. It had been during my junior year in high school that my parents had finally reconciled after their first legal separation, and at this point were still some years away from separating for the second and final time. They lived in the modest home I purchased for mom. It was 900 square foot, 3-bedroom, 1 bath, stucco home close to the city limits. Tuna was, of course, very familiar with my mother and father, as we had made the fairly short trip from Berkeley to Napa many times. I came home at least once per month to visit and, admittedly, to have my laundry done by my devoted mother. I saved up all of my clothes to wash until I went home so that I wouldn't have to spend time at college in laundromats. Also, it saved me money, which was important to a "starving" college student. Depending on the amount of time between visits this could amount to two or three large sacks of dirty clothes per trip.

I recall only one occasion when I did not bring bags of dirty laundry home on a quick trip to Napa. This was because Mom had remarked on my previous visit that she thought I only came home to get my clothes washed and for no other reason. This was the closest she ever came to complaining about doing my laundry, and I must admit it made me feel guilty. She was right. Laundry was a major reason I had been coming home. I decided I would make a point on my next visit by not bringing any clothes home for washing. I would show Mom that I did, indeed, come to visit her with no ulterior motive. Not that I actually went to the laundromats myself. Instead, I just bought more underwear and T-shirts. For several weeks, I kept opening new package after new package of Hanes or J.C. Penney's underwear and T-shirts.

I should not have been surprised when I discovered the message I had tried to send was not the one Mom received. Instead of being pleased not to have to spend long hours of the weekend doing laundry for her son, she indignantly demanded to know why I hadn't brought clothes home to be washed. When I explained I had been burdening her, she felt terrible and made me promise to bring all of my dirty laundry home on my next trip – no matter how many sacks there were. I have to admit I didn't expect this reaction. I realized she really liked and, perhaps, needed to continue to take care of me, even though I had moved into adulthood.

Being the generous young adult that I was, I submitted to Mom's request from that moment forward allowing her to do all of my laundry. I rationalized it was an example of good social policy coinciding with good fiscal policy. I got to visit my sweet mom and get my dirty laundry done without feeling guilty. That was a win-win situation, as it often was with her.

It was more than a year after my laundry epiphany when Tuna and I made what he doubtless assumed was another routine trip home to Napa. He was at this point just turning a robust and energetic two – and arrived without any clue that my aging, first-generation, Italian-American parents were about to take him into foster care.

During my trips home, my dad had gradually taken to calling Tuna "Dummy." This was in line with his penchant for nicknaming all of my friends. Of course, the nicknames were seldom complimentary. As an example, his most favorite names for my friends were "Shithead," "Dumb Shit," or "Numb Nuts." He seemed to fixate on bowel movements or genitals for his nicknames.

When my buddies were over, he liked to speak Italian to any of his friends or relatives who were visiting. Whatever he said always made them laugh at us. It could not have been more apparent that Big Al was making fun of us. I only got the best of him in this routine once. It was a weekend evening in my junior year of high school when I had some friends over, but Al didn't. Although he had no audience of his own, he didn't want to miss a chance to make fun of me in front of my friends. I had misplaced my eyeglasses. With my friends looking on, I asked my dad if he had seen them.

Big Al pounced, booming in English so that my friends would understand his artful wit, "Raymond, you would lose your head if it wasn't attached to your body, you idiot."

My friends gave sort of a courtesy laugh, but they had seen his act so often, I knew they would like it if I could nail him with a comeback. I did have to be careful because with Big Al, it always seemed you were one step away from the anger tipping point and things getting physical. But with my buddies there, I decided I had to respond.

Answering in as normal a tone as I could master – to contrast myself with my father's bullying condescension, I said, "Gee, Dad, you're right. What do you think the problem is? Could it be my environment or is it my heredity?"

My dad didn't understand what I meant, but my friends did, and they couldn't contain their laughter. Mike Kerns, a big 6'3" strapping young buck, loved to laugh, and this time he laughed so hard he fell to his knees. For once the tables had turned and it was my friends laughing at an insult my father didn't understand.

Big Al was beside himself. He knew he had been trumped, but he didn't know how to regain the upper hand. He instinctively responded by saying, "I'll give you environment or heredity," butchering the pronunciation of both words. I wish I could say he never tried to outdo me again, but no such luck. At most, it was a minor setback to him. More likely, he figured his reply really put me in my place.

It was fun, at the time, making fun of Dad's inferiority instead of the other way around. However, as I thought about it later that evening as I was falling asleep, it didn't feel good to me to make him feel bad.

In retrospect, I realize my father's character may not have been an enormous surprise. Big Al had had a tough life.

He was born in Chicago, one of three siblings, with an older brother and a younger sister. When they were very young, sometime in the 1920s, my grandparents divorced, and remarkably, my grandfather got custody. However, he decided he couldn't raise all three children by himself, so he returned his daughter to her mom and kept the two boys. He moved to a rustic one-bedroom cabin in an orchard in Healdsburg, California. My grandfather would leave the two boys in the cabin all day while he worked the land for the landowner. One day, while left alone, my dad's older brother (my uncle Leo) started playing cops and robbers with my dad. Leo was the cop and my father was the robber. The problem was Leo used my grandfather's double barrel 12-gauge shotgun as his play weapon. As the robber was trying to escape, Uncle Leo pulled the trigger and blew away most of my dad's left thigh. As an adult, my dad would recount a vivid memory of seeing blood and muscle spewing onto an old calendar on the wall of the cabin. He was very lucky to survive this accident, as it took my uncle some time to find my grandfather, who then had to load my father into the back of his old Model T Ford flatbed and drive him to the small hospital in Healdsburg.

My dad's education ended after the third grade, when he had to drop out to help his father with chores. It is an understatement to say that as an adult he suffered from serious self-esteem issues. I can only speculate as to the causes, but I do know he ran away once from his dad's home and went to live with his mother, who had remarried by then. Her new husband did not treat him well, so my dad ran away from his mother's home and returned to his father's home with his tail between his legs. I guess a person could feel a little unloved with that kind of background. This tough upbringing may explain his personality and character, but it didn't make it any easier to be around him.

To be fair, he wasn't without positive traits. He was generous to his friends, his relations, and sometimes even his children, although you always wondered if he was actually trying to curry their respect. He loved sports and social activities, and at some of these times he was actually enjoyable to be around. Those occasional moments showed there was more to the man than our daily life with him implied.

My mom was five feet nothing and very stout. She was a typical Italian mother. She was also a remarkable person. Some called her a saint. Others said she was a special soul. This was probably for putting up with not only Big Al, but also with two young boys, all of whom could be obnoxious from time to time.

She was kind and loving, and though she didn't believe it herself, she was very intelligent. Life had always been tough on her as well. Her mother died from pneumonia when my mom was 12 years old. She lost two siblings in their infancy. Her father was a gardener when he lost his wife. He collapsed into drinking, and although he continued to work, most of the caretaking of the home and her brother fell to Mom to handle. She dropped out of school in the eighth grade and began to take in laundry and keep the house. Her father died of alcoholism when she was 17. At this very young age she was left in charge of her only surviving brother, who was four years younger. She continued to take in laundry and found additional work cleaning houses, but barely earned enough for them to survive. Through it all she made caring for her only surviving sibling her priority. She insisted he stay in school. She would not allow him to work other than his paper route. Her paternal uncle, Johnny Bianchina, became their *de facto* guardian. He lived in San Francisco and would regularly check in to see if they were okay. Mom couldn't afford a phone, so Uncle Johnny checked in on her and her brother by having one of his San Mateo friends check on them or he would make the trip from San Francisco. He also provided them some food, and occasionally some money.

Yes, her life was tough, but she spoke of pleasant memories of school before she had to drop out. She was always proud of her academic success. She had won the San Mateo County grammar school spelling bee in the 8th grade. I always thought she would have gone far if not for the nasty breaks life gave her. Nevertheless, a hard life gave her the clarity to cherish her family and friends. I knew and felt her love for me in no uncertain terms. She was devoted, loyal, and dedicated to her children. She loved my brother and me unconditionally. We were the center of her universe, her entire life.

This extended to the point where she would ignore reality when it came to enjoying and encouraging her boys. I always had what doctors called a "weight problem." In grammar school, the other kids called me Butterball. But, according to Mom, "Raymond has a little tummy on him." That was as close as she ever came to saying I was overweight. She knew I fretted about my weight problem, so would remark it looked to her like my tummy was going down when, in fact, it might at the time be going up. I didn't doubt my mom's sincerity, but when you haven't lost any weight and you are still wearing "huskies" (the jeans for chubby boys), the compliment didn't make you feel any better, and tended to undermine your mother's credibility. My mom proved, beyond a reasonable doubt, the old saying that, "Beauty is in the eye of the beholder." To my mother, and only to my mother, I was beautiful. End of discussion.

At the time, I didn't know how my friends felt about her. I don't think I ever thought about it. I knew she was always kind to them, but I guess I thought all parents were that way to their children's friends. It was only later I learned they thought she was a saint. Over the years, many of my friends have praised my mother for her kindness to them. I have always found it amusing to talk with friends who had known both my mom and my dad. Trying to be tactful and never wanting to say anything negative about the dead, they would say, "Your mother was such a wonderful, kind and loving person. And your dad was interesting. Quite a character."

Tuna's and my separation came at the end of the weekend. It is debatable whether Mom was truly a dog lover, but this particular dog was her beloved son's dog and would be treated accordingly. I knew Mom didn't have a mean bone in her body, and treated man and animal with affection. Tuna would be in great and loving hands in her care. Still, it was a sad moment when I pulled out of the driveway from the modest little home in Napa, California, and started driving down the street. Mom was standing on the tiny front porch with Tuna in her arms, holding one of his paws with her hand. As I neared the corner, I looked in the rearview mirror and saw the paw waving good-by. I knew Tuna, who had so far lived his entire life with me, could not have any idea where I was going, why he wasn't coming with me, or what my parents wanted with him.

Tuna lived with my parents for the next two years. We were reunited during summer vacations, as well as weekend visits home during the school year. For a dog "doing time" in a place of confinement, Tuna's stay was not so bad. He had a cozy backyard to play in and to excavate. He continually explored and dug his way around the different parts of the yard. Mom had a bird feeder that she kept well stocked. This encouraged lots of birds to visit. Tuna was a maniacal bird chaser, so this was a match made in heaven. And, Mom took such good care of him.

Life was not bad. He had great food provided by Mom who was a renowned cook. Living with me, Tuna had mostly dry dog food as recommended by the vet. I would occasionally give him some meat as treats and anything that fell on the floor was fair game. Still, Mom's gourmet table scraps were better than anything he had ever sampled. Tuna also had plenty of places to roam, smell, pee, and dig. And, I came home for frequent visits. Still, Mom used to report to me that she could tell that Tuna missed me. She said that after every weekend visit, for several days Tuna would check my bedroom each morning to see if I was there. She said Tuna was always hoping to see me.

CHAPTER SEVEN

Law School with Tuna

At the beginning of my third year of law school, I finally found a place to live that allowed pets. This meant Tuna would move again, and we would be reunited. And, as fate played out, exciting adventures were in store for him.

Our new home was a second level flat in the Sunset District in San Francisco. I used to joke it was called the Sunset District because the sun was always set. The drawback of the location was it was not in the heart of the city, but on the plus side it was not too far from the ocean. There was no back yard, but Tuna could be reliably allowed outside the front door to roam, do his business, and return to the middle door of the three flats that made up this building. Tuna was a predictable creature of habit, asking to go out at about the same time each day and returning after about the same interval of time. This little routine happened once in the morning and again in the evening. If he needed to go at other than the usual times, Tuna would simply scratch at the outside door until I let him out. For almost two years we followed this unvarying ritual of Tuna being let out on his own to do his exercise and business, and it worked very well.

The flat consisted of four bedrooms, two bathrooms, a kitchen, and a living room. We had two male and two female roommates. We three guys each had our own bedroom, and we shared one bathroom. The two girls shared the other bedroom and bathroom. Having five people share this flat and its attendant expenses enabled me to reduce my rent to $37.50 per month. This was very low, even in 1970. My bedroom had the capacity and grace of a small tool shed, but what do you expect for $37.50 per month? These were our accommodations as Tuna and I started out life together in San Francisco. It was August 1970.

The day we moved into the flat was a significant day in Tuna's life, and a memorable one in my life as well. The morning started out predictably enough. Moving things into the flat was mostly work and no fun, but I had a big surprise in store for my trusted dog. After moving most of the morning, Tuna responded happily when I called him to come outside and get in the car. This was encouraging, because car rides were often somewhat troubling to Tuna until he knew where we were going. If the trip turned out to end at the vet, then it was not a happy day for Tuna. However, if it was almost anywhere else, then Tuna was a happy dog. He loved to go for rides. Car rides were especially enjoyable if I cracked the window enough for Tuna to stick his head out into the wind. It always amused me to see Tuna with his head out the window and his face distorted by the wind blowing through his jowls. His eyes would exhibit different stages of squinting depending on the velocity of the car and the strength of the outside breezes. Sometimes he looked magnificent – like a general leading his men into battle, while other times he looked like an old man or an evil scientist.

On this occasion, as a reward for moving into the new place, I was taking Tuna to Baker Beach. It was a beautiful sunny day in San Francisco, and, as San Francisco natives knew, and we transplants quickly discovered, one did not waste such a rare day by staying indoors if one could help it. Law students at Hastings were known to cut class to take advantage of the good weather. Not today, however, because school hadn't started yet. Tuna seemed particularly pleased to have me all to himself without having to share me with any of my buddies.

When we arrived at Baker Beach, I took out a big beach blanket and a six-pack of beer stored in a cooler. I clipped on Tuna's leash because I knew there would be other dogs at the beach, and I wanted Tuna controlled at least until we got settled, and I could attain some comfort level that it was okay to let him roam around on his own. We made our way down the rocky walkways until we arrived at the beach. A lot of people of all ages were already there, setting up to engage in the usual activities that happen in such settings: lying down on their beach blankets and listening to their favorite music on transistor radios; playing catch with a football in the sand; throwing Frisbees and having their dogs play catch and fetch – there had to have been a dozen or more dogs; assisting little children digging and building sand castles; and, running toward or away from foaming ocean waves. It was a rare opportunity for us San Franciscans (both human and canine) to enjoy the glorious weather and the beach.

After Tuna and I had picked out a promising spot to establish our beachhead (carefully selected to be near several young pretty girls who seemed to be without guys), I laid out our blanket, took off my shirt, applied suntan lotion, and broke out a cold beer. Tuna appeared to be settling in comfortably. He sat next to me gazing with mild interest at the neighboring sunbathers. Then he looked at me and leaned in for a scratch between the ears. When I unclipped his leash, he stood, wagged his tail a couple of times, and began to explore, sniffing here and there, making his way through the throng in the direction of the bushes and paths at the back of the beach.

I was feeling pretty happy. Our move complete, I was looking forward to a chance to relax in the fresh ocean air. I lay back on the beach towel, wearing my sunglasses to mute the bright the sun, took a wonderfully refreshing sip of cold beer, and stared out at the glorious ocean, with its foaming white waves breaking over the deep blue waters underneath. It was spectacular. And all around me there were youthful, good-looking, female bathing beauties. They were probably college or graduate students like me, or young secretaries, but to me, they seemed like gorgeous exotic dancers or Brazilian underwear models. As I sat on my beach blanket, deep in fantasy, I daydreamed, what might this day bring? Perhaps I would meet a woman who would become a significant part of my life? Would I meet some new friends and we would agree to rendezvous later that evening for a night out on the town? School hadn't started yet and I was ready for fun in my life. Gently reeling myself back in, I thought, no matter how the stars aligned or what the gods had in store for me, it was already a good day.

As I sat watching the sparkling sea and listening to the heavenly roar of the ocean waves, I felt a warm spray cascading over my bare back. My first confused reaction was to realize the spray I was feeling was not coming from the ocean.

In that first nanosecond, a dozen possibilities flashed across my mind. Was some punk spraying me with a warm beer? Was a little child dumping some liquid solution of some kind on me? Was it just an accident – a person tripping and spilling their drink on me? Even before I could move I became aware of laughter beginning to well up from the nearby towels. Turning to look over my shoulder, I was confronted by my Tuna, leg held high, peeing across my entire bare back. Tuna was staking out his property, letting all dogs know, in no uncertain terms, that this young man was his and would not be shared with any other canine.

The several dozen people around me were not only watching but thought the situation was hilarious. Rage and embarrassment overcame me. Without thinking, I made a fist as if to hit my own dog. Aghast, I quickly checked the impulse. Instead, I sprang to my feet and with an inarticulate guttural noise, chased Tuna off. I toweled off the warm and odorous urine, put on my shirt, and quickly packed up my beer. Like an unexpected gust of wind, I got out of there as fast as I could, desperate to get away from the laughter and humiliation. I walked straight to my car and threw my stuff in the back seat. I had taken off so fast to escape the demeaning laughter of the crowd that I neglected to put Tuna back on his leash. In my beeline to the car, I assumed Tuna was tagging along, as was his usual custom. But Tuna was not there. I glanced around more carefully. No sign of him.

I began to walk up and down the parking lot whistling and searching. Still no Tuna. That meant, of course, I had to go back to the beach and get him. I looked from the parking lot down to the area where the incident had occurred. He was not there. I continued along the top of the bluff surveying the beach below and looking for packs of dogs or dog fights. Still, Tuna was not in sight.

Skirting the area where Tuna peed on me, I once again made my way down to the beach. He didn't appear to be on the beach itself. I turned my attention to the steep hillside, with its paths and cliffs rising to the parking lot above. In one of the steeper sections, there was a ledge half way up the bank. Looking along the ledge, I spotted Tuna standing stock-still, gazing out toward the water's edge.

Torn between exasperation – I really wanted to get home and take a shower – and relief at finding him, I called out, commanding him to come so we could get the heck out of there. At first, I didn't think he could hear me, because no matter how much I called, he didn't make a move toward me. I decided if Tuna wouldn't come to me, I would go to him. As I began to clamber up the steep, rocky hillside, I called out to him, but again, no movement by Tuna. Finally, when I was no more than fifteen feet from him, I called out as loudly as I could. It was clear I was in earshot, even with the sounds of the wind and ocean swirling all around us. Still, there was no movement from Tuna. I called one last time. Barely turning his head, Tuna looked in my direction.

Tuna was not wagging his tail. This was always automatic when he saw me; it was unprecedented to see no wagging at all. As I stood on the ledge regarding the silent and motionless dog, I realized I had been calling Tuna in a voice that manifested the anger and frustration I had been experiencing over the past hour. Taking a deep breath, I began working my way along the ledge, speaking his name in a low, soothing voice. When I was within reaching distance of him, I stopped and murmured in the most comforting voice I could muster that he should come with me. Still, no wagging. In fact, he continued to sit frozen to the spot. Finally, I reached out. Tuna immediately bared his teeth and emitted a sharp and sustained growl. I quickly pulled my hand back. I couldn't believe it. He had never come remotely close to snarling at me before. In an instant, it was suddenly clear: Tuna was scared. No doubt about it, Tuna had gotten himself into a place where he could not figure out a way to return to safety. He was frightened for his life.

I didn't know what to do. As I stood there gazing at Tuna, I realized that, for the first time in our relationship, there seemed to be the distinct possibility he would bite me. I certainly didn't want to get bitten, but I somehow had to figure out a way to get us both down from the ledge and safely home. After letting a few more minutes go by, I slowly crouched down beside him and began talking to him softly in as comforting a tone as I could. Then I very gradually began to extend my open hand. I stopped with the palm up, just a few inches from his nose. Tuna stared at it intently. After what felt like an hour, he finally leaned forward and sniffed. Then his tongue came out and he gave me a single lick.

I took this as a signal that we were heading in the right direction. Still moving slowly, I dropped my hand a few inches and began to stroke his chest. He let me pat him for several minutes. Then I stood and gently picked him up.

Tuna was trembling but lay passively in my arms as I carefully picked my way down the steep rocky cliff to the beach. When I set him down on the sand, he stood motionless, tail down as I clipped the leash to his collar. Tuna walked obediently beside me as we made our way along the foot of the cliff until we found a gradual, easy path that led us back to the parking lot. I didn't begin to feel safe until we were in the car and heading toward home.

Emboldened by the sense of relief washing over me, as we drove I took the opportunity to give Tuna an earful regarding the propriety of peeing on one's owner. But I was careful to do this in the same kind and understanding tone I had adopted on the ledge. The truth was, I was by now feeling sorrier for Tuna than I was for myself. When we got home, I took a shower, rinsed out my shirt and towel, and, with a sigh, settled into a chair in front of the TV. After a few minutes, Tuna ambled over and flopped onto the floor by my feet.

Neither of us ever brought up the incident again.

Things settled in after that inauspicious start to our new life together in San Francisco. I started my third and final year of law school, and Tuna set about learning his neighborhood. Our routine was simple enough. I would get up every morning, let Tuna out to do his business, and then get ready for school. I would leave some food and water for the rest of the day. Tuna was almost always back at the front door of our flat by the time I was ready to depart for school. Sometimes he would arrive early and start scratching. If not an early arrival, then I would just call out for him, and predictably Tuna would return for a day of leisure in the house.

I was always amazed Tuna could find his way back. Ours was the middle of three flats in the building. The building was in the middle of the block surrounded by many other residential apartments, all looking pretty much the same. And this block of apartments was in the middle of many, many blocks of residential apartments, again all looking pretty similar. Still, Tuna always found his way back to the exact apartment.

Returning from school was also pretty much a set routine. Like a clock whose alarm is set for a certain hour, Tuna would be at the front door waiting for me. I could always count on a warm, excited greeting. In fact, it is understated to say his greeting was merely warm and excited. It was more like extremely high spirits, ecstasy, and unconditional love. Every evening it was as if I had been gone for years, the kind of joy humans reserve for the prospect of seeing a loved one after a long absence. Tuna greeted me with wild out-of-control jumping, and it seemed to me he was actually smiling. It was as if he had just won the World Series. It was something I got used to, but never tired of. On more than one occasion when I'd had a rough day in school or socially, it was Tuna's greeting that lifted my mood.

After the wild greeting and an exchange of hugs and kisses, Tuna went outside again to roam free, run, and do his business. This was his opportunity to do as he pleased. He took a longer time on his night run than in the morning. He was in sync with me and knew his liberty was more extended at this time of the day. It was usually an hour before I would hear Tuna scratching at the door signaling his return. I would feed Tuna his evening meal while I ate mine, with Tuna willingly enjoying some scraps of human food from my plate. Tuna was also very good at cleaning spillages from the meal preparation process. That is, unless he didn't like what was spilled on the floor (vegetables). Otherwise, he was better than a human at picking up scraps, because invariably he would, in addition to eating the scraps off the floor, lick the floor as well. Tuna was a vacuum and floor mop combined. He really earned his keep at dinnertime.

After dinner, I would sit at the desk in my bedroom reading law cases assigned as homework by one law professor or another, and Tuna would settle in for a nap by my feet. Study time over, I would relax with my roommates in the living room in front of the TV watching the news or some popular sitcom of the time. Tuna would once again join me by lying at my feet.

One of my roommates, Bob Trevorrow, was a recently returned Vietnam veteran who was attending San Francisco State College. He was my age, but not as far along in school because of his tour of duty. Bob was a great guy, and an exceptionally talented musician and singer. I loved hearing him sing around the house. He had a powerful voice and was also a compassionate person, lots of fun, witty, good looking, and a charming personality. My other male roommate was Tom Heuer. Like me, Tom was in his final year at Hastings College of the Law. Tom was a pleasant fellow, and a committed and dedicated law student. Every night he locked himself in his bedroom after dinner and studied until 11:00 p.m. Then he would come out to the living room to watch the Johnny Carson Show. You could set your clock by him. I enjoyed Tom's sense of humor and self-deprecating personality.

The other two roommates were young working women, not students. I didn't really know them very well. Bob had recruited them in an attempt to get our per-person rent down to a manageable amount of money. The two women shared the one remaining bedroom. Of course, living in the same flat, we gradually became acquainted and I got along with them well. The harmony of the group and the fiscal benefits all worked. I was very lucky. I had my own bedroom for privacy, so I could close myself off and study. I also was the only person to have a pet. Fortunately, Tuna was very well liked by all the roommates and it wasn't long before he became our arbitrator. If we needed to resolve a disagreement, we all looked to Tuna for an answer. For example, if Tuna was sitting, we would each pick how long he would remain sitting before he would invariably lie down. Whoever was closest to that time would prevail in the disputed matter. It was a reflection of Tuna's stature in the flat that everyone abided by this method of problem solving.

The remainder of a typical evening consisted of me getting ready for bed and then retiring to my room for some fun reading and bedtime. Tuna loved this time of the day. Instead of just lying at my feet, he joined me in bed and snuggled with me for the night.

The next morning the routine would start again. Granted, it wasn't very exciting, but I was grateful for the normalcy it provided to my life. I am not an optimistic person by nature and am definitely a worrywart. These negative aspects of my personality, coupled with the stress of law school, where everyone around me seemed like a genius, plus the loneliness I felt being a single person with no money in an expensive city, made life a downer at times. The weather in San Francisco didn't help either. It seemed like winter all the time. It felt bleak and gloomy and dark. Having Tuna with me allowed me to bask in the warmth of his loyalty and devotion. With him as my companion, I could imagine a far worse fate than being right where I was at this time in my life.

CHAPTER EIGHT

Parties, Social Life, and Tuna's Influence

My social life as a law student was not terribly exciting, but between my roommates and my own efforts, there were parties to attend and people to meet. Every so often, one of my roommates or I would host a party. It is not modesty that precludes me from bragging about my parties. It's that my parties were abysmal failures. Looking back, I realize one difficulty was I would invite friends from different points in my life. For example, I would invite my old high school buddies plus some of my college friends from Cal and, of course, my current law school friends. The result was that my Napa friends hung out together in one part of the house, and my college friends were huddled in another, and my law school friends were in yet another location. That left me to spend the evening worrying about everyone being happy. I scurried back and forth between the groups, trying to make sure everyone was having fun. I felt like a mediator facilitating different groups of people with separate backgrounds and interests, and trying to bring them all together to achieve the mutual goal of having a good time. Another problem with my parties may have been that the guys always outnumbered the girls by a 5 to 1 ratio, and the ratio was even worse if you eliminated the girls who were already spoken for. Being out of the game, so to speak, girls in committed relationships didn't really count, so there was truly a paucity of girls at my parties. And this was ironic, because the number one goal of my parties was for me to meet girls. Clearly, these gatherings were doomed from the outset.

The success of my parties was summed up by Mike Howard, one of my Napa friends. He had driven down for one of my dismal parties with Bill Murray and Del Domezio, and the three of them were sitting around the living room drinking beer. "You know, Ray," he said, "we could have stayed in Napa and done this." It was so true.

Although my own parties always left something to be desired, it didn't mean there weren't some exciting parties at our flat. The most memorable was during that third year, after Tuna had moved in. The reason it was so memorable was the entertainment Tuna provided.

It was a Saturday evening and my roommate Bob Trevorrow was the organizer of the party. As a result, I did not know many of the people at the party, since Bob was not a law student at Hastings, but an undergraduate student at San Francisco State. Most of the people at the party, therefore, were Bob's friends from his college, whom I'd never met. I was fine with this, because I figured I might meet some new people, and more specifically new girls.

Unfortunately, the evening did not go as I hoped.

The party started out agreeably enough. People arrived in stages with a few arriving at the start time and more showing up over the next hour or two. The guests were eating our chips and dips and drinking beer. Some were smoking pot and more than a few were starting to get high and buzzed. Then two guys I didn't know began to roughhouse. It started out friendly enough but developed into a full-fledged wrestling match. They were both still laughing periodically, but eventually one of the guys flipped the other one to the floor and was trying to pin him. The guy flat on his back on the floor had one leg sticking out with his knee bent and one foot partially on the ground.

The excitement of the match fascinated Tuna. He loved it when people embraced, and always wanted to be part of the celebration, the hugging, and, in the spirit and era of free love, the lovemaking. It was not uncommon for him, in such settings, to joyously and lovingly jump into and onto the people involved. He never waited for an invitation. From his view, a demonstration of love and happiness would always be welcome and that was enough for him to get involved. In this particular situation, the combatants were still vaguely acting like it was a friendly affair, and Tuna wanted to be a part of it.

Unfortunately, it was not wrestling that Tuna had in mind. It became apparent he was sexually aroused and because he didn't believe in foreplay, he leaped at the first limb he could find, and climbed aboard humping like a jackhammer. In this case, it was the leg of the combatant who was on his back. Tuna was on this leg like a Gila monster, his paws surrounding the shin so that he had a good lock. He was pumping on the shin with complete abandon.

The human participants of the wrestling match were so into their own struggle, they apparently did not even notice the amorous sideshow that Tuna had added to their athletic exhibition. As a result, no one attempted to kick Tuna off his lover, or more precisely, his lover's limb.

When the wrestling match started, I was hanging out in the kitchen (my favorite room in any house). At some point, the commotion caught my attention. By the time I came into the living room, the public lovemaking was just about over. Tuna's sexual activity rarely took very long because it was usually interrupted by the owner of the non-consenting shin or by me. But not this time. In fact, this was the only time I ever recall Tuna not being interrupted.

As a result of Tuna being allowed to continue his lovemaking to fruition, my visual image of those last brief moments have left me with psychic scars that I bear to this day. They were exacerbated when the "rape" victim angrily demanded that I pay for a cleaning of his Levis. I politely declined the demand, citing something about consent between a dog and a shin. The party ended shortly thereafter.

In addition to these quirky and largely unsatisfying parties at the flat, my social life included "keggers" at various local colleges – especially Lone Mountain College for Women (now part of the University of San Francisco). They were well organized, in part because I had nothing to do with putting them on. A women's college hosted them, so the only women attending were from that school. Since Hastings was a graduate school, many of my law student friends were already married or had steady girlfriends. Their resulting unavailability swung the odds in my favor. I needed all the help I could get. Being just under 5 feet 6 inches tall and always battling (and usually losing to) a weight problem, I really appreciated anything that improved my odds.

It had become apparent to me back at the beginning of law school that male law school students became more popular the further along in law school they progressed. It was not an uncommon question for a "kegger girl" to ask a law student what year he was in. If the answer was "first year," then the conversation might not last beyond that answer. However, if he was a third-year student then conversations became lengthier and more exciting. It appeared that some ladies thought the law student might then be worth dating. Once I figured out that the question of "what year are you in" would be asked in the first ten minutes of any conversation, I didn't mind the question at all. In fact, by the time I entered my third year, I had been proudly representing myself as a third-year law student for approximately two years. Anything that might improve my chances with females was something I wanted in my arsenal.

Although I didn't bring Tuna with me to the keggers at Lone Mountain, I did debate the possibility with myself. I knew Tuna would be attractive to women because he was so cute. However, I couldn't risk him launching into his jumping and humping routine which was such a turnoff to most human beings, especially, I feared, women. Also, I didn't want to spend a lot of time breaking up dogfights, which was another real possibility. I wanted to use my time meeting women.

Even with the advantage afforded by my perennial status as a third-year law student, the odds of meeting a woman and actually obtaining a phone number felt daunting. As I've already mentioned, I was short and stout. I had a friendly personality, but I rarely succeeded in bringing it out at these get-togethers. I was too shy. I could abstractly think about how to interact with girls, but when I came into their actual presence, my mind flooded with thoughts like "She is not going to like me," "No one wants a 'little drink of water'," "She's taller than me – I'm out." This led to me being hesitant to engage girls in conversations.

Notwithstanding these seemingly insurmountable challenges, I did succeed in meeting a woman at one of these events. This meeting was because of my buddy Paul Supnik. He actually met her first and then introduced her to me. But once I had my chance, I did everything I could to charm her. Apparently, it worked. She agreed to see me again, and after that we became an item. I really fell for her because she loved to have fun and experience things. We became close quickly and spent all of our time outside of school together. We went on picnics and other outings. She asked me to come to her family home in Ukiah to spend the weekend and meet her parents. Her dad seemed to like me. I met her two sisters and we got along great.

We had been going together for 5 months when one evening I took her back to the university to drop her off after a date. When I got back to my flat, I realized she had left her purse. One of my roommates suggested I go through it. He said I would probably be surprised what I would find out. I rejected his suggestion outright. It struck me as a complete invasion of her right to privacy and it violated the golden rule. I would not want anyone to go through my wallet. What kind of a person did my roommate think I was anyway?

Ten minutes later I found myself going through her purse. I was inspecting the contents like a farmer assessing a mare at an auction. Everything was under review. I found a photograph of a young man. On the backside of the picture were some romantic dribblings to "my girlfriend." The word "love" was in it and so was "forever."

Well, I didn't know what to do. To confront her would be to admit I had searched through her purse, but to not confront her would kill me. I had to know. I guess it could have been a past love. Maybe it could have been a picture of her brother. Especially if the two siblings were into incest. There was a range of possibilities. I tried to stay calm.

When we met the next day, I immediately blurted out what I had done. She didn't like it at all and became angry. I tried to redirect the conversation by agreeing it was not right to do what I did, and I apologized profusely. Then, with my apology accomplished, I asked about the picture. With disconcerting openness, she said it wasn't a past boyfriend or an incestuous brother. It was her high school boyfriend, who was in the Army stationed in Germany. They were engaged, but she dated because she wanted to have fun and experience a social life in his absence. They were going to get married upon his discharge from the service in a year.

A silence ensued, which I broke by pleading a gastrointestinal issue requiring my immediate exit. With that explanation, I left the campus. We never spoke again. I really liked this girl. But the moment she explained that our relationship was time limited, I realized I couldn't continue seeing her. I was looking for a relationship with the possibility of going all in.

I went home, where Tuna set about the business of restoring my mental health.

CHAPTER NINE

The Unanticipated Change

Tuna's routine of going out for runs each morning and evening continued. He was always excited about his free time, and also consistent in returning after he had finished his business and gotten some exercise. Otherwise he was completely content to be near me, and eager to do so as much as possible. Looking back, it seems strange and irresponsible for me to have just let Tuna run free; but he always returned on schedule and always managed to be safe. Except for one occasion.

This particular day started out normally enough. The morning was like any other in the budding spring of the year. It was Thursday, which meant it was a school day for me. Per our standing routine, I let Tuna out for his morning run. The difference from this usual custom was not apparent until Tuna did not return home promptly as he always had done in the past. In fact, Tuna did not return at all. At first, I went to the front door and called for him. When he didn't respond, I went inside to get dressed. Then I returned to the front stoop to once again call for him. Nothing. This was really unusual. I went out into the street and called several times. Then I walked around the block three times, still calling to him. Nothing.

By now seriously worried, I got in my car and slowly drove around the neighborhood, calling out the window. Again nothing. I drove a bigger perimeter. Still no sighting or response. I was up against the starting time of my first class. Reluctantly, I turned away from the neighborhood and drove to school. The first class was endless. The moment it let out, I hurried to the pay phone in the basement and called the animal pound. I was informed no dog matching Tuna's description had been brought in, nor reported injured or dead.

My last class ended at 3:00 that afternoon, and I again ran to the phone and called the pound. Still, nothing. I drove home as fast as the city traffic allowed. There was no sign of Tuna, so I once again set about driving slowly around the neighborhood, hoarsely yelling his name out the open car window.

By now, I was very concerned. I had such mixed emotions. I was anxious that I couldn't find him, but happy I didn't spot a dog that had been hit by a vehicle and left for dead on the side of the road. At last returning home, I rounded up my roommates and asked for their assistance. By this time in our cohabitation, my roommates had become close friends with Tuna, so they were more than willing to join in the hunt. We formed a search party. There were five of us, with three cars. The two female roommates split up into two cars, one with me and one with Bob. Tom drove his car solo. We divided up the entire Sunset District into three sections, one for each of the three vehicles. The plan was to search each person's district for one hour and then return to base. After an hour, all teams of roommates had returned to the flat, and each unit reported no sightings or any success. Tuna did not come home that evening or the next day. With the generous assistance of my roommates we continued to search, driving around the Sunset each evening when we got home.

After a couple of weeks, I stopped asking my roommates to help, but I continued to drive through the neighborhood each night, looking for Tuna. I continued to check with the pound every day or two. In fact, I checked with them so often I was on a first name basis with the people who ran the place. They were surprisingly kind and it became apparent they didn't mind my frequent calls. After another week or two, the calls evolved into something like, "Hi, it's me, any sign of Tuna?" They would say no and suggest I check back in a few days. They always made a point of saying not to allow a 72-hour period to elapse between my calls, so that there would never be a chance Tuna could be unclaimed for the period of time they retained dogs before disposing of them. I never let that 72 hours elapse without calling in.

All my efforts to find my Tuna were in vain. He had vanished.

Tuna's disappearance was a savage blow. But time moved on. After several weeks of daily searching and daily phone contacts with the animal pound, I finally began to gradually curtail my efforts. I left my name and number with the animal pound in case a dog was found fitting Tuna's description. I continued to keep an eye out for him. But the day finally came when I was no longer actively looking for him. My attention had shifted to the sad task of adjusting to losing him. I knew in my heart my dog was gone. I began to grieve. He had been with me through college and law school. Tuna had been my closest buddy and I had lost him.

It nagged at me that I hadn't found Tuna's body, nor was he ever picked up by the pound. However, when these thoughts flooded in, they only served to revive my anxiety and grief. I actively pushed them out of my mind. I still carried my little pal in my heart, but I told myself to accept reality. I admitted to my friends Tuna was gone, as opposed to saying, "Tuna is missing but we keep searching for him and hope we will find him." When a friend asked about my fun but quirky dog, I would simply say, "Tuna is gone. He disappeared some time ago and I never could find him." Or, if a conversation about animals came up with a new acquaintance who did not know Tuna, I simply would say, "I don't have any pets," without even bothering to mention my Tuna.

I was learning life is a series of adjustments. This was an adjustment I needed to make. Life needed to go on and, of course, it did.

CHAPTER TEN

The Big Surprise

It was late one sunny afternoon some three and a half months after Tuna disappeared. I was returning from law school with my roommate Tom in my 1961 Ford Fairlane – a four-door sedan with faded, sky-blue paint and lots of dents and rust spots. It had come from my dad's wrecking yard. The car was not a "chick magnet" in any respect. It couldn't have outrun a dairy cow overdue for milking. But then, as I've explained, not very many things about me could be described as a chick magnet, particularly now that Tuna was gone. We finally made it through the Friday afternoon traffic to our flat in the Sunset and were delighted to find a parking place just down the street. As we parked, I glanced across to the flat and spotted an unfamiliar dog by our front door. This was unusual, given the nature of this old apartment building. The building had three separate flats, which were on three different floors. Our flat was the middle flat and the entrance was the middle of three immediately adjacent doors sharing the same stoop. The dog was not only directly in front of the middle door, but seemed to be scratching, as if seeking to gain entrance. It definitely looked like this dog intended to be at this exact door. He was scratching exactly in the way my Tuna used to do.

There was a sudden resurgence of the old futile hope, but as much as I wanted to believe this was Tuna, from my vantage point, I could only see the dog from his backside. Still in the car, approximately 100 feet away, I remarked to

Tom with studied casualness that this dog appeared to look like Tuna but was larger, better groomed, and much huskier. In fact, this dog was fat. It bordered on morbidly obese. Tuna had been somewhat unkempt, with a slender build, even scrawny – more along the lines of a Tijuana survival dog. But otherwise, it was dawning on me the appearance of this dog was a spitting image of Tuna. It was as if they were twins, except one was fat, well groomed, and soft looking, and the other had been unkempt, skinny, and scrawny looking.

I climbed out of the car without taking my eyes off this pudgy dog. As I approached the staircase, I softly called "Tuna?" The dog turned around. Upon seeing me, he charged directly at me, jumping up in my arms, licking me wildly. I staggered backwards, bowled over by the weight of the dog. It was clear this fat dog in my arms WAS Tuna! This new version of Tuna weighed much more than I remembered. He had a huge, fat belly. And this Tuna was wearing a dog collar with a nametag.

The name on the tag said "Peter," and listed a phone number. Hmmmm? Was this still my Tuna?

I brought Tuna into the flat and re-introduced him to my roommates, who were not just pleased to see Tuna, but also palpably delighted to see me happy again. Tuna was deliriously overjoyed to be with all the people in the house.

After we spent some celebratory time at the flat enjoying Tuna's homecoming, I decided I should call the number on the dog tag and talk to the owner of "Peter" to explain the mistake. If there had been any questions in anyone's mind, by now I had decisive proof this was indeed Tuna: he had gleefully performed several of his tricks. The only possible conversation I could have was to tell this person I had found my dog. As I dialed the phone number, potential conversations raced through my head. I hadn't planned what to say. I didn't know how to explain I was sure this was my dog.

After a couple of rings someone answered the phone. The voice was that of a young girl. I said I would like to speak to one of her parents. The girl replied that neither of her parents was home. I asked if she had a dog. She responded immediately, "Why, have you found him? My doggie has gone missing and we have been searching all over for him. Do you have him?"

I explained I had a dog with a nametag with this number on it, but this dog was my dog. The girl asked me for a description. I described Tuna as he presently looked. The girl said in an excited, raised voice, "That's him, that's Peter, my dog!"

I said in as calm a voice as possible, the dog was mine. The girl started to grill me with a barrage of questions. She asked how old the dog was and what did he like to eat, and what tricks, if any, could he do. I explained the dog was about three years old. I could hear on the other end of the line the girl whispering to someone else, "He's lying, because Peter is only one year old. My dad told me so."

It was apparent the girl was not going to be persuaded Tuna belonged to me. I said I would come over to talk to her parents when they were home. The girl told me her parents would be home around 5:00 p.m. and I should come over at 6:00 p.m. I agreed and then got off the phone. The question suddenly occurred to me: should I bring Tuna to this meeting or not? Ultimately, I decided not to bring Tuna. I was not going to take any chances the girl's parents would try to resume custody.

I started to fantasize different scenarios playing out at this confrontational meeting between the rival dog owners, each claiming to be the true and correct owner of Tuna/Peter. I envisioned the girl wanting to put Tuna/Peter in the middle of the room, with the girl and me on different sides of the room. Each of us would call out to the dog. Whomever the dog went to would be the winner, and the owner of the dog forevermore. That match was not a risk that I was willing to take. It was entirely possible the friendly Tuna might go to whoever called him first. It was too unpredictable. Besides, Tuna WAS my dog, and I wasn't going to let any silly game determine who was awarded care, control, and custody of him. No. I decided I would not take Tuna with me on the visit to the girl's house.

At precisely 6 p.m. I showed up at the girl's house to call upon her parents. My sole purpose was to explain Tuna was mine and I was going to keep him. I would be diplomatic and acknowledge the girl quite understandably had grown attached to the dog and loved him; but I'd had Tuna from birth for 3 years – which meant 3 years, as opposed to her relationship with Tuna, aka Peter, for only 3.5 months. It was also my intention to let her know that I, too, loved Tuna, and would take good care of him.

An adult male opened the door and I introduced myself to this man. The man was indeed the father of the twelve-year-old girl. I described the situation, giving a brief history of the dog, which included pictures of Tuna as a puppy and later as a full-grown dog. This was to dispel the notion that Tuna was only one year old, and also to demonstrate I was intimately familiar with the dog, proving my ownership beyond a reasonable doubt. I guess I was trying to play lawyer.

The father was very understanding, but did not invite me in. I was glad he didn't, because I didn't want to stay any longer than I needed. The father seemed to be satisfied with the explanation I gave and indicated he was convinced I was the true owner of Tuna. I could see the little girl peeking out at me from behind her dad. I expressed my sympathies for the man's daughter and thanked him profusely for his understanding. The entire conversation lasted less than five minutes. It had gone better than I had dared hope.

As I turned away, I felt a flood of relief. There was no unpleasant confrontation. I didn't have to see or talk to the little girl, who must have been upset. The explanations were left for her father, as they should be. I hoped he would be comforting. I had walked to the meeting because it turned out Tuna had been living only three blocks from our flat. I was wondering if he had tried to get home. I guessed, given his weight gain, he was probably kept inside the whole time. I hadn't seen any sign of him outside on a leash when we were searching. As I neared our flat, I was so happy. I couldn't wait to tell Tuna and my roommates we would not be bothered again. Tuna was home to stay.

CHAPTER ELEVEN

A Return to Normalcy

Now that Tuna was back at home, he dropped right back into the routine – albeit a slightly modified routine. I did not let Tuna outside off his leash for the first month. Instead of just letting him out, I took him for walks in the morning and evening – before I left for law school and after I returned at the end of the day.

During this last year of law school, I had a couple of very good friends I hung out with all the time. One was my roommate, Bob Trevorrow; the other was Mike Low, a recent graduate of Hastings. Mike was a caretaker at Mt. St. Joseph's Orphanage. He lived rent free in a cottage on the grounds of the orphanage, in exchange for his services as a caretaker. Caretaking meant he had to do night checks of the grounds and buildings and be at the imperious summoning of the nuns if they needed any services for the children.

I idolized Bob and Mike. They were both talented musicians and singers. Mike was also a brilliant law student who possessed impeccable logic – like Mr. Spock from Star Trek. He could twist anything into a winning argument. He had an excellent sense of humor. Both Bob and Mike were quite successful with women. Most important, they were decent, kind people who always seemed to be rooting for the underdog. Mike was a mountain climber and Bob played in a rock band. They were always having fun while still getting their work done. What was not to like about them? And, as for friends, they were perfect for me. I have always had a reluctant side. I tended to be more of a passive recipient of life than an active participant. I was the ultimate couch potato. I loved sitting around with Tuna and watching sports, sit-coms, talk shows, and movies on TV. I loved going to the movies and I loved going out to eat. That was about it. The rest of the time I either worried about law school or did homework. These two guys would always try to bring me along to get me out of my shell.

Of course, Bob and Mike enjoyed my interests (such as they were) as well. The three of us would sit around watching TV or attend parties together. These interests were free, and all of us were without parental support and or significant income – all I had was a part-time job as a janitor at Hastings. We sought out activities that didn't cost much, such as going to the beach or hiking at Yosemite National Park, movies, parties, and ushering at plays that allowed you free admission.

Mike and Bob had become friends whom I trusted and relied on. Our enjoyment of each other's company was mutual.

By this time, it went without saying, anyone who hung out with me would have to accept the company of Tuna. Bob and Mike were not only okay with this – they embraced it. They regularly talked directly to Tuna as if he was a human being. It wasn't long before they had invented a make-believe gang with Tuna as their rebel leader. The gang consisted of Mike, Bob, and me.

They dubbed Tuna the Generalissimo. Whenever we introduced him to new people, we would say in enthusiastic unison: "The Spanish call him, *El Fabuloso*; to the French he is known as *Le Magnifique;* but to his

American friends he is known as Tuna the Wonder Dog!!!!"

We, his loyal minions, would then extend a special hand salute to the Generalissimo, which consisted of a symbolic hand wiping of our butts, followed by sniffing our fingers, and extending our arms in what can only be described as a Nazi-like salute.

This admittedly disgusting introduction was often the prelude to Tuna performing his tricks, including Sitting Up, Rolling Over, Jumping into My Arms, and Looking for Airplanes. Tuna always executed them with precision and to the complete delight of his audience. By now, Tuna had become a veteran, accustomed to performing in front of audiences large and small.

On weekends the gang favored recreational events out of town. Trips to the Sierras were particularly thrilling. Mike was really into mountain climbing, had all the right gear, and had taken several lessons. On one particular occasion, Mike and I took a trip to Yosemite National Park.

I hadn't ever taken Tuna on any of these trips to the mountains. But I felt guilty leaving him alone, especially after coming so close to losing him. I knew Mike wanted to hike and do some rock climbing, and since I had neither experience nor equipment, I wasn't sure if I would have anything to do. I thought it would be nice to have Tuna along in case I needed somebody to hang out with. Plus, I always found nights camping in the mountains to be really cold and thought Tuna might be an impromptu heater. I decided to take him on his first trip to the mountains.

We arrived at the trailhead in Yosemite in my '61 Ford Fairlane. It was in the mid-morning hours on a Friday. It didn't take long to pull together our gear and we were underway, lugging rope, pitons, and camping equipment, together with wonderful selections of beef stroganoff, macaroni and cheese, and chicken and rice cacciatore – all of which had been scientifically freeze-dried. But dinner proved to be a long way off. The hike was lengthy and hard, straight up a mountain that was mostly steep. Where it wasn't steep, it was "rich in exposure," meaning, while possibly a little less steep, there were no trees or big boulders for shelter or, more important, to grab on to – you were "exposed" to the heights with no safety net.

As we made our way up the mountain, Tuna was constantly running circles around us, and then careening off by himself, up and down the mountainside sniffing rocks, marking trees, chasing chipmunks, and harassing other hikers. He was always in running mode. It became pretty clear Tuna would get exhausted. Tuna had never been in the high elevation of Yosemite and had not had time to adjust.

Sure enough, after running around like a mad dog, Tuna finally settled back with us as we continued our slow but steady ascent. Before long, even our steady deliberate pace became too much for Tuna. He was so wiped out that he began to dry heave, forcing us to take a break on the mountainside, still far from our goal.

It was a long break during which Tuna reclined, panting at the rate of a wild colt shooting out the gate. At length he began to recover, his breathing steadied, and he gave the appearance of finally being ready for more. We resumed our trek up the mountainside, observing a measured, even pace. After another couple of hours, we came to a clearing where we would break for the night. By now, it was dusk. Tuna flopped down and appeared to go to sleep. As soon as we began setting up our cooking equipment, he once again sprang up, looking as if he was completely restored and perky. The plan was to pitch camp, make dinner, and get to bed early so we could get an early morning start on the balance of our climb. We needed to reach the cliff Mike had picked out by mid-morning, which would leave us the rest of the day for rock climbing (pitons, rope, and all) and lessons in rappelling down a steep mountainside.

The pitching of camp consisted of finding the most level area possible within this amazingly unlevel site where we had stopped for the evening. Settling on a rocky incline, we put out our sleeping bags (neither Mike nor I brought a tent) and set up our camp stove fueled by propane. We fanned out under the surrounding trees and gathered wood for a fire and chopped some of it up for kindling. Then there was a great dinner of beef stroganoff and Michelob beer. Dessert was brandy straight from our respective flasks (neither of us forgot our flasks; we had more than enough alcohol). With no other menu choices available, Tuna also had beef stroganoff and fresh water from our canteens. After this satisfying dinner, we sat around the fire sipping our brandy and talking about the adventure that would start tomorrow morning. Tuna sat half on and half off my lap. A pleasant feeling of contentment came over me. I was warm, Tuna was with me, and there was no more strenuous climbing for the evening.

Finally, it was time for bed. We retired to our respective sleeping bags for our slumber. Tuna immediately joined me by slipping into my sleeping bag. I was more than happy to share my bag with Tuna. Unlike Mike's goose-down bag, which could carry its occupant through sub-zero weather, I had a modest sleeping bag from Brewster's Army-Navy store in Napa. But with Tuna burrowed down by my feet, both of us were cuddly warm the entire night. As we went to sleep, I basked in the warmth of my dog's fur and stared up at the blanket of beauty provided by the brightly shining stars. What an incredible way to go to sleep.

The next morning arrived with a cold crisp wind hitting me in my face, as well as the rays of the sun, minus the warmth. Mike, Tuna, and I rose and somehow managed a hearty breakfast of cold cereal and coffee. Tuna feasted on Milk-bones and fresh water. We packed our gear and set off.

Soon the journey became more earnest as we moved up the mountainside. Steep climbing, with the aid of ropes and pitons, commenced. As the three of us ascended the mountain, it became apparent Tuna was experiencing gastrointestinal problems, possibly caused by the delicate cuisine of freeze-dried stroganoff. The odor proved incredibly foul, causing Mike to audibly complain and me to gag. Finally, after overcoming great obstacles of steep climbing and odorous air, we arrived at the summit of the mountain, where a vast, vertical slice of pure rock awaited us. Mike pointed at the rock and said, "Welcome to Rock Climbing Country." He also pointed out other rock climbers scaling similar sharp, high-rise, slabs of rock, hundreds of yards away. They looked like little ants on a wall.

I tied Tuna to a scraggly alpine bush so that he could safely observe my prowess in mountaineering. Mike gave me some basic climbing lessons – the part about going up – but neglected to give any instruction on how to descend a mountainside. The art of descending a steep slope is called rappelling, and without proper knowledge, it can be treacherous. So, with no lessons and no practice in descending, I started my climb with rope and pitons in hand. I was excited, yet nervous. The climb up was fairly easy. Mike had gone first, hammering in the pitons for us both, so I only had to worry about climbing the rock and securing the rope. I did this well, with only a couple of slips. Mike climbed all the way up and then secured a rope at the top of the mountain. It took me another 10 minutes to reach the top. I was sweaty and tired, but exhilarated, as I peered down from the ledge on top. The view was magnificent with the large expanse of majestic rocks, trees, other vegetation, and crisp blue skies with beautiful clouds. I could see Tuna, like a speck tied to the scraggly bush below.

After we had regarded the expansive view for a few minutes, Mike said it was time to climb back down. Before we set out, he put his hand on my arm and gave me a one sentence instruction. "Ray, lean out as you descend."

As I commenced descending, I immediately began to feel the need to get close to the surface of the mountain for security. This turned out to be exactly the wrong thing to do. It was the opposite of what Mike instructed, which was to lean out. It was counter intuitive for the naive climber. I felt a strong need to be close to the mountainside. From the start, I did not keep my weight and body out. Within a few moments, my feet gave way, and I quickly realized I was losing my grip. I began to slide, desperately trying to lock onto the rock. I felt the rocky slope slipping by as I began to twist on the rope. Then I was in full freefall. As I spun around I could see how close I was to the rock. The velocity of my twisting increased, and I smashed my head against the rock. I heard Tuna barking frantically below me.

When I hit the ground, I felt queasy and disoriented. Incongruously, I noticed my hat had flown off of me. What I saw alarmed me – blood! I put my hand to the back of my head where a troubling lump was beginning to form, as well as an open laceration that felt warm and wet. Mike was scurrying down the side of the mountain. Tuna was still barking incessantly but couldn't get loose. The moment he was down, Mike began attending to me. I was left with an indentation on the back of my head that is still there to this day. After Mike completed his first aid efforts, I went over to Tuna to reassure him.

In truth, he comforted me as well.

Once the commotion had died down, Mike blamed himself for the lack of appropriate instructions, and apologized. But he insisted I get back up on the horse and attempt a proper and appropriate descent. I wanted to decline this tempting invitation to risk my life again, but Mike said I would be terrified of mountain climbing forever if I didn't try again and conquer the descent. I was perfectly happy with the notion of not mountain climbing or descending ever again, but Mike would have none of this.

Mike gave me more instructions, stressing that leaning my body outward would result in a successful descent. He told me that hugging the surface, while feeling instinctively safer, was never going to result in a successful descent. I was still ready to call it a weekend, but with Mike's not-so-gentle nudging and encouragement, I again scaled the mountain. Once more on the top, we carefully reviewed the proper procedure on how to rappel, and then commenced the descent.

This time everything went smoothly. I leaned way out and "walked" down the mountain, sometimes even hopping or bouncing as I descended. Everything went perfectly. I did the rappelling over and over that afternoon. I would never again forget this skill.

The day had started out rough but ended with a gratifying breakthrough. To my great surprise, I actually enjoyed rappelling down mountainsides.

Mike, Tuna, and I hiked back to the base of Yosemite and loaded our gear in the car. Off we went back home to San Francisco, readying ourselves for another week of law school.

CHAPTER TWELVE

Employment at the Psychiatric Center

Most of the time, life for Tuna and me consisted of the monotony of studying during the week and lying around during the weekend, except for the occasional jaunt to the beach (weather permitting) or hiking around in nearby woods. These experiences were usually unremarkable, but memories of these unremarkable times are some of my most cherished recollections. It was peaceful and wonderful to just enjoy life with my dog.

In the summer between my second and third year in law school I deviated from my usual routine of working at the Kaiser Steel Fabrication Plant in Napa. It had been a great job with great pay, but that summer I had an adventure. I bummed around Europe for most of the school vacation. Normally, I would not have been able to afford European travel, but I spotted an advertisement in the newspaper for a round-trip ticket from San Francisco to London for $299.00. Even in 1970, this was incredibly inexpensive. After further research, I purchased Arthur Fromm's *Europe on $5.00 a Day*, which turned out to be my Bible on the trip. It told me that train travel would be the cheapest and safest way to journey, so I purchased a Eurail pass covering the whole time I would be in Europe.

Spending money for travel was not something I had ever done. I was very frugal. But because this was such an inexpensive way to travel to Europe, I carefully reviewed my savings to see if I could find a way to go. I knew this could be a trip of a lifetime. I created a budget based on staying at youth hostels and on overnight trains (with a Eurail pass I could stay on board all night for no extra charge). I also planned to make it a point to eat at inexpensive cafes as recommended in Fromm's book. I compared this budget with the savings from my janitor job at Hastings, as well as my previous summer's Kaiser job. I decided I could afford the trip.

Next, I asked Mom if Tuna could stay with her and Dad in Napa. Mom had no objections, because she wanted to make this trip possible for me. She was pleased and excited I would be able to see my relatives in Italy. She even asked my Nonni (Dad's mother) to write a letter to all of my Italian relatives explaining who I was and how I was related. Nonni did this for both my paternal and maternal relatives. With my family's blessing, off I went.

For two months, I crisscrossed Europe by train, visiting my relatives in Italy, and staying in youth hostels in other parts of Europe. I was constantly consulting Fromm's book, which led me to theaters, where I could watch a first-class performance in London for $1.00 American or discover a five-course Indian dinner for $2.00 American. Of course, I didn't heed the author's warning about the spicy nature of the food and ended up purchasing about $15.00 worth of Coca Colas to put out the fire. Cokes were prohibitively expensive, but definitely necessary that evening.

When I returned to San Francisco, it was too late in the summer to work in Napa at Kaiser Steel. But, for the first time, I had experienced spending money during summer vacation, instead of earning it. I had stuck to my budget for most of my travels but ended up spending more money for gifts than I intended. I bought a nice piece of jewelry for Mom, a Swiss clock for Dad, and clothes for my brother Eugene. I should have saved the

$40.00 for the clock I toted throughout Europe, because when I presented it to Dad he said, "Boy, did you get taken!"

It was clear I needed to find a job in San Francisco for the balance of the summer, so I could earn some money before school started. That was my state of mind when I read in the paper that the Langley-Porter Psychiatric Center was offering to pay people $2.00 per hour to smoke marijuana. This late in the summer, I didn't have many job options. Law school was going to resume in a few short weeks. This was only a temporary job. It seemed made to order.

I applied and was accepted for the job. The job turned out to be as amazingly easy as it sounded. On my first day, the lab staff directed me to a room full of the other accepted applicants, some of whom I knew as fellow law students. One, in fact, was my good friend, Mike Low. After about ten minutes of waiting, the hall door opened, and a nurse came into the room. She was dressed in a white uniform and was absolutely beautiful. She was followed by a markedly less beautiful 50-year-old male doctor dressed in a white lab coat. One by one they took each of us into small adjoining separate rooms. My name was called, and I went into a small room that was painted all white. It had a couch with an armchair next to it. Across the room was a stainless-steel table that had a stack of papers on it. The doctor was the only person in the room. He had a clipboard in his hand and was looking down at it as I entered. He looked up at me and smiled, introducing himself. He asked me how I was and how to pronounce my name. With the social amenities out of the way, he explained the program, telling me I would be expected to come to the Center three times a week. I would be there a total of four hours a day. Some of that time I would be smoking marijuana, and some of the time would be for interviews about my experience including the effects of the pot on me. The interview sessions would be both before and after I smoked. This sounded too good to be true. I was being paid to smoke a popular drug that most of my friends had to purchase to enjoy. The best part of the program was that it was completely legal. I felt like I was getting away with murder.

The doctor asked if I had any questions. I responded that I did not, except to ask when we started? He said right now. He then handed me a sheaf of papers, which turned out to be consent forms and waivers of liability, which I signed without reading. He gathered up the paperwork and shook my hand, telling me it was nice to meet me. He told me to wait in the room.

Shortly after he left, the nurse entered the room carrying a clipboard. She was stunningly gorgeous, with a shapely figure and an air of elegance. She seemed kind as well. She had silky, shoulder-length black hair, olive skin, big brown eyes, and a smile that lit up the room. She was probably about my age, which was 24 years old, and she was shorter than me, which filled my heart with hope. Her all-white nurse's uniform complemented her olive skin. In short, she was a knockout. It is important to note I felt this way about her before I got higher than a kite.

The nurse introduced herself and began the interview. She asked me if I worked or was in school. I proudly told her I was a third-year law student and would graduate next May. She then explained she would ask me questions before I smoked the marijuana, and then supply a marijuana cigarette for me to smoke while she left the room. She would then return to ask me post-smoking questions. She asked, "Do you have any questions before we begin?"

I didn't have any questions, but I wanted to continue to talk to her. So, I asked her how many cigarettes I would be smoking each day, and she answered usually only two, but it could be more. I asked if I could read books while I smoked. She said it was fine and, if I wanted to, bring some books or other material to occupy my time. I asked if I got so high I couldn't drive home, would the Center provide transportation? She said they would not, but she reminded me not to drive if I was under the influence of drugs. She was so polite and engaging, I couldn't tell if our conversation was going well, or if she was just a kind soul who liked people in general.

She rose from the armchair and picked up a silver rectangular box from the stainless-steel table. Opening the box, she took out 2 marijuana cigarettes already rolled like commercial ones. She walked over to where I was sitting on the couch and handed them to me. She gave me a book of matches and told me she would be back in 45 minutes. Smiling warmly, she said, "Enjoy," and left the room carrying the clipboard and silver box. I was hoping she didn't see the *Sports Illustrated* magazine I had brought with me to read. I decided next time I would bring a Hemingway novel or something that might impress her. I made a mental note to purchase more sophisticated reading material.

At some point after I finished smoking the marijuana, the nurse returned with clipboard in hand. She administered the "after" questions and I answered them as best I could. They all dealt with the effects of the marijuana, such as, "Do you feel the effects of smoking the marijuana? On a scale of 1 -10 with 10 being the best marijuana ever, how do you rate this marijuana?"

I answered these questions at some length. As subsequent sessions unfolded, I always enjoyed this question and answer period because it was time I could spend with the nurse, time that I treasured. Not being very pleasing to the senses myself, it was a pleasure to see someone so beautiful and cute. I enjoyed making her smile or even, occasionally, to laugh. I was delighted it was the nurse, and not the doctor, who was in charge of conducting the interview.

My job had me smoking pot three days per week. Each workday I would smoke marijuana and be interviewed by the alluring nurse. Unfortunately, for me, Mike Low was in my group, so the nurse was also assigned to him.

Mike was six feet two inches tall and well built. He was dark haired and handsome, a brilliant guitarist and composer, and a talented singer. After smoking marijuana in the sterile room each work day, our jobs required us to remain on site. There was nothing to do, so Mike asked permission to bring his guitar to play in order to pass the time. While I smoked and then read books, Mike smoked and played the guitar and occasionally sang as well. I always speculated Mike wanted to display his exceptional talent to the nurse, although I couldn't be sure of his motive since Mike truly did love his music.

As things turned out, the enticing nurse loved the entertainment. Mike was also personable, quick-witted, and well spoken, so it was not surprising to learn Mike had received an acceptance to his invitation for a date with the beautiful nurse. It was clear I had lost out to my buddy for her affections, but at least, I still had frequent opportunities to see this exquisite creature and talk to her. I was sure she liked me, if not in "that way." I intended to enjoy our friendship to the hilt, as I really loved her company.

After a couple of times when I encountered Mike and the nurse out on dates, my crush dissipated, and I was no longer jealous. In fact, I found myself genuinely happy Mike had a new love interest, and I hoped they would be happy. I believed he had found a keeper.

At the end of this three-week job, we all went in to smoke our final marijuana cigarettes and pick up our pay checks. On this day, the nurse came in at the commencement of the session as usual, and, of course, was extra friendly to me because we had become platonic friends. She gave the usual instructions about the smoking and asked the standard pre-smoking questions. She set out my marijuana cigarettes and left me to my own devices.

After a hazy, indeterminate period of time, the nurse returned and questioned me for the final time. Again, questions like before – "Did you smoke the marijuana cigarettes back to back and over what period of time? Do you presently feel the effects of the marijuana? How do you rate the marijuana on a scale of 1-10, with 10 being the best? Do you feel the effects of smoking the marijuana? Do you think you are under the influence of the marijuana? If so, how much? Do you feel it is unsafe to drive an automobile? Do you feel you need to be driven home?"

I answered all of these questions in a bleary affirmative. This weed was the best ever. I gave it a 10 but would have given it a 12 if the rules permitted. I rated this particular marijuana as the "best stuff I ever smoked." I was unsteady in my gait, slurring my speech, and stumbling when I walked. I said I was so under the influence I needed to be driven home. In fact, I was so messed up I could barely walk. I asked the beautiful nurse if they had waited until the last day to give me the granddaddy of all weed. She smiled but slipped out of the room without answering. After about twenty minutes, she returned. This time the doctor accompanied her.

He started by thanking me for being part of the study. He then informed me in such an experimental study there are two groups. It was imperative that they have a control group and a test group. The doctor informed me I was in the control group that was given a placebo – that is, marijuana that had the active THC chemical extracted from it. The marijuana I smoked was phony – it wasn't real. It wouldn't mess up anyone. You could not be under the influence of those particular phony marijuana cigarettes any more than you could be drunk by drinking a twelve pack of near-beer. It was not the real McCoy.

The doctor explained all this with the beautiful nurse standing right next to him and both of them looking at me. All she did was smile. They had to be howling with laughter inside, but outwardly they both wore polite smiles. I thought she was a nice person, and wouldn't want to cause me any pain, but this only made it worse. If she had laughed at me then I could at least have written her off as a cruel person who I wouldn't want as a friend anyway. But no, not this particular beautiful nurse. She was classy all the way.

The immediate embarrassment that I felt, realizing everything I'd said previously to this woman about the sensations of being high were just figments of my imagination, is beyond words to describe. She had known from the beginning my answers were based on my assumption I was ingesting real drugs. It dawned on me how suggestive I must have appeared to her. This was more embarrassment than I wanted to endure.

My mind was flooded with all the stupid things I must have said to her. I remembered telling her on several occasions I should be driven home because I wasn't a safe driver (I wondered at the time why no one from the hospital drove me home). My head was swelling from these humiliating thoughts, like an old tire about to explode from over-inflation. I thought I was going to burst with embarrassment. The totality of these recollections had the cumulative effect of making me want to rush from the room. Instead, however, I thanked them both for the opportunity to earn some money and then quickly walked out of the room.

When I got back to the apartment, I was still numb with embarrassment. Tuna was there to greet me but, although I hugged him, I didn't tell him what had just happened. Normally, I told The Wonder Dog everything, but I didn't even want my dog to know what a gullible fool I was.

This experience reinforced my conviction that I was not a smoker. I had never been interested in regular cigarettes. The phony marijuana probably made me dizzy just because of ingesting smoke. I remembered being high once from smoking a cigar on an experimental basis in college. But being fooled by the phony weed didn't comfort me at all. The only thing that consoled me was that I would never have to see the gorgeous, sweet nurse again. This was certainly cold comfort but at least things couldn't get any worse. At least, not until the next day when Mike Low came over to see me. He told me he had rated the marijuana as "terrible" and hadn't felt any effects. Great, I thought to myself, Mike was not fooled and, as a result, must have seemed even cooler to the beautiful nurse.

My feeling the lovely nurse probably felt pity for me was confirmed when Mike told me she had actually told him she felt sorry for me. She could tell it was embarrassing for me to learn I was so off base and completely wrong about the marijuana. Great, now I knew she was telling people about me, the bozo who couldn't tell fake marijuana from the real stuff. And, then, as a further low, Mike couldn't help but make fun of me by talking about how I may be able to start a business selling fake marijuana. That way I could make money and it would be perfectly legal. Alternatively, Mike suggested I should be the representative of our group of friends to always sample alcohol or marijuana to make sure it was of the highest quality. Of course, he was just warming up. Over the ensuing weeks Mike directed many more digs and barbs of this nature at me. This was not surprising because this is what we friends did to each other. We made fun of each other's mistakes and foolishness. I deserved it. If the shoe were on the other foot, I would have unloaded on him.

Still, this incident stung. The "grass is always greener" syndrome (excuse the pun) started to haunt me. I couldn't help thinking of how this hand played out. Let's review the facts: Mike was in the same control group as me. He was cool enough to know real marijuana from the fake stuff. He could sing, and play the guitar, and he was tall, handsome, and very smart – and he got the girl. Me? All I did was make a complete fool of myself in front of a girl I coveted and ended up pitied by her. I really wanted to remember this day (as if I could ever forget it) because I planned to one day tell my analyst about it when I started my inevitable therapy. I just couldn't afford it yet.

CHAPTER THIRTEEN

The Incident at the Psychiatric Center

The psychiatric center where I had been so busy not smoking pot was surrounded by a wooded, park-like area. I sometimes explored these woods after my smoking sessions, thinking it was a good idea to walk off the effects of the "marijuana" before I drove my car. During these "clearing my head" walks, I found these woods beautiful and very peaceful. I realized this would be a nice place to walk Tuna.

In the fall, with the sting of my summer embarrassment still fresh in my mind, I returned to law school and began my final year of studies. I also started dating Bonnie, a secretary from law school. I met her when I worked in the mailroom, another part time job I had in addition to my janitorial duties. She was a college graduate from Wisconsin who had come out to San Francisco to do graduate work in political science. She had a great sense of humor, and I liked her and her friends as well. Besides work, we occasionally bumped into each other at Harrington's bar, a popular hangout around the corner from school. One day, we sat together at the bar waiting for our respective friends to arrive. We really hit it off, and soon after, we began dating.

One autumn Sunday morning, Tuna, Bonnie, and I arrived early at the woods. A hilly enclave surrounding the Psychiatric Center, and surrounded itself by residential housing, the steep, heavily wooded hillside was an attractive site for people living in the city to exercise and walk in a peaceful forest setting – a refuge set squarely in the heart of San Francisco.

As we approached the entrance to the woods, I decided to let Tuna off his leash. I knew he would want to bound ahead into the woods where there were plenty of trees, bushes, and shrubbery for him to sniff and lift his leg on. It certainly appeared to be a safe place to let him roam free, as there was nothing but forest ahead of him and the dangers of vehicles were behind us.

Before he could take off running into the woods and up the hillside, Tuna's attention was caught by a bird soaring above us, sailing gracefully in the direction of the nearby Psychiatric Center. Now I don't know what exactly was going on in Tuna's head, but perhaps it appeared to him he could pursue the bird in a straight line by simply jumping over a small barrier between the park and the Center that looked like a two-foot high cement curb. The curb, however, was actually the top of a retaining wall protecting a driveway into the Center. On the other side of this seemingly minor barrier was a drop of about 25 feet straight down to a cement roadway.

Before any of us realized what was happening, Tuna took off running at full steam ahead with his eyes focused on the bird. In one beautiful leap, he easily cleared the minor curb-like cement barrier. However, instead of quickly landing on the other side to continue his pursuit, Tuna suddenly found himself in mid-air with no landing in sight, except for the long drop below. Not that it helped, but all four of his legs kept running, a desperate dog paddle, as if to swim his way out. Unfortunately, Tuna quickly learned he was unable to fly, and instead plummeted to the cement driveway below. Horrified, I ran to the cement barrier and looked down, fearing the worst.

Tuna was lying motionless on his side on the cement roadway.

As I dashed down the hill to the sidewalk and then up the driveway, my heart was pounding. I was praying Tuna was still alive. Illogically, I was at the same time hoping he was not terribly hurt. I felt an imperative need to get to my dog before a car entered or exited, because Tuna was lying right in the middle of the road.

Puffing from the run, I slowed to a walk as I approached the motionless form of my beloved dog. I bent over and spoke his name, hoping to see a response. Tuna's eyes were open, and he was panting rapidly, but otherwise not moving. I petted Tuna on his head, and softly asked him how he felt. He seemed to be listening. This encouraged me. After a few minutes, Tuna attempted to get up on his own. I was glad to see this, because I was very reluctant to move Tuna myself. I feared he might have some internal damage. I worried that broken bones could puncture vital organs, and I did not want to make matters worse. At last, Tuna got up and started to walk toward me. His equilibrium seemed a little off. After looking at me for a few seconds, he turned and began to slowly walk on his own toward the street.

At this point, I stopped Tuna and, as gently as I could, checked for injuries by touching him and inspecting his paws and sides, tummy, and head. There was nothing evident. It appeared Tuna might have had a miraculous escape. I saw no obvious injuries or any bleeding, but he was moving very slowly, and seemed disoriented.

I decided to take Tuna to a veterinarian to ensure nothing was wrong. Unfortunately, this was a Sunday, in San Francisco. Sunday meant emergency services, which everywhere meant an expensive visit. In San Francisco, it meant a ridiculously expensive visit. Nonetheless, in this situation my usual frugal tendencies were not a consideration. It would have to be a San Francisco veterinarian on an emergency basis. When we arrived at the vet's office, it seemed like a positive sign that Tuna threw the usual instinctive fit that began any trip to a vet's office (growling and baring his teeth). The vet examined Tuna and determined he may have had some internal bleeding, but otherwise was medically sound. He could come home. I was to watch him closely over the next few days.

Except for the charges for the emergency visit, the news was spectacularly good. This was the first, and last, trip to the woods in that particular location of the world that I ever made with Tuna. I was concerned the driveway with its steep drop off might always be a trap he couldn't avoid, should he see another bird. Tuna had irrefutably shown the sight of a bird in flight gave him an irresistible impulse to chase after it by taking off like a vulture flushed from a kill. My poor dog had proven he just couldn't help himself. It was like telling the wind not to blow, a flower not to bloom, gasoline not to burn, a baby not to poop. Tuna HAD to chase birds.

CHAPTER FOURTEEN

Seclusion

In May 1971, I graduated from Hastings Law School. I now had to devote myself to studying for the California Bar Examination. Hoping not to work while studying for the exam, I stumbled onto an opportunity where I could live for free in San Francisco and keep Tuna with me. There were some drawbacks to this situation, but somehow, I convinced myself it made sense.

I had only been paying $37.50 per month for my share of the flat, so rent had not really been a concern. However, this arrangement was ending because my roommates were all going elsewhere for the summer. I could not afford the whole flat on my own. One day when I was moaning about this predicament to Mike Low, he told me about a lead on possible free housing, which he didn't need since he already lived rent-free as a care taker at Mount St. Joseph orphanage in the Bayview district.

Mike was a year ahead of me, so by this time he held his caretaker job for several years as he finished college, attended law school, and now was beginning to practice law. During this considerable period, he had proved his trustworthiness to the nuns who ran the orphanage. When their order closed a convent located in the Hunter's Point area of San Francisco, the nuns asked Mike if he could recommend someone who could live at the decommissioned convent. It was located in a high crime area and the nuns had decided it would discourage vandalism to have someone living on the premises. They must have realized there might be some challenges because they were proposing to let the right candidate live at the convent for free. In the nuns' minds, the right person would of course, like Mike, be a good Catholic boy.

The convent had been housed in a three-story building. The third floor had been a dormitory for the nuns. The second floor was a fully furnished two-bedroom apartment. The first floor was a garage that contained clothing and other goods. On Sundays, the Church would open up the first floor and distribute these items to the needy.

Mike decided I was the right person to mind this building and invited me to his cottage for a meeting with the head nun at the orphanage. The appointed Saturday morning was warm and sunny. I arrived to find the front door of Mike's modest one-bedroom stucco cottage wide open to let in a mild June breeze. I had decided to bring Tuna to the meeting, because I was sure the nuns would recognize my dog as a source of extra security for their convent building. I had arrived a little early and Mike and I were sitting around shooting the breeze when Tuna spotted a dog that lived at the orphanage. A very old dog, beloved by the orphans, he was allowed to roam the entire premises unleashed. His name was Moses, which was fitting because he was as old as the Hebrew prophet himself. His reactions were so slow that it took him a long time to cover any substantial ground. Mostly he stayed close by the big orphanage itself, near his food and the affectionate orphans. On this sunny morning, however, he had wandered a bit and was right outside Mike's cottage.

Tuna had been looking out the living room window with his hind legs on Mike's couch and his front legs perched on the windowsill behind the couch. Like a shot, Tuna spun, streaked out the open front door and mounted

Moses sidesaddle. This was not a fight but rather a sexual encounter of the strangest kind. Poor Moses didn't even react until Tuna had completed what he was doing, hopped down, come back inside, jumped back onto the couch, and resumed gazing out the window at Moses. It was at that point that Moses slowly turned to regard a soiled part of his coat in the middle of his body. He was clearly mystified.

I was suddenly seized by the fear that perhaps the head nun had seen this sexual assault on their beloved Moses by a perverted dog. If she had, and I acknowledged Tuna as my dog, I might be kissing away a free-living arrangement. I scanned the yard through the window. There didn't seem to be anyone nearby who could have seen the incident. I quickly locked Tuna in a bedroom and Mike and I waited uncomfortably for the nun to arrive.

Sister Jean arrived exactly at the agreed time. A member of the Order of the Daughters of Charity, she wore a calf length blue dress, with her head covered by a trim white headdress and a blue coif. Her appearance was so different than what I remembered of the nuns at St. John's School in Napa. They all wore the cumbersome garb from the 17th century. Sister Jean was ancient, dour, and intimidating. After Mike made the introduction, Sister Jean focused on me directly. She told me Mike had highly recommended me, but she wanted to hear from me why I wanted to live in the convent. She explained it was not far from the orphanage, but it was in Hunter's Point, not Bayview. Did I realize Hunter's Point was considered more poverty stricken, with a high crime rate? She asked me if I remembered the riots and shootings in the Point in the mid-60's. It was clear to me she wanted me to fully comprehend the dangers of the area, so I would make an informed decision, and maybe to clear her conscience. Her disclosures, made in such a dogmatic manner, made me nervous. Maybe this opportunity was not as good as it initially sounded.

At this point in the interview Tuna had started scratching at the closed door of Mike's bedroom. I anxiously wanted the interview to end before the barking commenced. I asked when I could move in and how long I could live at the convent. Sister Jean told me I could move in immediately and stay throughout the summer. She assured me I could stay beyond the dates for my bar examination. With that assurance I had no more questions. Sister Jean said based on Michael's recommendation, and my assurances I understood the potential risks inherent to living in Hunter's Point, I would be acceptable to the Mount (as the orphanage was called). She extended the keys in her open hand. Quickly, I snatched the keys, shook her hand, thanked her, and bade her a quick goodbye. I never mentioned I had a dog, let alone a horn-dog.

As Tuna and I drove back to the flat, I felt a vast sense of relief. We had been up against a deadline to vacate the flat. We hadn't found a place to live. I needed time to study for the bar examination, which meant I had to keep expenses down, so I wouldn't have to waste all of my time working. The convent would be ideal, because the rent was zero, which would allow me not to work at all. I had enough savings for food. The Church even paid the utilities. It was the best job in the world. All I had to do was live there.

Clearly, there were some drawbacks to this living arrangement. It was located on Quesada Avenue in Hunter's Point in the southern part of San Francisco – an urban neighborhood with predominantly African-American residents. By the 1960s the neighborhood had become increasingly segregated from the rest of San

Francisco. Pollution, substandard housing, declining infrastructure, limited employment, crime, and racial discrimination were notable problems. In 1966, just a few years earlier, racial tensions had sparked the race riot in Hunter's Point that Sister Jean had alluded to.

Despite my assurances to Sister Jean, nothing to this point of my life had provided me with any experience or understanding of the gang and drug activity, as well as the high murder rate, which plagued the district. I had a superficial knowledge of problems in the projects, but I mostly dwelled in my own world of getting through college and law school. My naiveté also left me unaware of the tremendous anger in this region toward white people. Maybe I was blinded by the fact that free rent and utilities solved my immediate problems. I could study without having to work. One thing is certain, I was disconnected to the times, the area, and the intense racial tensions.

CHAPTER FIFTEEN

The Birds

When law school ended in May of 1971, my roommates and I said our goodbyes and vacated the flat in the Sunset. I immediately moved to the convent, with help from Mike Low and Bob Trevorrow. We all had cars and packed all of my stuff easily in a single caravan. I didn't need much because the second floor of the convent building was a fully furnished two-bedroom apartment. I had my typewriter, stereo, clothes, canned goods, motor oil (which the '61 Ford drank like water) and dog food. The apartment was spacious and comfortable. Upon entering, there was the living room, complete with a television set (a necessity of life, in my opinion). Beyond the living room was the formal dining room and the kitchen, fully stocked with dishes and glasses in the cupboards. The drawers contained silverware, knives, a can opener, and various other kitchen implements. On the kitchen counter was an old coffeemaker. In every room of the house, including both bedrooms, crucifixes hung on the walls and ashtrays lay on the tables. Inside these walls, I had everything I needed (well, maybe apart from the ashtrays and crucifixes).

This being the beginning of the summer months, I saw many young people out on the streets during the day and even during the evenings. In Hunter's Point, it was not uncommon to see large groups of young black men moving through the neighborhood. I felt it was their area, the only thing that belonged to them. Despite the warnings of Sister Jean, it had not sunk in about any possible danger for me. Gradually, however, I found I was no longer thinking about what a "cool free place" I was moving into. I was experiencing, rather, a realization of what Hunter's Point really was. I didn't know if the groups of men would accept me if they saw me walking Tuna on the street. Would I be hassled? Threatened? Physically assaulted? Was I going to have to be holed up in my apartment to be safe? These questions gradually flooded my mind. I had no experience living in such an environment. I came from the lily-white community of Napa, and now resided in an area where I was apparently the only Caucasian for blocks around. I had never thought I was a racially bigoted person, but now I was afraid for my safety because there were large crowds of African-Americans on the streets at night, who did not know me except for the color of my skin. It was an uncomfortable feeling.

I had signed up for a review course, designed to help students pass the bar. This course met once a week on Sundays and was usually the only time I left the house except to walk Tuna. The rest of the week I needed to study full-time for the next bar class.

One of my favorite places in the three-story convent building was the roof, where I had placed lawn furniture and tables, so I could enjoy the outdoors without actually leaving the building. To be honest, I felt safe there.

One morning not long after moving in, I took my coffee, newspaper, legal outlines, and a securely leashed Tuna up to the roof to enjoy the fresh air. I had already developed a routine. I set everything on the table, and then freed Tuna from his leash. My previous experiences on the roof had been peaceful times. They were almost always in the morning and allowed some private time for rest and relaxation before I commenced with my serious study for the day. Tuna roamed on the rooftop while I enjoyed my paper and coffee. Then I started reviewing my notes and reading through the course outlines.

This time, however, as soon as I released Tuna from his leash, a bird flew over the rooftop. In the blink of an eye, Tuna was off and running after the bird. I immediately had a sense of deja-vu from the incident at the Psychiatric Center. There was a small curb–like wall to jump, but an unforeseen drop below that Tuna could not anticipate. And this time, instead of a 25-foot drop, there would be a treacherous fall from a three-story building.

I immediately yelled out, "Stop!" in a loud-as-thunder shout. To my great relief, Tuna realized my yell meant business. Despite how often he disobeyed similar commands, he abruptly pulled up short of the edge. Maybe it was because I yelled louder than I had ever yelled before, and in a tone that sounded urgent with conviction. Maybe it was because Tuna remembered what had happened the last time he jumped a short curb. Whatever the reason, Tuna stopped short of the wall.

It's certainly possible his prior in-air experience had taught him to think before he chased and to look before he leaped – but I couldn't afford the risk of finding out. I couldn't believe how careless I was with Tuna. How could I have once again put him in a situation that could have put his life at risk?

With panicked haste, I rushed over and threw my arms around Tuna. I immediately put him back on his leash, packed up the coffee, paper, and legal outlines, and took us back to our apartment on the second floor.

Tuna never saw the roof again without being on a leash.

CHAPTER SIXTEEN

First Degree Residential Burglary

Living in an empty three-story building alone with one canine companion was often peaceful and quiet. Sometimes, however, it was downright scary. Late at night Tuna and I would hear creaks coming from the third floor dormitory where the nuns used to bunk. Sometimes it sounded like there were people on the first floor, where the used clothes and shoes awaited distribution to the poor every Sunday. Because I went out so infrequently, and with noises above and below me, I developed a mild case of agoraphobia. My fear of intrusion grew to the point that I started to barricade the front door of our apartment.

After a month or so, I began to become acclimated to the quiet stillness of the three-story building and the occasional punctuating eerie noises, although I continued to barricade the front entrance. But just when I was coming around to the possibility that maybe I was being overly reactive, I learned my concerns were justified.

Returning from a weekend trip to Napa one Sunday evening, I entered the apartment, and immediately sensed something wasn't right. Walking from room to room I noticed the spare bedroom I had been using as a study was missing my typewriter (my beautiful manual Royal Typewriter). In my bedroom, my stereo was missing. Searching more thoroughly, I discovered the coin collection from my childhood was also missing. None of

120

these items was valuable monetarily, but they had sentimental value.

This was the first time I had been burgled. Nothing like this ever happened to me in Napa, Berkeley, or in three years of living in San Francisco. I felt so vulnerable seeing my stuff strewn all over the place with drawers pulled open and clothes hanging out. My first reaction was to search all three stories to ensure there were no other people on the premises. I went to get my large hunting knife, but it was missing as well – another memento from my childhood gone. I found my wooden baseball bat and brought that along on the search of the third-floor dormitory. I let Tuna go first so he could sniff out anyone still up there. The third floor was clear. Then I went to search the first floor and the garage. Tuna was again at my side, and my bat was in my hand. Again, the results of the search led to no one. In fact, there was not a trace of anyone being on the first or third floor. Nothing was out of place. Whoever did this knew, or had soon discovered, the only items of any value were in the apartment on the second floor.

As I stood there surveying the mess in my apartment, it dawned on me I was not really safe. Maybe I would be burgled over and over. The shock I experienced from being burgled was magnified because of the pressure I already felt from studying and worrying about the bar examination. Maybe my no-rent deal was not such a good deal.

The typewriter was important. I had been using it every day for my studies, typing my notes from the bar review course, and then creating outlines to help make sense of it all for the examination. The stereo was equally important. I used it to listen to music in the evenings to force myself to relax. But most devastating was the loss of the knife and coin collection. The knife wasn't valuable, but I had saved my money as a boy and bought it at Brewster's Army-Navy Surplus Store. I could still remember my surprise that the store had been willing to sell such a large knife to a kid my age. I loved the knife. It had a flat butt at the base of the handle that could be used as a club or hammer.

The loss of my coin collection was also profoundly disturbing. Like the knife, it wasn't really valuable, but over the years I had saved my money to purchase these coins one by one. I had some nice pieces, too. I acquired them in the late 50s and early 60s, and they included a United States half-dime, many buffalo nickels, and many Indian head pennies.

As I stood there that night, I realized I was mad at myself that I even brought my collection with me to the apartment, instead of leaving it safely in Napa. It was just something from home I'd wanted to have with me; now I was paying the price.

Determined to find out what happened, I tried not to disturb anything in the apartment, hoping to get the police to take fingerprints. I hoped they would treat this as a major crime. I pictured several squad cars outside the convent with a team of investigators and evidence technicians scouring the apartment for clues. I went to call them but did not pick up the phone. The visual image of swarms of police made me realize this would be very time consuming. I might have to go down to the station and give a statement. That would not normally bother me, but I was feeling a growing pressure to study, as the bar exam was drawing nearer. I sat down on the couch and started thinking about whether I wanted any police involvement at all. I knew the few missing items I really cared about would have probably been pawned or sold on the street already and I would never see them again. As I pondered what to do, my feelings of being violated and my outrage were outweighed by the uncomfortable realization the bar exam was the highest priority for me and getting mixed up with law enforcement might derail my preparation. After much agonizing I finally decided the most I could risk would be to contact the director of Catholic Charities, which was the organization running the clothing distribution center on the first floor. They were the only other people besides me who had a right to be at the convent. They were open for business on Sundays, which meant they had been on site that very day.

I had met the director previously. He seemed like a nice person. Maybe he could help me get to the bottom of this. I decided I could spare a half hour to talk to Director Tim. Tim, who didn't live far from the convent, came over to see me in person when I called him the next morning. I showed him the mess in the apartment. I asked him if anything unusual had happened yesterday that might explain how I was burglarized. Tim said he didn't know of anything. Something in the tone of his denial though made me press on: I asked him if he was only person running the program yesterday or did anyone assist him. He admitted he had two new people helping him. His demeanor made me think there may be more to his story than he was saying. How well did Tim know these people? Tim admitted they were new to him and had been assigned under a program to help ex-cons reintegrate into society. I was excited. I asked if these two people were in his view at all times. Tim said they were – except for a brief period when he sent them upstairs to look for scissors and paper supplies.

"You mean you sent them to the apartment? Do you have keys to the apartment upstairs?"

Tim answered yes to both questions. I couldn't believe it. I had hit pay dirt. Tim, as the Director of Catholic Charities, had ordered these two people into my apartment. I was elated. I asked Tim for the names of the two men. Tim said he couldn't tell me. He had to protect their privacy. I countered by asking him to go to them himself and get my stuff. Tim became more reluctant to talk. He said he could make some inquiries, but he wasn't convinced they took anything.

I told Tim if my things were put back I would not call the cops, and there would be no questions asked. He responded he really couldn't arrange for that. He said he didn't have any contact with the two guys anymore and reiterated he would not give me their names. His attitude had noticeably changed from personable and cooperative to dour and scornful.

I wasn't willing to let it go. I couldn't accept him telling me there was nothing to be done. An injustice had occurred. There is a difference between what's right and what's wrong, and I decided to draw a line in the sand (I fear my being a fresh lawyer had a bearing on my passion for a righteous remedy). The director of the church-based charitable organization (my church!) was avoiding looking me in the eye, and clearly trying to end the meeting.

I made a proposal: I told him he was responsible for the people who were in his charge and who he allowed into my apartment. He was therefore civilly liable to me for the damages caused by the men's conversion of my property. I also said the monetary cost to me and ultimately to him would be in excess of $500.00, but I would accept the sum of $500.00 in full satisfaction if he paid me in a timely manner. Otherwise, I would file a small claims action to recover this sum from him. Tim was no longer contrite but scornful. He turned my offer down with a scowl and stood up to leave. I told him I was sorry he didn't want to settle out of court. That ended our attempt to settle this matter.

I weighed my options. If I called the police now, a few days after the burglary, it would probably not get my property back. I concluded the best avenue was to pursue a small claims action for money damages. This course was not risk free. It would take time – time I didn't have. Equally important, initiating legal action against the director of Catholic Charities might result in hard feelings with the Church, perhaps leading to a request for me to vacate the premises. Getting ready for the bar exam was of paramount importance. The answer was plain.

But not to me. Against common sense, I decided no one – not even the Catholic Church – was going to rip me off.

I sued them – the director and the entire Catholic Church. It was my first lawsuit as a budding lawyer – a small claims court for the maximum monetary damages of $500.00. I went to the small claims division of the municipal courthouse in downtown San Francisco, filled out a form explaining what the case was about, and paid the $5.00 filing fee. The clerk explained I had to send notice of the hearing to the Catholic Charities director by mail. First, I had to select a hearing date at least three weeks away to allow time for notice and also for the defendant to prepare for the hearing. On the day of the hearing, I set my studies aside and went to the small claims courtroom, being careful to arrive a half hour before the scheduled 2:00 hearing time. It was adorned with dark walnut paneling and theatre seats for the audience. There was a gate running the width of the courtroom about three-quarters of the way to the front of the courtroom. Beyond this gate were two tables for the litigants, and a majestic bench centered in the back of the room, which rode high over the rest of the court furniture. On each side of the bench were flags. One was the flag of the United States of America and the other was the California Bear Flag. I checked in with the clerk and sat in the audience area to wait for court to begin. By 1:45 p.m. the courtroom was packed with people there to have their cases heard. I spotted director Tim in the audience. I was sitting on the opposite side of the room. Our eyes met once but he didn't even acknowledge my presence.

I did not have a good feeling about my chances. The reason? The director of the Catholic Charities in the Hunter's Point area was African American. The notice of hearing indicated the case had been assigned to Judge Kennedy, who I knew was an African American judge. I had heard only good things about Judge Kennedy. Still, I did wonder if I would get a fair trial when I was suing an African American who was the director of a charity serving an African American neighborhood when the trial was before an African American judge. I was sure many African Americans must regularly feel this way when things were reversed.

I knew I could file an affidavit to have the judge removed from the case. Law school trial classes had taught me a litigant has the right to disqualify one judge without proving cause. You just need to say you don't believe the judge will be fair to you. I decided against disqualifying the judge. He had a reputation of being fair. I didn't believe I could in good conscience sign an affidavit stating Judge Kennedy could not give me a fair hearing. I had no basis. Also, I had a naïve belief in our legal system. I believed justice prevails if you have proof of your claim – I had proof. However, when I actually walked into the courtroom and found myself in front of a judge and an opponent, both of whom were of a race different than mine, I felt powerless and suddenly fearful the hearing might not be fair. It was an unexpected lesson on how people with little power must feel most of the time when interacting with power.

The case was called. Tim and I went through the gate and took our respective places at the table. The left side of the table was for the plaintiff – the person who brought the suit. The right side of the table was where the defendant sat. I was wearing the only coat I owned – a brown corduroy sport coat. I also wore my best shoes, my best slacks, and a white shirt and necktie. Tim was more casually dressed, but he looked appropriate, in an open sports shirt, tan slacks, and polished leather shoes.

As Plaintiff, I presented my case first, simply alleging men under Tim's supervision had stolen my belongings. Tim presented his response denying all responsibility. Judge Kennedy said it seemed to him I should be at the District Attorney's Office, making a criminal complaint. He said the case did not seem appropriate for small claims court, because it appeared a crime had been committed.

Realizing I had not explained Tim had given these men express permission to go into my private apartment, I asked to supplement my argument. Judge Kennedy granted me permission. I argued the clothing distribution center was located in the garage of the building separate from where I lived on the second floor. The director was in charge of the men who had been working at the clothing distribution center – they were his agents. He gave them permission and furnished them with keys into my private apartment where they took my belongings. Judge Kennedy asked the director if it was true he had allowed them to go upstairs into my apartment. The director admitted it was true.

At that moment things seemed to change. There was a long pause as Judge Kennedy quietly looked over his glasses at the defendant and then directly at me. Judge Kennedy awarded me $200.00 against the director personally. No award was made against the Catholic Church.

I pursued an ideal of fairness in my inaugural voyage after law school and prevailed. That was satisfaction enough for me. A good thing too, because I never collected the money from the director.

CHAPTER SEVENTEEN

Tuna Becomes Tuna

At this point in Tuna's life I was still calling him Kingfish after the character on the *Amos and Andy Show*. The role of the character Kingfish was that of a scoundrel. He was a habitual cheater. He lied to his friends. He was presented as lazy and unable to hold a job for long. He was always trying to con someone out of something and seemed to work harder at anti-social behavior than he would have worked in any legitimate business or job. He had poor grammar and was clearly uneducated. The show was a comedy and portrayed the African American as stupid and antisocial. Even the fairly conservative NAACP, hardly a radical or militant organization, put the *Amos and Andy Show* on its list as a racist TV show and succeeded in having it banned from the public airways in the 1970s. It was dawning on me that my new African American neighbors in Hunter's Point might not look kindly on a black dog named Kingfish owned by a young Caucasian fresh out of graduate school.

Summer was here, and it could get fairly hot in this area of San Francisco. I routinely walked Tuna in the morning and evening. When we set out, I would let Tuna off the leash because there were no rooftops to fall from, and Tuna liked to run and get his exercise.

One evening, about two weeks after the burglary incident, we started on one of these walks. The only thing different from the usual routine was the time of the walk. It was later than usual. In fact, it was about 9:00 p.m. It was still warm out. After a couple of blocks, I let Tuna off of his leash. As usual, Tuna took off.

When Tuna bounded across the street, I saw he was headed straight toward a large group of young black guys walking along the other side. There were at least fifteen people, all in their late teens and early twenties, spanning the sidewalk and spilling into the street as they sauntered along. Even in my first glance, I realized most of them were wearing black leather jackets and several were casually twirling lengths of shiny steel chains.

Tuna (then still known as Kingfish) charged straight toward this group and began barking madly. Before I knew what I was doing, I began to shout at him to stop and get back to me. But in the split second it took me to call out my dog's name, I realized it was well known to have racial overtones. I hadn't had a clue about this in 1962 when I watched the show, but I fully realized it in 1971.

Without thinking I changed Kingfish's name in mid-call. What came out was "King-Tuna"! To my amazement the dog sensed the urgency in my voice. Tuna stopped in his tracks, turned, and looked at me. After what seemed like a very long, awkward moment, Tuna heeded my call and came bounding back. Without making eye contact with the fifteen sets of eyes gazing from across the street, I clipped Tuna onto his leash, turned, and strolled casually back to my apartment.

I had generated a new name for my dog based on survival needs. The demographics of the neighborhood demanded Kingfish no longer be Kingfish. In that brief moment, I decided my dog would thenceforth be known as "Tuna fish." Or just "Tuna" for short.

Oddly enough, the new name didn't seem to matter to my dog. Tuna obeyed, or didn't, depending on the circumstances, not on the name he was called. If a bird flew past, he would not listen to me, no matter what I called him. Without a distraction, he would respond to the name Tuna just as much as he had responded to the name of Kingfish for all of his prior years. His adjustment to the new name was instantaneous.

Notwithstanding periodic moments of sheer fright about the impending exam, I continued to study. The routine of the days went on. Coffee and paper on the roof with Tuna on a leash. I continued to type up my notes and outlines on a used typewriter I had borrowed to replace my stolen one. And, of course, more coffee.

Before I knew it, the summer was coming to an end. The bar exam was set for the last week of August 1971. I completed the bar review course and concluded my studies. The week leading up to the exam was the longest week of my life, second only to the week of the exam itself. But at last the time came – the moment I had hoped for and dreaded, not just through the intense summer, but for the entire past three years: it was time to take the bar examination to become licensed to practice law in the State of California.

CHAPTER EIGHTEEN

The Bar Exam

The bar exam consisted of morning and afternoon sessions for three consecutive days. At the end of each day, I would go home to review and speculate on what areas of the law I might be tested on the next day. This routine was short-lived, but very intense. During each day of the exam, I did my utmost not to listen to anyone who was discussing the test questions during the lunch hour. I knew if I heard someone discuss an issue I had forgotten, it would demoralize me, and very likely distract me during the sessions of the test that still lay ahead. I was determined to maintain a positive attitude, as it would be easy to get down on my chances if I felt I had messed up on the first day. As it happened, I was successful at this for the three days of the exam.

Except for one occasion during the noon break of the second day.

The exam was being administered in the library of Hastings College of the Law – the law school I had just been attending. The library was on the third floor. On this particular day, when the lunch break arrived I made the mistake of taking the elevator to the cafeteria on the first floor. During this short but crowded elevator ride, I was a captive audience to the discussions of the other occupants. The moment the doors closed, I began to feel claustrophobic. We were packed like sardines. I was the shortest person on the ride with everyone towering over me.

Sure enough, a couple of fellow students on the elevator started talking about the questions. One guy asked his friend if he had spotted the crossover issue in one of the questions. This meant that there were at least two different areas of the law covered in one question. If you missed one, it would be a serious setback. It might even result in your failing the entire bar exam.

As soon as the student's question was uttered, someone else in the elevator angrily shouted, "Don't talk about the test. Shut the hell up!"

I was in complete agreement with the protestor, but at this point in the day, didn't have the guts to join in. Instead, I put my hands over my ears, turned to the wall, and loudly started singing the Beatles tune, *It's Been A Hard Day's Night.* Everyone on the packed elevator broke out laughing. They understood my somewhat bizarre response and used it to release the pent-up, nervous, strain. Even the original blabbermouth and the student who had yelled him down were laughing.

My awkward behavior notwithstanding, I couldn't take a chance on any further disruptions to my mental game plan. Any conversation raising the possibility I had missed a legal issue might completely derail my attempt to maintain a positive attitude. Whether or not I missed an issue, there was not a thing in the world I could do about it. I had to look forward and put the past questions out of my mind.

So, I never took the elevator for the balance of the exam. I was successful in maintaining a positive attitude during the three days of testing. Afterwards, I felt I had done well on the test, and in fact believed I had passed. At least, that was my feeling right after the three-day test. By the time the bar results were released three months later, my confidence had evaporated. I was convinced I had flunked. I was so certain of this that, a few weeks before the results were due to arrive, I went to a bank to arrange a loan to support myself while I prepared to take it again.

There were varying theories floating around about whether the results would come in a thin or thick package. One rumor was if it was a thick envelope it meant you had flunked the examination, because the envelope contained an application to re-take the test. Another rumor had it that if the envelope was thin, it meant you had flunked because all they would send was an abrupt, succinct notice you failed.

These pointless speculations added to the enormous anxiety building up during the three months it took the State Bar to grade the exams and process the results. At last, rumors began circulating. The results would be out at any time. By now, I was going crazy with the waiting. A superstitious person by nature, and somewhat ritualistic by virtue of my Catholic upbringing, I was plagued both by dreams of passing and nightmares of flunking. I found myself daydreaming as I was driving about whether I passed or not. On more than one occasion, as I approached a green light at an intersection, my mind would entertain the thought that if I made it through the intersection before the light turned red, it would mean I had passed the bar. But, God forbid, if the light turned red, it meant I had flunked. I found myself barreling through some intersections at 90 miles per hour, just to ensure I passed the bar.

On a crisp, sunny day in December of 1971, the mail containing the bar exam results was delivered to my parents' home. I happened to be in Napa that day, home for an appointment with the family dentist. My mother heard the mailman drop the day's mail into the mailbox affixed to the wall by the front door. We had been sitting together in the living room catching up when she stood and went to let herself out the front door to get the mail.

But before she opened the door, my very Catholic mother withdrew her hand and, looking back toward me, still sitting in the living room, said, "Please, dear God, please let today's mail have among it the bar results, and let it be that Raymond passed the bar exam."

I had never seen my mother do anything remotely like this in my life. An objective bystander who had been subjected to my constant whining and witnessed my anxiety over the cruel wait for the results, might well have wondered whether she was praying for me or for herself.

But I knew my mom. She truly was praying for her son.

Turning back to the door, my mother went out and then reappeared, looking through the stack of letters and ads she had retrieved from the mail- box. When she reached a cream-colored legal-size envelope – it was thick – she stopped and, without a word, handed it to me.

I slowly stood, walked into the dining room and laid the envelope on the table. After taking a deep breath, I picked it back up and opened it. My mother watched anxiously as I began to silently read. I was so nervous that I was most of the way through the first page before realizing what I was reading. It was something about where I could be sworn into practice law. I went back to the opening paragraph. There it was in black and white: "Congratulations, you have passed the California Bar

Examination." What beautiful words. What wonderful words. What great words.

I put the letter down, looked at my mom, and softly said, "Mom, I'm a lawyer."

She screamed and hugged me. Tuna started barking and jumping up and down as we all shared the moment together. It was one of the best moments in my life.

CHAPTER NINETEEN

A Lawyer's First Days of Practice

After I passed the bar, Tuna and I stayed on at the convent for the sole reason it was rent and utilities free. I still felt unsafe at the apartment and didn't feel comfortable going out at night. But I had no other place to go. I didn't want to go back to Napa because I wanted to get started practicing law in San Francisco as soon as I was sworn in. At length, I decided the benefits of the apartment outweighed the downside, at least for the short run. Tuna and I would stay until I could figure out where to live next – or until they asked me to leave.

As soon as I was sworn in as a lawyer, I started to practice law with Mike Low, who was working as a sole practitioner in San Francisco. The cases he handled were few and not lucrative. Mike had been one class ahead of me at Hastings, so he had been a lawyer for only one year. His cases were almost all of the legal aid type. That is, they were not substantial cases and the clients had little or no money to finance their cases. Still, it was real law experience and an important service to this underserved clientele. Also, I could afford to take these types of cases because of my free rent situation.

My first client was a young lady with three young children. She and her husband had incurred significant debt, and under the financial stress, their marriage had failed. The husband abandoned the family and walked away from his responsibility to support his wife and children. As a result, my client was besieged with debt collectors and lawsuits. On her behalf, Mike had contacted all of the client's creditors, and every creditor except one – the phone company – agreed to defer collection of these debts until her financial situation improved. This was when Mike assigned the case to me. The telephone company had already sued my client and obtained a judgment for approximately $5,000.00. This meant she legally owed the debt. The phone company was now pursuing collection by bringing my client to court on a wage garnishment that, if successful, would entitle them to get a court order requiring 25% of my client's earnings go to them to pay off the phone bill, plus legal interest at the rate of 10 percent per annum.

Mike's, and now my, law practice was such a bare-bones operation that we had no offices. We did our legal work at home or in the law library at the court. This arrangement presented some challenges when it came to client meetings. For this first client, I decided to meet with her at the courthouse to establish an appearance of professionalism. It also occurred to me that, as a single white woman, she might not feel entirely comfortable coming to my apartment in Hunter's Point.

After the interview and some preliminary research, I decided to first call the creditor, even though Mike's initial phone call had provided no relief. I figured there was nothing to be lost in making another attempt to work out an arrangement to repay the debt, perhaps deferring collection for a period of time and then setting up a payment plan my client could afford (the sound of the term "my client" felt good to me). And I was hoping to avoid going to court, which was always a risk, especially when one is a newbie lawyer who wasn't even sure where to stand in a courtroom. If we lost and 25% of my client's wages were sent to her creditor, she wouldn't have enough left to support herself and her three children. If I could get them to consider a settlement and avoid court, we might be able to work out something she could afford.

Unfortunately, I was no more successful than Mike. I could not work out a successful compromise. The representative of the phone company clearly felt they were in the driver's seat and were going to get 25% of her wages, so he rejected outright any offer to compromise.

My next move was to file what was called a "claim of exemption" with the court, asking that the phone company not be allowed any of her wages because of her severe financial situation. As expected, the phone company opposed the claim of exemption. A court hearing was scheduled.

In preparing for the court hearing, I discussed the law with Mike and the facts with Tuna, who seemed to enjoy discussing my new legal cases. I also went to the law library at the courthouse and researched the case law in this particular area. Fortunately, it was not a big complex case with many legal issues. This was a very narrow area of the law, which made it considerably easier for a new lawyer.

The first thing I learned was that I did not have a slam dunk winner. My research revealed it might be possible for the judge to deny the entire garnishment, meaning the creditor would not be allowed to garnish any money to reduce the legal debt. This would require me to successfully persuade the judge to rule that a phone bill was not a "necessity of life." If this could be proven, then the judge could deny the wage garnishment in its entirety. My client would still owe the money, but the creditor would have to wait a statutory period of time to collect it.

If a phone was a deemed a necessity of life, the creditor's case would be strengthened, because providing a necessity is favored under the law and the creditor will usually be allowed to collect its debt for providing the necessity. The challenge was that a phone could be a necessity of life under certain circumstances, and *not* a necessity of life under other circumstances. When the phone is needed to summon emergency services, for example, one could argue it *is* a necessity of life. But in many other circumstances, a phone is not a fundamental necessity of life on a par with food, shelter, or clothing. I did not have much experience on which to base an opinion – actually, I had no actual experience – but I guessed the judge could go either way on this question.

CHAPTER TWENTY

My First Court Hearing

The day arrived for the court hearing. The claim of exemption was a routine and insubstantial case for the judge who heard the "civil law and motion" calendar. But for me, it might as well have been a death penalty criminal case before a jury. Our hearing was set for 8:30 in the morning.

Having been wished good luck by my wonder dog, I arrived extra early at the courthouse to meet my client and make sure I knew where the courtroom was. I wanted to locate it before I met the client, so I could show her where it was, as if I had been there many, many times before. This was deceptive, but I wanted my poor client to have some confidence in me. On reflection, it must have been evident I was not experienced. She had to have noticed I had no office, because we always met at the courthouse. She was paying (nothing) for what she was getting – a complete rookie. I did not own a suit, so I had put on my best (and only) sport coat, the brown corduroy jacket, and I wore my only pair of dress slacks. I thought I looked professional. The trousers, unfortunately, were a little tight. I remember thinking when I had gotten dressed that I'd had to bungee cord myself into those pants.

I met my client at 8 :00 a.m. on the stairs of the courthouse. I had stressed the importance of being on time, and she was. I smiled at her as she approached. She asked me, "What's wrong?"

I said nothing and asked her why she asked me.

She said, "You looked so worried, I thought you must have learned something bad about our case."

I assured her everything was fine, making a mental note that in the future I should not show fright in front of a client. From there we walked together to an elevator and took it to the third floor. From the elevator we went down the hall until we found our courtroom. There was a piece of paper posted outside with a list of the morning cases. I checked it to make sure our case was on this calendar. We were there, about three-quarters of the way down.

"Okay, we are set, let's go in."

I opened the courtroom door for my client and we took a seat in the back. The courtroom was already beginning to fill up. Precisely at the stroke of 8:30 the judge came in and took his seat on the bench. I stood up along with everyone else when the judge made his entrance. I noticed the judge was an older gentleman with a full head of thick white hair. I estimated his age to be 60-plus years old. He showed little emotion and walked with a demeanor of quiet deliberation. He seemed very relaxed, especially for someone who was facing a room full of attorneys and litigants. When seated, he said good morning to everyone in a calm voice. Before he commenced calling the cases, he told us we should attempt to settle our case. Anyone who successfully settled their matter would be called first, so the parties could put their settlement on the record and leave. The same applied to agreed-upon continuances. After taking up the settlements and continuances, he would hear all of the contested matters in the order they appeared on the calendar. He jumped right into calling cases and dispatching them as quickly as possible.

Everything seemed to be going so fast. I was nervous. Suddenly, I heard myself starting to gag. This occasionally happened to me – my doctor said it was due to post-nasal drip. I started to let out random sudden coughs, which I tried to stifle, with my hand clamped over my mouth. I was concerned my client might recognize this behavior for the case of nerves it was and start to lose whatever faith she might have in me. Between gags, I whispered to her that I must have eaten something bad the night before. My client's eyes widened, and she seemed to edge away a bit on the hard bench. It never crossed my mind to come clean by telling her this was my first case ever.

Late in the morning, our case was finally called. I popped up like a piece of toast from my seat in the audience. I quickly approached the counsel table and announced my appearance.

"Your Honor, I am Ray Guadagni, and I am appearing for my client in this matter. It is our claim of exemption."

Opposing counsel was about 5 feet 10 inches tall with a medium build. He was conservatively dressed in a dark brown suit and a striped brown and yellow tie. He appeared to be 40 to 45 years old with greying black hair. He was clean-shaven, and very serious.

He stood and announced he was appearing for the collection agency on behalf of the phone company and that his clients opposed the claim.

"Your Honor, we are ready to proceed with the hearing," he calmly stated.

Gazing at me over the bench, the judge told me to present my case, as it was my motion.

I commenced my argument by summarizing the pertinent sections of the code of civil procedure and the case authority I had found in support of the position that a phone was not a common necessity of life. Therefore, a phone bill could not overcome the exemption provided in the code allowing a debtor to keep her paycheck, as long as she could show she needed all of the check to live on.

I felt my argument went well. I finished by rolling out several examples of when a phone is not a necessity, like talking to friends or calling the theater to see when the movie starts. In these situations, the phone was just a convenience. I thought these examples would be persuasive to the judge.

Now it was the opposing counsel's turn. The lawyer stayed with the law and argued the evolution of the law clearly showed how some debts had, at one time, been considered not incurred for a common necessity of life, but as time went by the case authority evolved and the law had extended the "common necessity of life" definition to these very items which had once been considered not a common necessity of life. For example, a car was originally not considered a common necessity of life, but today it was. The opposing counsel gave example after example. At last, he did admit he had not found a case addressing the specific question of whether a phone service was, in all circumstances, a necessity of life, but he argued the law was evolving, just as it had in the example of the automobile he had cited earlier.

"In today's day, one must have a phone. It is a necessity of life. People live far away from essential services for health and safety and it is imperative they have a phone."

He closed his argument by pointing out the burden was on my client, the debtor, to show she was entitled to the exemption. He said we had not carried our burden of proving phone service was not a common necessity of life, so we should lose.

At the conclusion of the opposing counsel's testimony, the judge looked at me and said, "Do you have any final comments or is the matter submitted?"

I didn't really know what the judge meant, but it sounded like he was asking me if I had anything else to say. I had been impressed by the opposing attorney's comments, so I decided it might be a good idea to argue some more for my client. However, I also knew the judge had a big calendar and wanted to get on with the rest of his cases. He had remarked to other lawyers in their cases about being brief, such as, "Give me the abridged version, counsel." I knew I had to make my comments short, and I had better not repeat myself. I had to give the judge something different.

I responded I did have some final comments. The judge said he would allow them, but to make them brief. I began by saying it was the opposing counsel's burden to show the service his client furnished to this lady was a necessity of life. I said phone service was *not* clearly a common necessity of life. The judge interrupted to say I was starting to repeat myself, and I should conclude my comments. I felt the pressure to wrap it up, but I also sensed I had not persuaded the judge to rule in our favor. The opposing attorney's closing remarks were still hanging in the air: straightforward, factual, and persuasive.

I suddenly felt desperate. I was going to fail.

But then out of nowhere, I remembered what a law professor, in my trial practice class, had advised. When you have the law on your side, argue the law. When you have equity on your side, argue the equity.

The realization washed over me that the equities favored my client much more than the affluent phone company corporation, and I hadn't even argued them. I quickly shifted gears and argued the equities. I told the judge, pleading in a very emotional manner, that my client was in a hopeless financial situation. Her husband left her with well over $5,000.00 worth of debt and then ran away. She was the sole support of her three children and was doing all she could to stay off welfare. She was desperate, and she needed all of her income to live. She could not spare a dime.

I would probably still be talking to this day if the judge had not interrupted me to say, "Counsel, I am going to grant your client the full exemption, but you should really consider taking her through bankruptcy."

The way the judge said it, you could have substituted the word "son" instead of "counsel."

It was overwhelming. I was so thrilled to win my first case and delighted my poor client could keep her full paycheck. Without thinking, I responded to the judge, "Yes, Judge, thank you so much, Judge. I will put her through bankruptcy as soon as I learn how to do one."

Everyone in the courtroom broke out laughing – including the judge and opposing counsel.

As my client and I were leaving, I could see other lawyers and clients looking at us. My over-the-top emotional argument on the equities of a minor case, as well as my ecstatic reaction and remarks of happiness after winning the case, earned me the smiles, winks, and nods of veteran lawyers still seated in the audience waiting for their cases to be called. One grizzled lawyer gestured with a thumbs-up, mouthing the words, "Way to go!"

I still remember the excitement and satisfaction of winning that case. Even more, I remember the happiness of my client. It is true I had served as entertainment for the more seasoned lawyers and perhaps the judge during an otherwise routine and boring civil law and motion calendar. But for me, it was the thrill of a lifetime.

When I finally got home to my apartment, Tuna greeted me like I was a rock star (the usual greeting) and I, of course, immediately set about telling Tuna how I had won my first case. I may have exaggerated how good I was, but Tuna was very impressed, going so far as to jump into my arms. I hugged and kissed Tuna. Then we went out for a celebratory afternoon walk.

Mike Low continued to feed me a smattering of matters much like that first case. They were not always wage garnishments, but they were all small potatoes by any lawyer's standards. I did not mind, however. They were cases I could learn from, even though they did not have much value. I discovered I was not motivated by money, but by a personal determination not to be the lawyer who cost his client their case. That more than anything else drove me to win my cases. I had to go all out so there could be no second-guessing by anyone, especially by me. I would not have to wonder, if I had said or done something else, would the result have been different, and would my client have prevailed?

Anyone as desperate as I was to win, usually will do pretty well, because they will put in the time and energy necessary to properly prepare their case. Of course, they still need to have some facts on their side. There is not much one can do if the facts are against you. However, I was convinced that if everything else is equal, then the lawyer who works the hardest would prevail.

Before long, it became clear that Mike Low's leftovers were not going to earn me enough money to live independent of the free rent at the empty convent. The arrangement with the Church was already past the time I had expected I would have to move. Winter was approaching and 1972 was just around the corner. In late October, the Church finally got definite. They called, thanking me for living there, and followed up the call with a formal written notice to vacate in thirty days. It was time for Tuna and me to move again.

CHAPTER TWENTY-ONE

Job Hunting

Coinciding with the receipt of the thirty-day notice to vacate, I began applying for jobs everywhere I could find openings. I knew a job would probably require a move to someplace out of the City. I loved the City, but it was time to begin the serious practice of law. I applied to several legal agencies in counties in and around the Bay Area. A veteran attorney back in Napa had also contacted me. Joe Peatman was a partner in Dickenson, Peatman, and Fogarty (DP&F), at the time the largest law firm in Napa. In 1972 it had half a dozen lawyers. Most firms were either two lawyer firms or sole practitioners. DP&F was one of the most successful law firms in town. Both Howard Dickenson and Joe Peatman were former County Supervisors, and both had excellent reputations in their particular areas of the law, as did the third partner, Jim Fogarty. Howard Dickenson was a civil law attorney; Jim Fogarty handled probate law and estate planning; and Joe Peatman was the foremost authority on land use law in Napa at that time. All three partners were well connected in the community and their services were much in demand.

A job offer from DP&F was not one to lightly disregard. The offer coming from Joe Peatman himself meant a lot to me. Joe had been a friend of my family. My mother often babysat his three children. Joe loved my mom, and she loved him and his entire family. He had watched with interest my path from high school to college to law school. When he extended the offer, he told me he knew I was personable and believed my Italian heritage would be a benefit to the firm as well. The partners wanted me to practice in their small satellite office in the quaint town of St. Helena, about 20 miles north of the city of Napa. In this affluent up-valley location, there was a large population of well-to-do Italians. The firm believed they could place a young Italian lawyer in St. Helena writing wills and trusts, cornering the market for a lucrative probate/estate planning practice.

Money wasn't really the issue with me, but I couldn't help but notice the money offered for this job was pretty generous. I would start at $850.00 per month, which by Napa standards was an excellent starting salary, and to me, personally, a huge amount of money which would help pay off my student loans.

Around the same time Joe Peatman called me, I heard from my friend Joe Flax, who informed me there was a job opening at the San Joaquin County Public Defender's Office in Stockton. Joe was from Napa and had also attended Hastings Law School, one year ahead of me. Joe had learned of the public defender position when he himself was looking for work. However, he had just been offered a position as Deputy City Attorney in Stockton, so he was no longer considering the Public Defender position. Joe wanted to help me in my job hunt. Also, although he was married, he felt it would be fun having a buddy in Stockton with whom he could hang out.

The job sounded intriguing. It was in the field of criminal law and would give me important trial experience. Criminal attorneys spend most of their time in court and lots of time in trial. I had noticed that civil litigators, on the other hand, have less trial work. They made their money by settling cases. Further, I liked the idea of representing people accused of crimes. I had recently read a book by Attorney General Ramsey Clark in which he explored the disparity in prosecution rates of middle class Caucasians compared to low- income minorities. He posited that the root cause was poverty and its consequences. This made sense to me. I realized that, if given the choice, I would rather be using my new skills as a lawyer representing poor people.

But I wasn't ready to shut the door on the DP&F job in Napa. I called Joe Peatman, told him I greatly appreciated the job offer, and asked if I could have some time to think about it. I explained I had some other interviews to complete first. I asked for two weeks to make a final decision. Peatman graciously agreed.

I immediately contacted the Public Defender's Office in Stockton and submitted an application. A few days after I mailed the application, someone called to offer me the opportunity to interview for the position – in early March. The interview was not within the two-week grace period given to me by Joe Peatman. I either had to get a further extension or turn down his job offer.

I turned down the offer. I realized I didn't want to go back to Napa yet. I didn't want to be near my obnoxious father, I didn't want to just write wills, and I wanted to get the trial experience a Public Defender's Office would offer.

Joe was gracious and understanding. Later, when I did come home to Napa, he welcomed me as a friend, and on many occasions referred business to me when his firm could not handle a case because of a conflict. Some people might have held resentment toward me, but he did not. He tried to help me as much as he could. He was a real friend.

But I digress. I had turned down Joe's offer to come to Napa. Now I needed to get a job.

CHAPTER TWENTY-TWO

San Joaquin County Public Defender's Office

The day of my interview finally arrived. I knew from talking to Joe Flax he had met Public Defender Robert Chargin when he interviewed there. Even though Joe took the Stockton City Attorney job, he had done his research on Chargin. Joe told me he was a longtime resident of Stockton and a well-respected attorney in the area. Mr. Chargin was a caring and sentimental man who was very loyal to his deputies and staff, which in turn earned him the loyalty and admiration of his employees.

The interview was scheduled for 10:00 a.m. I left San Francisco at about 7:00 a.m. to make sure I had time for unanticipated mishaps, flat tires, or whatever else could go wrong. I was not going to be late for this appointment.

I arrived more than two hours early. I was wearing my best corduroy light brown jacket with khaki slacks and new brown loafers. The past few years I had sported a full beard, but I decided my interview chances might be better if I shaved, so now I only had a great-looking (in my opinion) moustache. It doubtless looked silly, but I thought I presented a clean-shaven appearance.

After locating the Public Defender's office, I decided to kill some time walking around the surrounding area. The first thing I observed was how poor and run-down this part of the city seemed to be. Every building was at least 50 years old and the entire area seemed dilapidated. The Public Defender's Office was housed in a three-story building converted from an old hotel. The area also held a hint of danger. Across the street from the Public Defender's Office was a dark, dirty bar called the Owl Club. It had an ancient neon "Schlitz" sign in its barred window and a larger neon sign sticking out over the sidewalk with an owl perched next to the word "Club."

Next door to the Owl Club was a little hole-in-the-wall shoeshine shop of a type not much seen anymore. A one-man operation about the size of a telephone booth, the shop was equipped with two chairs for two customers. I later discovered they were used mostly for the old proprietor and a buddy to sit and pass the time of day philosophizing about the troubles of the modern world.

The little shop had no door but rather a rusty iron gate (similar to old elevator gates) which could be used to close shop at the end of the workday. Even with the gate closed, you could still see the chairs, shoe shine box, rags, and polish.

Next to the little shoeshine shop was an Italian deli. It had the name "Angelina and Ferrari" painted on the plate glass window. Like the shoeshine shop, an ancient sliding metal gate was locked in place across the front of the deli when it was closed.

By 8:30 a.m. it was already hot. I had a fleeting thought of going to the Owl Club for a shot of whiskey, but instantly dismissed it as absurd. I was not going to have any alcohol on my breath during my interview. Besides, it was barely 8:30 a.m. The only reason whiskey even occurred to me was because I was nervous about the impending interview and would have loved to have been able to calm my nerves. I decided to keep strolling.

Proceeding south down South San Joaquin Street, I observed more of the same. Xochimilco's Mexican restaurant stood right next door to the Public Defender's Office, and adjacent to it was a corner store named Calcagno's Liquors. I later figured out the proprietor was the brother of my mother's godson. Small world.

Across the street from the liquor store was a dry cleaner's shop. Everything looked decrepit, faded, or tired. Further south was an old Catholic Church and a park where groups of people were just sitting around or lying on the lawn. They apparently had nothing to do. It dawned on me they were probably homeless. Or maybe they were just killing time until they drifted down to the Owl Club for a drink.

There didn't seem to be anything else of interest in a southerly direction, so I decided to turn north. I came upon a coffee shop called Emma's Café that was reminiscent of the old breakfast/lunch diners which have mostly faded away due to fast food and chain restaurants. There was a movie theatre that had once been a majestic palace showing the premier movies of its era. The theatre was still adorned with multitudes of little Christmas lights on the ceiling and neon signs on each side of the once magnificent entrance, but it too, had become a run-down relic of a time past. It was no longer showing conventional movies, but rather films not suitable for family entertainment.

Across the street and a little further north, was a tall, newer-looking building. Seven stories high, it stood out from the run-down one and two-story structures in this area. It was the Stockton Courthouse. There was still an hour before my interview, so I decided to go into the courthouse and look around.

The courtrooms were located on the upper floors of the building. After checking the directory, I headed to the second floor to see what was going on in the Municipal Courts. These were the courts that heard small claims, traffic cases, and misdemeanor criminal matters. I discovered this floor was extremely crowded around 9:00 a.m. From my few months of law practice in San Francisco I recognized lawyers in the hall talking to other lawyers, trying to make deals and settle civil cases. Young deputy district attorneys and deputy public defenders were also out in the halls, trying to negotiate last-minute plea bargains. The noise in the hallways was a steady drone. I made my way into a courtroom where it was less noisy, but still chaotic, as the judge had not yet taken the bench, and there was still a buzz of talking going on. I didn't have time to wait for the action to start, so I left the courtroom and quickly went up to the third floor to see what was happening in Superior Court. This was where the felonies, big money personal injury cases, and family law cases were being tried.

I opened the door to a family law courtroom and couldn't tell if I had missed the case already, or if it hadn't even started. There was no one in the courtroom but a bailiff, a court clerk, and two lawyers with their clients, presumably the husband and wife, because this was, after all, divorce court. I asked the bailiff if the case had been heard yet. He said it was about to start, so I quietly slipped into the back row of fold down, theater-style seats, and sat down.

A few seconds later, an older black-robed judge seemed to appear out of nowhere and took his seat behind the elevated walnut paneled bench which housed both himself and a clerk, who was busying herself with paperwork and otherwise apparently ignoring the proceedings. A uniformed, armed deputy sheriff was to her left at a desk. He appeared to be sleeping with his eyes open.

Both attorneys walked over to the counsel table accompanied by their respective clients who dropped into seats next to their lawyers. The court calendar posted by the courtroom door hall said the case name was Carpenter vs. Carpenter. The woman appeared to be in her 40s. Although it was only March, she was wearing a brightly colored floral print sundress. She wore her hair in a throwback style, sort of an early Jackie Kennedy look. She had accessorized with a bracelet and necklace matching the colors of her dress. Her husband also looked to be in his 40s and was dressed in the latest fashion of the day, including a lavender shirt, a wide matching lavender tie, and a loud plaid sport coat. He had frizzy black hair and long side burns, with a neatly trimmed mustache. He looked ridiculous – like he was trying hard for a sophisticated, debonair look but came out more like a circus clown. He had definitely missed the goal he was shooting for by a very wide margin, assuming the goal was not to look like a clown. I found myself wondering if Mr. Carpenter was having a mid-life crisis or merely a complete lack of fashion sense.

The attorneys were also dressed smartly. Mrs. Carpenter's attorney was slick-haired, with lots of styling gel, and was wearing a double-breasted glen plaid suit. He was the younger of the attorneys, perhaps in his late 30s. Mr. Carpenter's attorney was in his 50s, with long silver hair that also had lots of product in it. He was wearing a thinly striped seersucker sport coat with burgundy pants, held up by a white belt. His shoes were also white. He looked like an ice cream salesman. It made me want a Fudgesicle.

The judge peered over the bench at the lawyers. "All right, I will call the case of Carpenter and Carpenter. May I have appearances, please."

Each attorney introduced himself, first the attorney for Mrs. Carpenter, who was the petitioner in the case, and then the attorney for the husband, Mr. Carpenter, the respondent in the action.

The judge said he had reviewed the file and noted the case was on for a motion to establish spousal and child support for the wife and their three children. He also noted the husband had filed opposition documents contesting the amount of the support being sought. The judge asked if the parties were both prepared to proceed. It was obvious the judge was ready to get the hearing started and commence with the evidence.

The husband's attorney spoke first. "Your Honor, we are pleased to announce the parties have reached a resolution in this matter as to all issues. We have reduced to writing our oral agreement and would ask that the court review it and if it meets with your approval, Your Honor, make this agreement the order of the court pursuant to our stipulation."

The judge seemed pleased he would not have to spend the morning hearing another divorce case with two squabbling parties, each quarreling over who was the real victim. He turned to the wife's attorney and asked in a perfunctory manner, "Is this accurate, counsel, that is, have the parties reached an agreement?"

The attorney for the wife replied, "Well, Your Honor, if it please the court, I would like to state for the record the respondent, Mr. Carpenter, has deserted his wife, leaving her with three children to care for and support, as well as her own support. She is unable to work as she has the full-time care, custody, and control of the three children, one of which is not even in school yet. Now, Your Honor, she is not complaining, mind you, she is a wonderful mother, and loves being a mother, it is just that she has no viable means to support herself or her three young kids. Mr. Carpenter just took off with his 28-year-old secretary, and left Mrs. Carpenter and the three kids high and dry, twisting in the wind, with no financial means to support themselves and no way to contact him. As to visitation, Mr. Carpenter never visits his kids except on…"

"Objection, Your Honor," interrupted Mr. Carpenter's attorney, in an attempt to stop what appeared to be an unexpected filibuster from opposing counsel. "I have no idea where counsel is going with this. We have reached an agreement, a stipulation as to all the issues regarding support, both future support and back arrearages, which are the only issues before the court at this time. I do not know why we need to get into these issues. If it makes counsel feel any better, I will stipulate my client is no good. May we now proceed?"

The judge turned back to Mrs. Carpenter's attorney and said, "Yes, counsel, I agree with the respondent's position. If an agreement has been reached, then there is no need to go into any of these issues. They are no longer relevant. There is no longer a need for a hearing. So, I ask you again, counsel, because you still have not answered my original question, have you and opposing counsel reached an agreement as to all of the issues or not?"

Mrs. Carpenter's attorney thought for a moment and then finally said, "Yes, Your Honor, we have an agreement."

The judge said, "All right, give the written stipulation to the bailiff and I will review it."

After skimming through the stipulation, the judge spoke directly to the wife and then the husband, asking if they each understood the terms of the stipulation and were entering into it voluntarily. Then he asked if they were willing to abide by the terms of the agreement. Each time the judge asked one of these questions, the husband and wife answered in the affirmative. His questions complete, the judge approved the stipulation and said he was making it a court order. He signed the original document and handed it to the clerk for filing. He thanked the parties. The brief hearing was over. The lawyers and their clients filed toward the door.

As I was about to get up to leave the courtroom, the gray bearded judge noticed the only person sitting in the audience and called out, "You lost, son?"

"Ah, no sir, just watching," I stammered, instinctively rising from my seat.

The judge chuckled, "We don't get many interested observers in family law disputes. I figured you were a friend or relative of one of the parties."

"No, Your Honor, I'm killing time before I have an interview with the Public Defender's Office at 10:00 a.m."

The smile disappeared from the judge's weathered and lined face. "There seems to be no end to you new fellows. How does Bob Chargin do it? Where does he find it in his budget to keep hiring?" After an awkward silence, he added, "Well, good luck, young man." He rose, stepped down and disappeared into his chambers.

It was time to get to my interview at the Public Defender's Office. I quickly walked back to the old building across the street from the Owl Club.

Entering the reception area, I introduced myself to the receptionist and said I had an interview with Bob Chargin for the position of deputy public defender. She told me to have a seat and said she would let the Public Defender know I was there.

After a few minutes, Mr. Chargin emerged from the office area with a big smile on his face. After a friendly greeting, he invited me into his office, which was located on the first floor of the old building. Once inside, I immediately observed that everything in the small cramped office appeared oversized and out of place. If Mr. Chargin was trying to portray a county department head that was not in luxury, but rather getting by on a shoestring budget, he was succeeding. He settled into an oversized brown executive chair which was weathered and worn. It reminded me of the old, torn, Naugahyde brown chair in our living room where my dad sat, wearing a wife-beater T-shirt and boxer shorts, while watching wrestling on our Zenith black and white television.

Like his chair, Mr. Chargin's desk looked like it may have been expensive when new but had long since become worn and scratched. The wood didn't come close to matching anything else in the room, including the fake walnut veneer paneled walls. The green shag carpeting also matched nothing, and, as far as I could tell, it was the only carpet in the whole place. The waiting room and the hallway were floored with 1950's-era linoleum. The entire office looked run-down and slapped together. Clearly, no one gave any thought to interior decorating.

It didn't take me more than a minute to realize Bob Chargin was a smart, kind, and sentimental man. He asked how I was doing and how traffic was driving over from San Francisco. He joked about the office not being a palace, but explained it was functional for him and his employees. I assured him I was most comfortable in the office. After a momentary pause, I told him I had mailed my resume and asked if he received it. He said he had and pointed to it on his desk. He said he hadn't had a chance to review it but was looking forward to doing so with me during the interview. With that, he picked up my resume and started to read through it. I sat anxiously watching him. At length, Mr. Chargin looked up and asked, "Well, why do you want to be a public defender?"

I told him I was convinced poverty was the root cause of most crime in America. I wanted to be part of the solution, and on the side of these poor people. However, as the words were coming out of my mouth, I realized what I was saying might be coming across as a standard, politically correct response.

What the heck. I decided to go with a more complete answer. "Also, I need a job, and my friend, Joe Flax, told me about this opening."

He laughed and seemed to appreciate the candor. Then he glanced at his watch and invited me to have lunch with some of the deputies. I figured he wanted to get some input from the lawyers on his staff. I would have to pass the peer test at lunch.

The one-on-one office interview was over. We had been in his office for less than 15 minutes when he rose and said he wanted to take me around to meet some of the staff, including some of the deputy public defenders who might not be able to attend lunch. Suddenly, my spirits began to sag. Based on the brevity of the interview, it seemed likely it hadn't gone well. Thinking back to the mental challenge of the bar exam, I resolved to stay positive.

Our first stop was the secretarial pool which was immediately adjacent to Chargin's office. There were six ill-matching desks crowded into the room. On each desk stood a huge, cumbersome IBM Selectric typewriter. Young women were seated behind each of the desks, some typing quickly, some flipping through the pages of legal files. The room fell silent when Chargin ushered me in and we were suddenly looking at six faces, all regarding me with frank curiosity.

"Ladies, this is Raymond Guadagni from Napa who has just finished up at Hastings and is interested in coming to work with us."

They smiled and seemed to be giving me the once over. I smiled back at them, feeling very awkward and uncomfortable. Then we were gone, heading briskly upstairs to the library where I met a couple of attorneys who were assigned to research. Then Chargin introduced me to a couple of deputy public defenders whose offices were also on the second floor. Both deputies greeted Chargin with the succinct appellation "Boss," which I soon learned was how Chargin was referred to by the vast majority of both the staff and the attorneys. After the brief introduction, Chargin told the deputies to take me around to meet other deputies, and then to come downstairs to the lobby at 11:45, so that all the available lawyers could go to lunch.

As I walked around with the two young attorneys, meeting yet more attorneys, I quickly realized just how out of my element I was. There were constant digressions involving questions about pending cases. The lawyers were casually throwing around jargon that made absolutely no sense to me. After listening to their easy legal banter for several minutes, I at one point mustered up the courage to interrupt.

"Excuse me, but what is a 245?"

"ADW," one of the attorneys said pleasantly, as we turned into yet another small, cramped office to meet another deputy.

Not knowing what an ADW was, either, the answer made no more sense to me than "245" had. But I decided not to press the matter – there were more people to meet.

At last, it was time to gather for lunch. It developed the Boss liked to bring the interviewee to lunch with as many deputies as were available, so they could evaluate the candidate on a visceral level. Mr. Chargin wanted to know if his deputies liked me and would want me to be part of their team.

We gathered in the lobby. There were six deputies and myself. All of the deputies were male. All of them were dressed in lightweight slacks, sport coats and ties. One of the deputies said Mr. Chargin would not be joining us, so we should leave now. He led the way, opening the glass door of the office. I was hit with an immediate inferno-like blast of heat that burned my face before the door had swung closed behind me. I felt like I was baking in an oven as we walked to a Chinese restaurant that was only about 500 steps away. I was dripping with sweat by the time I gratefully lunged through the door into the swamp-cooled humidity of the extremely…casual…establishment.

As I dropped into the plastic-covered chair, I found myself silently wondering, "What am I doing to my life? It is 110 degrees in March and I am eating chow mein. Is this what I really want to do?"

But, I needed to keep an open mind and, even more, I needed a job. We ordered, the food arrived quickly – I could see why busy lawyers on a budget might frequent the place – and I began to relax a little. All the deputies were about my age, and, coincidentally, almost all from the Bay Area. I discovered myself feeling comfortable. We seemed to be relating.

After lunch, we headed back to the office. Chargin met with me in private one last time and explained the remaining process – when recruitment would end and when decisions would be made. After we shook hands, I made my way back out to the sidewalk, where it was even hotter than it had been when we returned from lunch. But as I climbed into the blast furnace that my car had become, I was hardly noticing the heat – I was too busy sorting out my feelings and weighing my options.

Safely home in my peculiar – but cool – lodgings in Hunters Point, Tuna listened carefully to my detailed description of the day, including the exploration of the courthouse and surrounding part of the city. I wasn't completely sure Tuna really was listening when I disclosed the terribly intense heat. He should have listened. It was less than two weeks later I received a call from Mr. Chargin offering me the job. I was to start in one week. I had to find a place to live in Stockton as soon as possible.

CHAPTER TWENTY-THREE

Stockton, California

Stockton is located in California's San Joaquin Valley, one of the richest agricultural areas in the United States and possibly the entire world. It is big, flat and perfect for producing abundant crops, with its alluvial soils and the blistering heat of its afternoons. The valley is very wide and developed, including half a dozen cities. Stockton is the largest and most substantial city in San Joaquin County.

The valley's summer heat is intense, but dry and so much more tolerable than the stifling humidity of some other parts of the country. The evenings are relatively cool compared to the nights in, for example, St. Louis at a similar time of year.

I was moving to Stockton in early 1972, and air conditioning had immeasurably improved the livability in the valley. Simple swamp coolers were very popular, less expensive, and actually somewhat effective because of the dryness of the air. The shade trees in the older parts of town had grown tall and eased the worst of the summer heat, when afternoon temperatures above 100 degrees were as much the rule as the exception. This was the very same heat that provided the ideal growing conditions for the valley's multitude of crops.

I thought I would hate the intense San Joaquin Valley heat, having grown up in the much more agreeable climate of the Napa Valley. Air conditioning, however, made the heat manageable, and I learned to tolerate it. What I found more disagreeable than the heat was the dense ground-hugging tule fog. In the winter, stagnant high-pressure systems would clamp down, locking in the fog and shutting out the sun for weeks at a time.

The impact of the fog on valley life was far-reaching. The Highway Patrol regularly had to lead long lines of traffic down the highway at maddeningly slow speeds to avoid the chain reaction highway pile-ups that commonly occurred without the Patrol's intervention. Airports occasionally had to close, and this, together with the slowing of vehicle traffic, resulted in business slowdowns. Schools were put on "foggy day schedules" with busses and classes running one or two hours late. But for the farmers, the persistent blanket of fog had the positive effect of providing protection for the citrus industry from the damaging frosts that clear, cold winter nights might otherwise bring.

A lot was going on in the world during the early 1970's, just before, during, and right after Tuna and I took up residence in this central part of California. All the chaos of the 60's, which included the war in Vietnam and social change, seemed certain to continue in the 70's. There was clearly an evolving trend toward disillusionment with government.

The war was dragging on and dividing our country. President Nixon vowed to bring the conflict to an "honorable conclusion" – in effect, promising to end the war. Visible signs of this promise could be seen when our boys started to come back home. And, thank goodness, most of them were coming home alive and not in the dreaded body bags the country was used to seeing on the nightly news. Still, until the war was over, it wasn't over. We were used to seeing this war continue, despite the rhetoric of politicians. It seemed as if no one believed any politician anymore. And of all politicians, why would you believe that Richard Nixon, with his hawkish background, would end this war? Admittedly, there were now some encouraging signs, but the fact remained, one of the consequences of this war was to change our country significantly in terms of the government's credibility with its citizens.

There were events occurring here and abroad that affected us besides the war in Vietnam. An Arab-Israeli war was causing grave concern to our country. It spilled over into the Olympics, when the Arabs took and killed hostages while the world watched on television. There were oil boycotts and skyrocketing gasoline prices. American citizens were lining up their automobiles in depression era bread-line fashion, waiting hours to fill up their tanks. People were getting in physical fights over gas hogs who topped off and then filled extra containers. There was trouble and unrest on both the foreign and domestic fronts.

But not everything was negative in our country in the early 70's. We also saw advances in civil rights, increased influence of the women's movement, a heightened concern for the environment, and breakthroughs in space exploration. Ideas which seemed so radical in the 60's were now gaining acceptance in the new decade and were mainstreamed into the culture and life of America. Powerful events and ideas can inspire music, literature, and entertainment, and the early 70's reflected its times.

Sandwiched around the war and social change was routine life. In 1972, in Stockton, California, that meant life went on as usual. People went to work and came home. They watched the top TV shows of the times (*All in The Family*, *Sanford And Son*, and *Hawaii Five-O*) and they enjoyed the TV premiers of *The Bob Newhart Show*, *MASH*, and *Maude*.

They listened to new pop songs like *American Pie* by Don McLean and *The First Time Ever I Saw Your Face* by Roberta Flack.

They went to movies like *The Godfather*, *The Poseidon Adventure*, and *The Candidate*.

They heard, without at first understanding the significance of the news, that five burglars had been arrested on June 17, 1972, inside Democratic national headquarters in Washington DC's Watergate complex. The citizens of San Joaquin County, California, like the vast majority of the people in this country, didn't realize this was the beginning of the end of President Nixon's presidency. Six days later, President Nixon and White House chief of staff H.R. Haldeman discussed a plan to use the CIA to obstruct the FBI's Watergate investigation. Revelation of the tape recording of this conversation sparked Nixon's resignation in 1974.

Of course, they closely followed the news on the war, and could hardly be blamed for being skeptical about the news on August 12, 1972, reporting that the last American combat ground-troops left Vietnam.

They watched the Dallas Cowboys win the super bowl and the Oakland A's win the World Series.

And, amid the hostage-taking violence of the 1972 Olympics, America watched with pride as U.S. swimmer Mark Spitz, on September 4, won a record seventh Olympic gold medal, in the 400-meter relay at the Munich Summer Olympics.

As for fashion, in 1972 around the courthouse in Stockton, California, it would be commonplace to see lawyers dressed in leisure suits, with women being fashionable in everything from ankle-length granny dresses to micro-miniskirts.

These were the times. This was 1972.

CHAPTER TWENTY-FOUR

Tuna Moves to Stockton

Tuna had to stay with Grandpa Al and Grandma Anne in Napa, while I searched for our new home in Stockton. House hunting took some time, so for my first few weeks in the new job, I arranged to stay with a friend from law school who had also found work in Stockton. The accommodations with my friend weren't convenient for him or for me. I didn't want to overstay his hospitality. He had a new wife and I felt like I was imposing on the young couple.

The problem was, I didn't have a lot of time to house hunt because I had plunged into the new job the day after I arrived in town. I reluctantly decided on a short term, month to month tenancy of an apartment in North Stockton. It was the only affordable option – but pets were not allowed. I asked Mom to continue to watch Tuna. To my vast relief, she was happy to do so because it helped me.

I continued my search for the right place to comfortably house me along with Tuna. Not only did I miss his companionship, but Mom reported he was sharpening his excavation abilities in the back yard. I began to worry he might escape.

After about three months of searching, I located a flat on the second story of an old Victorian house for $110.00 per month. It was very spacious, with a kitchen, back porch, bedroom, and large living room/dining room area. It was fully furnished. And, crucially, the landlady allowed dogs! Another plus was that the old house was on Center Street, not far from the Public Defender's office. Notwithstanding their close proximity, the difference between the neighborhoods surrounding this old Victorian house and the Public Defender's Office was stark. I felt safe in my new home and its immediate surroundings. There were old but nice houses in the area, as well as a city park. It would be a great neighborhood for strolls and walks with Tuna.

In contrast, the neighborhood surrounding the Public Defender's office was a different story altogether. It was a seedy depressed part of town, where people gambled in the alleys alongside the rundown storefronts. There were drunks rolling other drunks in the park south of the old stores. There were lots of drunks in old bars like the Owl Club, across the street from the Public Defender's Office. The Owl Club was pitch dark inside and inhabited by people who would settle in as soon as the club opened in the early morning hours. The ambiance was not suitable for bringing a date, and, in fact, was not even suitable for stopping by yourself. One would want a gang of guys with oneself, for self-protection.

There was a weedy lot south of the Public Defender's Office where you could park for free all day. Free parking appealed to me. I was frugal by nature and had school debts to pay, so anything free sounded good. It was about a ten-minute walk to the office from the dirt lot. The only problem was, the neighborhood around the lot was even more run down than the area surrounding the Public Defender's office. The place was desolate, sporadically decorated with dilapidated shacks that looked like they were falling down. These shacks appeared to be abandoned, except for vagrants who crashed there from time to time. I soon learned law enforcement considered this area to be a high crime rate location, which spoke volumes, considering it was located in the City of Stockton.

This high crime rate area had to be crossed each morning and evening as I went to and from the office and the free parking lot. After parking in the lot a few times and returning to it in the dark of the evening, I decided I would stop parking there, free or not. Since I could get to the office on foot from my home in just over ten minutes, I decided to walk and eliminate any risk of danger going into that area.

Tuna and I moved into the upper story of the old Victorian on Center Street on a sunny weekend in early September. In anticipation of the move, I had driven to Napa to pick up Tuna, so we could move in together. Upon seeing me he was ecstatic – jumping into my arms and licking me all over my face. He was ready to move anywhere with me.

The house was huge and gave Tuna plenty of room to explore. This was a far cry from being cooped up in a small home like my parents' 900 square foot bungalow in Napa. The rooms were spacious, with tall ceilings. After our years sharing the crammed student flat in San Francisco, Tuna and I felt like we had moved into a mansion. This was the previously-mentioned home with the beautiful old large dining room table finished in a very shiny black veneer adorned by a sheer, elegant, embroidered, yet understated white tablecloth. More specifically, this was where Tuna's most famous and requested trick, Clear the Table Tuna, was born.

Tuna and I were comfortable in this lovely Victorian and immediately got down to the business of enjoying Stockton, California.

By the time we had moved out of the San Francisco flat, Tuna had once again proven himself sufficiently trustworthy to resume exercising with free runs morning and evening. These were relieved by weekend leashed walks with me when we would explore new parts of the city. I had gradually stopped worrying he might once again disappear for three and a half months and be named Peter by the time he came home.

We both wanted to get back to this routine in Stockton, but I was concerned. Center Street was a busy downtown thoroughfare, and the surroundings were unfamiliar to Tuna. For the first few months, I didn't allow Tuna to roam – all of his outings were on the leash. Then I began to release Tuna from his leash while we were on our walk, but I kept a vigilant eye to make sure he would not disappear for long periods of time. The day finally arrived when I felt confident Tuna had developed a thorough knowledge of our neighborhood. But I still felt some anxiety as I brought him out to the front porch and, instead of clipping on the leash, simply released him. He glanced at me once, and then trotted up the street and disappeared around the corner. After approximately half an hour, Tuna returned home to find me still sitting on the porch. The experiment had been a success. It seemed like things could go back to the San Francisco routine of giving Tuna the large degree of exercise he required. My decision was influenced by the fact I was no longer living the life of a graduate student. In my new job, I simply didn't have the time to walk Tuna on a leash for the number of daily hours he craved. I had to balance the risks of his daily solo walks against the health and mental health benefits of his getting sufficient exercise.

As it happened, my decision worked out well.

Except for a couple of times.

CHAPTER TWENTY-FIVE

Tuna and the Chicken

After a few months, the routine of releasing Tuna from the house to wander on his own was working out perfectly. No matter where he ventured, Tuna would return thirty to sixty minutes later, unscathed and happy. We were back in our San Francisco routine, and it felt like a return to normalcy for both of us.

This feeling of normalcy continued until the day when Tuna, unbeknownst to me, reverted to some primeval, ancient type of canine pathology and became a hunter of his food. Apparently, the canned and dry dog food and scraps I was feeding him were not really what this dog needed to sustain him.

Tuna would eat what he killed, and he would hunt what he ate. I learned this, in no uncertain terms, when one Saturday morning around 7:00, I released him to take his usual potty and exercise run. Nothing in his personal history or in these routine dog runs had given the slightest hint of what happened next. After setting Tuna free on his run, I went inside to have my coffee and read the paper. As was my custom I checked outside after half an hour to see if Tuna had returned. He hadn't, so I went back inside and didn't check again for another half hour (now one-hour total time elapsed). Again, no Tuna. This was a bit unusual. I called out but there was no response. Again, I went back inside to drink more coffee. I continued checking every half hour after that.

I was on my sixth or seventh round, at about 10:30 a.m., when I once again threw the door open. This time Tuna had indeed returned and was waiting for me on the front porch. However, my relief quickly changed to horror when I saw Tuna had a mangled, dead, full-grown chicken in his mouth. Panicked, I quickly looked up and down Center Street to see if there were any angry people following Tuna or other potential observers of this incident. I pictured a horde of angry villagers with lighted torches and pitchforks coming after my dog.

No one was on the street, but there was a distinct trail of chicken feathers coming around a distant corner and leading directly to the porch where man and dog stood. They could not have been more obvious. These feathers appeared to be planted carefully and perfectly, forming a direct path to the killer's doorstep. Did Tuna want to be caught? Was it a cry for help by my beloved dog? Or was Tuna proud of his accomplishment and hoping the neighbors would come see his prize? As soon as the thought occurred to me, I knew that was it: he would have gladly used chalk to draw an arrow on the sidewalks to our house if he had been able to.

My panic grew. On the one hand, I needed to clean up the chicken feathers before some angry farmer came running after me. Until those feathers were gone, there would be no mistaking where the culprit was. Based on my sketchy knowledge of angry farmers, I was certain he or she would want Tuna dead. On the other hand, if the truth be known, I wanted to kill Tuna myself for setting us both up for trouble.

Fighting to stay calm, I decided the first thing to do was get the dead chicken out of Tuna's mouth and dispose of the body. How to disappear a mangled chicken? Put it in the trash? Would that be too easy to discover? Put it in a garbage bag and then in the trunk of the car and drive it out to the country and bury it? This felt like a scene out of a mobster movie. Was I now an accessory after the fact to the crime? Wasn't I aiding and abetting the murder of a chicken? But first there was a threshold problem to resolve – getting the chicken out of Tuna's mouth. I had no idea how to solve this issue. Tuna was prancing around like a macho bullfighter with the horns of his kill, obviously determined to enjoy the rewards of his hunt.

Perplexed, I stared down at this complete stranger, who had begun to gorge himself on the chicken. Getting it out of his mouth now seemed not only difficult, but possibly dangerous. I realized anyone who saw Tuna at that moment would not soon forget the horrifying visual image. He looked like a zombie feasting on a decaying body. Unable to come up with a better plan, I reached out and grasped at one wing, seemingly flapping as Tuna shook the bird's body from side to side. It was as if Tuna had received an electric shock. He jumped away and screeched a frantic warning growl, bubbly with chicken blood. At that moment, I was terrified of my dog – he was unrecognizable to me. I had seen Tuna in some odd, high stress situations, but I had never seen this side of him before. As he stood there, facing me off, guarding his prey, I seriously considered darting back into the house and slamming the door.

I was really worried Tuna might run off with his victim, at which point, there would be no hope of protecting him from his crime. Reaching for his leash, I quickly grabbed Tuna by the scruff of his neck. His growl increased as I snapped the leash into place and standing back, pulled it tight. I wrapped the leash around a banister of the porch, figuring he couldn't run from me. Talking calmly, I explained it was me – his buddy – his friend who loves him. I told him I was not an animal competing for his kill. I sat on a chair on the porch and waited, continuing to talk to him.

After a while he sat down himself, all the while gnawing at the chicken. I tried getting up from the chair, but Tuna immediately stood up, growling and watching my every move. This went on for fifteen minutes. Eventually, Tuna set the chicken down on the porch, but carefully laid across his two front paws. The passage of time began to have its effect. I once again rose from my chair and went over and just stood by him. He remained lying down and no longer seemed so agitated. Suddenly, he knew me again. He started to wag his tail as I continued talking to him. I pulled him away with his leash, the chicken remaining on the porch, and brought him in the house. Inside, I grabbed some old newspapers, rushed back outside, picked up the bird, and wrapped the body in the newspaper. Darting out the back door, I buried it in my garbage can. Then I got the broom, dustpan, and garbage bag, and carefully swept up the long trail of chicken feathers that spanned the block.

When the evidence was swept away, I crept back to the house, unable to believe I had been able to clean the entire street without anyone coming along to see what I was doing. As soon as I was back in the house, I put Tuna in the bathtub and carefully washed away the incriminating evidence of blood and feathers matting his coat.

At last, I sat Tuna down in the kitchen and gave him a long lecture. To my great relief he seemed to be his old self – very affectionate, and not at all like the hideous monster who had been out on the front stoop only minutes before.

As I sat looking into Tuna's guileless, adoring eyes, the questions began to settle around us. Where were we to go from here? Could Tuna ever again be released to roam the streets of Stockton on his own? Could he be trusted to not raid a chicken coop? The answers to these questions remained unknown, at least for a few weeks. After the cold-blooded murder of the innocent chicken, I reverted to allowing Tuna to go outside only on a leash and in my personal custody. He was on probation, with terms and conditions that he not hunt, hurt, or kill any more chickens. I had no way of knowing whether Tuna understood these terms or, more importantly, whether he was willing or capable of abiding by them, so I walked him on his leash every day for about two weeks. I found myself wondering if things could ever return to normal? Was there really a bustling chicken coop nearby? If he ran free again, would Tuna bring home another mangled, partially dismantled chicken? Would he get caught by the infuriated farmer who so worried me? Would he be taken prisoner by the animal control officer? Would he not return at all?

I finally decided the only way to learn the answers to these questions would be by allowing Tuna to leave the house without a leash. So, one Saturday morning, with much trepidation, I let Tuna off his leash to run for what I hoped would be just a normal morning airing for my dog. After about a half an hour, Tuna returned unscathed, and without any dead animals in his mouth. There were absolutely no signs of a struggle, nor any indication anything out of the norm had taken place. But this did not give me complete comfort. Had this run only been successful because Tuna didn't find any chickens or other small prey? Perhaps he was just on a reconnaissance mission setting up his next murderous heist. Assuming there was a chicken coop nearby, did Tuna avoid violence and thievery only because there was someone watching said chickens? Was Tuna just lying low until conditions were primed for a successful hunt? Over the ensuing days, and then weeks, these thoughts haunted me, but I ultimately decided the chicken incident was indeed an isolated incident. I would have to trust that Tuna had returned to his non-violent, law-abiding ways.

CHAPTER TWENTY-SIX

Riddle

After the chicken incident, life was quiet for quite some time. Each morning I let Tuna go out for a half hour run before I went to work. Early each evening I took Tuna for a walk. During dinner, Tuna listened to the significant events of my workday before settling in to watch TV or snuggle with me as I read my files for the next day's work. Then, before bed, he would have another half hour on his own outside.

Meanwhile, on the work side of life, I was assigned to the library. The Boss believed every new hire should start in the library as a research attorney to learn how the justice system worked. Then, when Boss felt the time was right, the young lawyer would be moved into the court, joining fellow deputies in the rotation of lawyers. Once in the court rotation, the lawyer would start out working with the misdemeanor deputies, receiving cases from "El Jefe." El Jefe was the chief deputy in charge of the lawyers handling cases involving misdemeanors. It wasn't long before I figured out El Jefe was in fact not a specific person, but just the young deputy who had been in the rotation the longest of the misdemeanor lawyers. Promotion to El Jefe occurred when the previous El Jefe was promoted to the felony rotation of lawyers.

As an attorney in the library, my job was to research legal questions and write appellate briefs for cases we had lost at trial. The job had its peaks and valleys. Sometimes, you would be very busy as the trial attorneys assigned a multitude of issues to research and motions to be written which the trial attorneys would then argue in court. At other times the attorneys assigned to the library had very little to do. One of the reasons for this was there were quite a few researchers assigned to the library at any one time. When I arrived, there were two law students from Humphrey's, Stockton's local law school, doing research work as interns, plus at least two other new lawyers doing their "library time" before they got into the court rotation.

The library was ten feet wide and twelve feet long. In the center of the room was a large rectangular table with six chairs, placed three on each side. The walls were lined with bookcases containing law books, evidence books, treatises, Bells Compendium – the bible on search and seizure law – and form books. It was a well-equipped library for the field of criminal law. Usually the room was not crowded. Most of the time there were only the two or three research attorneys plus the occasional interns. However, from time to time, the trial lawyers would visit the library to research their own issues. The table was kept neatly ordered except for the one or two projects that the research attorneys were working on.

The library stint was not the most exciting assignment for a new lawyer dreaming of getting into the courtroom and trying cases, but it was one the Boss believed was necessary. Library duty was the foundation for competent trial work.

One minor blessing of library work was you could depend on going home at 5:00 pm. This gave my life stability and predictability. When I got home, Tuna and I could move into our regular routine: I got out of my "court clothes" and into my comfortable stuff, and we went outside for a walk or run. It was relaxing and fun and sometimes invigorating. I was never big into exercise, but these little jaunts helped both of us to stay in shape. After our exercise, we retired to our house for the evening, which included dinner for two and usually a movie on TV.

It was during library duty that I met the person who would become my best friend at the office. When we met, he was one of the interns. His name was Patrick David Riddle. I eventually realized Riddle was the most amazing guy I had ever met. He was smart, handsome, and quick-witted, with a superb sense of humor. A great athlete, he was captain of his high school football team at Lincoln High in Stockton. At Fresno State, he was the starting middle linebacker and captain of the defense for the freshman team. When I arrived in Stockton, Riddle (as everyone called him) was within a few months of graduating from Humphrey's Law School. He planned to take the bar and become a deputy public defender at the office. Riddle and I were the only bachelors in the office. We became best friends eventually, not because of our mutual bachelor status, but because we made each other laugh. Not just laugh, but belly laugh – the kind of involuntary laugh that comes from way down in your soul and can't be suppressed.

But that was down the road – it would be an understatement to say our relationship did not start off on the right foot. Unbeknownst to me, the Boss had shared with Riddle that the new guy (me) played the accordion and would doubtless be bringing it to staff parties. Riddle instantly decided I must be a nerdish accordion geek with whom he could not possibly have anything in common. As a result, from the moment I walked through the door, Riddle pretty much ignored me. Admittedly, there was little in my overall appearance to contradict Riddle's preconception. I was short and chubby, Catholic, and had a broad face with very curly black hair. I looked just like a

cheeky accordion-playing Italian who had never managed
to outgrow the decade of the 50's, a kid whose parents
gave him accordion lessons, so he could play the tarantella
for his cousins at Italian birthday parties. I had been
ridiculously easy to stereotype. As Riddle later explained,
"You were a runt who played the accordion and looked
like Buster Brown. What was there to like?"

On my first workday, Boss took me around the office to
introduce me (or re-introduce me) to everybody. When we
got to the library, there was Riddle. He was wearing slacks
and a sport shirt. It wasn't required to dress up in the
library, especially for Riddle, because he wasn't a lawyer yet,
and therefore couldn't be called on to go to court to fill in
for one of the regular attorneys, even in an emergency. I
was, of course wearing the only sport coat I owned, the
brown corduroy. I had dress slacks on, a white shirt and my
psychedelic tie – a wide necktie with a colorful swirling
pattern. I had convinced myself that everything went with
the corduroy coat. Even if it didn't, I had no other office
clothes. This made dressing for work easy.

As we walked into the library, Riddle rose from the
table where he had been reading through a pile of
casebooks pulled from the tall, dusty shelves. After a brief
introduction, Boss wished me luck on my first day and
went back downstairs, leaving me alone with Riddle.

After silently regarding me for a few moments, he said,
"Well, Boss wants me to show you the ropes around here,
so here goes – better pay close attention because this will
be pretty quick, and I am only going to say it once."

I was armed with a yellow legal-size pad and clutched
pen in hand. I needed Riddle to give me the Cliffs Notes
on the library assignment. A solid introduction would be
invaluable.

I had no idea that Riddle already disliked me. In fact, the dislike had been festering since Boss's inadvertent remark, and Riddle's opinion of me had become intense. The library was a small intimate room, and to get stuck in it for hours on end with a nerd was a fate the impatient Riddle didn't look forward to. He already envisioned me playing *Lady of Spain* on my accordion at office parties. The Boss, it happened, was a sentimental fool who loved to throw parties for his deputies. Attendance at these awkward affairs was not officially mandatory, but unless they were dying, the staff felt obligated to attend. Thanks to my arrival, Riddle would now have to also endure accordion music.

"There are the blue books, there are the brown books, and there are the red books," Riddle said, motioning to the bookcases holding the multi-colored law books.

Riddle then picked up a fat manila file from the table. "This needs a motion to exclude," he said.

Riddle tossed me the file. Then, without ceremony, he walked to the furthest end of the library, picked up another file, and buried his head in the pending case he was working on. He had given me no detailed instructions; he had offered no assistance; nothing! I could not believe what had just happened. I was outraged and immediately realized I didn't want to spend a moment of time with this disrespectful person ever again.

That evening it took most of an hour to describe the interaction to Tuna and run through my seething thoughts about it. It was clear Tuna agreed with my assessment and hated Riddle. After considerable processing with Tuna, I decided I would just have to get along without Riddle. Others could assist me until I learned the ropes.

After I had been working a couple of weeks, there were still no substantive discussions between the two of us, even though we were cooped up together in the relatively small library. There were some punctiliously polite conversations, but they were minimal. Outside of work we didn't speak at all.

Two more weeks passed in this fashion. I would walk into the library each morning, hang my one brown corduroy coat over the back of my chair, and settle into the law books and files. Whole days would go by without our exchanging more than a word or two.

It happened these long periods of silence were punctuated by the sound of ringing bells which banged out a short song, each hour on the hour, and then the time. The bells were assertively loud and one morning, without thinking, I suddenly asked Riddle, "What's with the bells?"

He said they were on the top of the Bank of Stockton, only one block away from the Public Defender's Office.

I went over to the phone, pulled out the phone book, and began thumbing through the pages. I could feel Riddle watching me from the corner of his eye. Finding the number I was looking for, I dialed. When someone answered, I said, "May I please speak to the person in charge of the bells?"

After a few minutes, someone came onto the line and I asked, "Are you the bell lady?"

"Yes, I'm in charge of scheduling the bells."

"Do you take requests?"

Now I had Riddle's full attention as he eavesdropped on the conversation.

"Well…yes, of course…if you have a request, we will be happy to try to accommodate you. What would you like to hear?"

"I'd like to hear the *Theme from Exodus* and, let's see, *Wipeout* by the Surfaris."

I hung up the phone, returned to my seat and picked up the brief I had been working on. There was a silence for about a minute.

"That was fucking unbelievable," Riddle declared in an excited voice. "Un-fucking-believable!"

It was immediately clear that Riddle had formed a new opinion of me based on this incident, just as quickly and with the same conviction as when he had condemned me on the basis of the accordion. In an instant, I somehow was okay, and from that second on, Riddle and I were best friends.

Three weeks later, the phone rang in the library and the caller asked for me. It was the bell lady.

"Are you listening?" she asked.

She was playing the *Theme from Exodus*. She went on to say she was sorry, but she hadn't been able to find "that *Wipeout* song" in bells. She promised to keep searching until she found a playable version of it. It was clear the bell lady was thrilled someone was actually listening to her bells and was sufficiently interested to call in song requests. Riddle and I could only imagine the bell lady telling her friends about the "keen interest the bells generated in the community and how appreciated they are by the locals."

After Riddle finished law school and passed the bar, it soon became apparent he was the real deal as a lawyer. He was smart and very quick-witted. He could think on his feet and carry more information in his head than anyone I ever knew. He was unstoppable in front of juries. He won trials in the initial stage of voir dire (which is jury selection, the initial stage of a jury trial when the jury is first being questioned). He was so charming that older men and women jurors saw him as their son. Young men wanted to be him, and young women wanted him. He owned the jury before any evidence had been presented. I was always amazed at how he would get the jurors to start talking to him and immediately feel comfortable. He would start by drawing them out about their jobs, because everyone seemed comfortable with what they did in their jobs, and soon they were talking freely on all manner of topics. He also was a chameleon. If the juror was a hunter, then so was Riddle; or, at least, he was a fisherman – he would quickly find some similarity with the prospective juror, so they had something in common. He made friends with jurors better and quicker than anyone I ever saw. Some years later the legislature actually changed the law to prohibit these wide-ranging questions during voir dire. This was in response to lawyers like Riddle, who could befriend jurors in such a short time. Riddle became close with people, fast.

Riddle reminded me of my Italian cousins. He was loud and obnoxious and funny and loyal. He had a big heart. I also loved the fact that we thought alike. In jury trials, there was often a moment, mid-way through, when he would finally untangle the mystery to the case, discover a winning strategy, but he would still act like the case was a loser. He loved to "lie in the weeds," as he put it, and then surprise the district attorney with an ambush toward the end of the trial. He never disclosed what trick or theory he had finally come up with unless it was a legal requirement. He loved to wait as long as possible and then, in the final stages of the trial, hit them over the head, as he would say, with a "two by four." He would win his case. Riddle never lost a jury trial during my three years at the Public Defender's office. He was a public defender. Most public defenders lose a lot.

Riddle had a mysterious background. He was of Irish descent, but Italians raised him. It was difficult to extract details from Riddle himself because he didn't like to talk about it. However, Big John and Dorothy Mazzilli raised him, and there was an occasion when Mama Mazzilli told me about it. She said his parents couldn't be bothered with raising Riddle to adulthood, so they abandoned the little five-year-old boy. He was handed over to his grandmother in Kansas, who raised him until she died. Mrs. Mazzilli said that after Riddle's grandmother died, the authorities could not get Riddle away from her body at bedside at the Kansas farmhouse. Finally, after some long period of time, a uniformed policeman came in and convinced the boy to leave her in peace to "go to heaven."

Riddle was 12 years old when he was sent back to his parents, who were by then living in Stockton. That only lasted two years. When Riddle was 14, his parents decided to move again. Riddle refused to go. Thanks to his friendship with Paul Mazzilli (the son of Big John and Dorothy), he moved in with the Mazzillis for the rest of his high school years, and beyond. The Mazzillis became home base for Riddle during school breaks and over the summer months, when he worked at the local tomato canners. Riddle grew up in Stockton with Big John, Dorothy, and their children, Paul and Patty. They took him in completely and loved him as their own. This was the only taste of true family life that Riddle experienced. He called Big John and Dorothy mother and father and referred to Paul and Patty as his brother and sister. Until the Mazzillis, Riddle had been constantly shuffled around between his parents and his grandmother, and back to his parents again, which resulted in a profound undermining of his sense of security. I had had it easier, but I had had enough to understand why Riddle wrestled with demons for the rest of his life.

I had a high regard for Riddle, but it gradually dawned on me that he didn't have any future plans. He lived in the present. So, I decided to plan for the both of us. Riddle, with his crappy upbringing and insecurity, had no map, no compass, and no safety net. He was a leaf in the wind, blowing wherever life took him. I decided he would come to Napa with me, if and when I made the move back to my hometown.

This was just my personal sense of the man. Outwardly, he never lacked confidence. In fact, he seemed incredibly confident, even overconfident. Riddle couldn't be wrong like the rest of us. When Riddle was wrong, the world made less sense. Riddle was so supremely confident and positive, it was difficult not to be influenced, even convinced, by his articulate, logical, self-assured analysis of any subject. It was like you were stupid if you didn't agree with him.

His confidence manifested itself in Riddle's bets. Riddle and I would bet on everything and anything. We bet on the monetary amount our groceries would total at the register. We bet on football and baseball games. We attended and bet on prizefights. When Riddle picked a team, it seemed like it was a sure bet. Riddle couldn't lose. If it turned out Riddle's team didn't win, you had to re-evaluate everything you knew about sports, men, women, relationships, God, and the universe.

I hadn't been working at the public defender's office for more than five or six months before we reached the point that Riddle and I had something going on every weekend – a Giants game, a 49ers game, out of town dates with women. Riddle was so personable, he could get us into any party. There was never a dull moment. I loved sports, and Riddle was a superb athlete in football and baseball. He could even play basketball, though it was more of the guts kind of basketball – a very physical, under-the-boards kind of basketball. In baseball, Riddle was a great third baseman, and a skilled hitter. Baseball was his game, and he loved it. Riddle used to analogize baseball to life: the ups and downs, the luck, the near misses, the agonizing defeats, the sweet victories.

When I learned we had a mutual love for baseball, I decided someday I would start my own softball team in Stockton, a team of buddies who would win some kind of championship. Of course, as an athlete I wasn't close to Riddle's class, but as a fan, I was every bit his peer: I followed every sport and played in pickup games.

In law, Riddle quickly established himself as the rising star of our office, and I believed him to be the rising star in the larger legal community as well. He was so incredibly bright, and such a determined winner. He didn't rely on the police reports in the cases he was assigned. As Riddle often said, "Why would I rely on the police report? It has nothing but bad news for my client."

Riddle did his own investigations. He had grown up in Stockton and had tons of connections. His "brother" Paul Mazzilli was a Stockton policeman, and he would occasionally provide Riddle with inside information that was useful in defending his cases. Riddle always came up with a plausible theory of what could have really happened. It wasn't that the cops were lying (Riddle never blamed the police – he always praised them), it was just that they weren't aware of this additional information, which, at the very least, raised a reasonable doubt about his client's guilt. He never once lost. Not one time. Only a fellow public defender can understand the rarity of this feat. As a result, Riddle was feared by the prosecuting deputies of the District Attorney's office and greatly admired by the defense bar in Stockton.

My strengths were less substantive. People did seem to enjoy being with me; they were drawn to my friendliness, openness, and good humor. Also, I seemed to be the Teflon man – just as Ronald Regan would later be called the Teflon president. Nothing negative ever stuck to me.

Riddle once told a mutual friend he thought I was a natural empathizer. He said, if someone was hurting or sensitive to something, then so was I, and it was genuine; it oozed out of my pores. Everyone was comfortable with me – it didn't matter what color, creed, race, or ethnic background. Riddle said I was someone who did not look down my nose to anyone – he said I was the "Real McCoy." While Riddle's assertions about me are greatly exaggerated, Riddle loved, admired, and respected me as I loved, admired, and respected him.

He was right, to a certain extent. I did try to be kind and friendly. But usually I was working some kind of angle. For example, my friendship with Riddle was genuine – probably the closest friend I had ever had. But even with Riddle I had some selfish motives. From the moment I had arrived in Stockton, I knew I would one day move back to Napa to practice law in my hometown. While my friendship with Riddle was real, I also discovered myself thinking about leveraging it to bring Riddle to Napa with me. My long-term plan was to come home and be a powerful force in Napa, and my secret weapon would be Riddle. No one else knew of this secret plan except Tuna. Even Riddle didn't know of it. But I was sure – we would be rich and famous.

At least that was the plan. What is that saying about the "best laid plans..."

CHAPTER TWENTY-SEVEN

Sports

As I settled into my new law job, I found my mind turning regularly to sports. I loved sports and my life outside the office was a little boring, so I considered whether I could find a competition sport to join in. I found myself mulling over touch football, basketball, and the newly – emerging soccer. Then I wondered about possibly a softball team in the city league, but it wasn't baseball season yet.

Around the office, there weren't any sports or other organized activities. Some of the deputies played in pickup basketball games on Monday nights at the local community college, where they were always killed by local jocks skilled at the round-ball arts. Traveling across town to lose to superior talent was still better than not playing at all.

One sunny afternoon a week before Easter, Boss came into the library accompanied by a robed priest from the nearby St. Mary's Catholic Church. St. Mary's was a rundown parish in the worst part of town. The Boss introduced Father Ronald, and explained he was having trouble with the local sheriff, who wouldn't let him use real wine at communion on Good Friday and Easter Sunday Masses in the chapel at the county jail. The Boss, himself a Catholic, was obviously upset. Stepping in front of Father Ronald, he said he wanted us to take an emergency writ to the Superior Court and obtain a court order allowing the Father permission to use wine in the services.

There were several deputy public defenders in the library at the time, including two who particularly enjoyed any cause opposing an unreasonable abuse of authority. They both spoke up enthusiastically in support of filing suit.

Boss beamed at the response and was turning away to usher the Father out of the library, when I had an irresistible urge to speak. A great idea came upon me and it couldn't wait. To this day I cringe when I reflect on my choice of words. Just as Boss and the Father were reaching the door, I said, "Not so fast, Padre." I hadn't had time to think the situation through, but I had a sense that using the government resource represented by the Public Defender's Office to sue over the right to serve wine in a Catholic Communion service might be outside normal boundaries. This in turn activated my sensitive nose for working the angles.

Everyone in the room had frozen. The Father turned toward me with a dumbfounded look on his face and said, "What?"

"You have a gym at your church?" I asked.

"Yes, we do," said the priest, not connecting the dots.

"Our attorneys here at the office are looking for a place close by to play basketball, and we've been wanting to talk to you about the opportunity to play at your church. What do you think, Father?"

He paused before answering. "Well, yes, the gym has basketball hoops, I think; but we don't use it anymore because the school has been closed to the public for quite some time. We keep it locked, except for special occasions like luncheons or meetings, things of that nature."

"Certainly, we understand," I said, as if I were speaking on behalf of a formally organized group of public defenders. "What we'd like to propose for your consideration is that we be allowed to use the gym at lunchtime several days a week. If we can help you not only with this present legal matter, but with any future legal matters, we would be pleased to do so."

There was a pause while this seemed to sink in. The priest finally replied, "The bathrooms in the gym work, but the showers don't have hot water." We had him.

"We understand, Father, and we'll adjust to no hot water," I said. Extending my hand, I asked, "Do we have a deal, Father?"

"Yes, of course," said the priest. "I'll tell my secretary about our arrangement. You should work with her on the details of access to the gym, locking the facilities afterward, and returning the keys."

"Yes, sir, and thank you so much," I said, easing myself around the boss and the priest, returning to the rest of the deputies crowded around the library table.

The Boss looked shell-shocked. He was speechless. He locked eyes on the priest, who was determined to exit before the deal broadened in a detrimental way to the Church. Boss' look to the priest was sort of an, "Oh well, what can I say." The priest smiled while descending down the stairs, shaking his head and disappearing from sight.

After the Boss and the priest had made their way out of the library, an astonished silence descended on the deputies, all of whom were staring at me as if they were seeing me for the first time. Riddle was the first to come around, his mouth breaking into a smile, his head shaking in disbelief. "This is way better than the bell lady," he finally said.

I was the informal CEO of our basketball organization. Though informal, it was a position of great power. There were no written articles or by-laws. There were informal oral by-laws which I developed myself and periodically adjusted to fit my purposes. If I didn't want a guy in the gym, he didn't get in. We were usually at "full capacity," but when I wanted to add a good guy whom I liked, then, what do you know? We all of a sudden had an opening. I doubtless abused my power from time to time; however, I figured but for me, there would be no basketball at all. I made up a procedure to gain admission. It went something like this: a prospective member would attend as a guest a few times. Then, if everyone agreed, he would be allowed to join. Of course, I maintained complete veto power – a power not mentioned to prospective new members.

As we settled in to our new relationship with the church and its gym, I started collecting from the regular members a small contribution to be given to the church on a monthly basis. This was a good move, because soon the church became dependent on the contributions. Before long, not only did the church not resent us, but the priest and his staff actually welcomed us as a sort of client. They wanted us to be happy because they were now getting over $100.00 per month – a good deal for them, and a great deal for us. Where else could you have full club membership down the street from where you work, with shower facilities (albeit showers cold as creek water) for $10.00 per month?

Basketball at St. Mary's quickly became an institution. Attendance grew as we added deputies from both the district attorney and public defender offices. Forty years later, the county attorneys still play basketball in that old gym, under the same arrangement as we snookered on that fateful morning in the library.

While basketball was a daily routine all year round, some of the jocks around the office also wanted to play softball when the city leagues opened in April. I didn't consider myself a jock, but I did like the idea of playing competitive softball. Based on my experience getting the basketball program going, I knew it was up to me to organize a team – especially if I wanted to play myself.

Back in Napa, my dad had sponsored a recreational softball team called "Al's Auto Wreckers," after his junkyard business. Al was a complex guy in many ways, but when it came to sports, he was simple: Big Al loved sports of all kinds and softball in particular. With this in mind, one evening after work I called my dad and asked if he would consider sponsoring an "Al's Auto Wreckers" franchise in Stockton. He loved the idea and agreed immediately.

This was perfect. It not only gave me the ability to outfit the team and supply the equipment but more importantly, it naturally led to my becoming the player-coach of the team. This was important because it gave me the final say on who was on the team and who started at each position. If I wasn't the coach I might not be the starting catcher. In fact, I might not make the team.

There was one initial problem. I of course, vetted the idea of an office team playing in the city league with Boss. Boss supported the idea. The problem was how Boss thought the team should be run. "All-inclusive" was the word Boss used. Boss, who had never played organized, competitive sports in his life, was enthusiastic about the

Raymond A. Guadagni

idea of an office team because he envisioned everyone from the office being on the team. His vision was something along the lines of a pickup softball game at the company picnic, a team organized for socializing, its main goal being to include everyone and have fun.

Among other things, this meant the Boss did not want anyone to be cut from the team. He believed cutting players could have a demoralizing effect on his close-knit office. He had spent years putting together the right people, and he did not want to do anything to hurt the collegiality.

While I appreciated and understood Boss' firm convictions on this issue, complying with his wishes could not have been further from my mind. I wanted to win and had no use for people who wanted to play just to be part of the activity. This team would not play for fun; it would not play for exercise; it would not play for the camaraderie; it would play for one reason only – to win. Every position would be filled with the best player for that position (with the exception of catcher). A championship would be our only goal.

Even as the sign-up sheet was being thumbtacked to the bulletin board in the staff break room, word of my management philosophy was spreading like wildfire through the office. This was okay with me, because I wanted people to know not to sign up unless they were serious and capable players. This team would not just win; we were going to piss down our opponents' throats. The word-of-mouth discouraged most of the "just for fun" types from signing up, though, as in all sports, some people rated themselves better than they really were and signed up anyway. But I knew the coach (yours truly) would take care of those who did sign up but were not

198

skilled enough or fully dedicated to winning. The term for those people would be "bench players."

By the time we held our first practice on a warm Thursday evening after work, I had already scouted the players and discovered the positions they had played in their previous baseball careers. From this research I had figured out we were so weak (or non-existent) at some of the positions we would have to recruit additional players from outside the office if we were going to have a winning team. I went to our more accomplished players who were native Stocktonians, or who had at least lived in the Valley for a long time, asking them to suggest people they knew who were superior ball players. This effort brought in some real refined talent – including my friend Joe Flax who, like me, had grown up in Napa, and was now working as a city attorney in Stockton.

Our first season went well. Boss was not aware of the "win at all costs" philosophy I was instilling in the team. I had been straight with him from the moment he had shared his vision of friendly, inclusive softball. He wasn't enamored at my approach, but he recognized the huge amount of time I was pouring into the team's development and gradually reconciled himself to the more competitive culture. He came to all of our games and became quite dedicated to the team. We finished the first season high in the standings, but because we did not win the championship, we were assigned to the same division for the next season. This ranking was just what we wanted. We wouldn't be moved up to a higher division to play against higher caliber players, who would all be new and unknown to us. Staying in the same division, we knew our competition well. Some players on the team developed scouting reports on the opposing players – things like where they hit the ball, if they were a high ball or low ball hitter, and so forth. I also recruited some even better jocks for the second season.

The second season started with a run of consecutive wins. Things were going along well until Pete Kelly, our first baseman, had his knee go out. The team finished the game with a substitute first baseman. We eked out a win, but I knew that unless we could find a better replacement, the next game was unlikely to be another "W." It happened I had envisioned the possibility of this type of situation arising when I was developing the player roster for the second season. This had led me to begin throwing out feelers to one of my best childhood pals, Mike "Kid" Kerns. Kid Kerns was a Golden Gloves heavyweight boxing champion, as well as an all-around athlete. Mike did not reside in Stockton, so I listed my address as his residence. It was likely a violation of the rules, but I rationalized this would be for one or two games at the most. As soon as I got home from the game in which Pete was injured, I placed a call to Mike, and he immediately agreed to step in for Pete.

The next day we were relieved to learn Pete's injury was not as serious as we had feared – he would need about two weeks to heal. That meant Kid Kerns would be substituting at first base for Al's Autos until Pete could return to the lineup.

I probably didn't do Mike any favors by bragging around the office all week about his power and defensive ability at first base. By the time his first game rolled around, the team expected to see the second coming of Babe Ruth. Mike did not quite live up to expectations, but he did play a superb game defensively at first base, grabbing everything that came his way. He hit, too, but not with the power I had forecasted. For whatever reason, Mike turned out to be a singles hitter that evening. The main thing, however, is we won. Mike served his purpose, the team survived for two weeks without Pete Kelly, and the winning streak was kept alive.

When Pete returned to the lineup, the team continued winning most of its games. As the season progressed our attention was increasingly drawn to the one other team in the league with proven hitting, fielding, and experience. Dreaded by many of the other teams, "Mr. D's Pizza" had won the league championship in several recent seasons. Not only were they a seriously good team that hit with power, but their sponsor made the best pizza in town. This created some problems for Al's Auto, because we had to find a place to celebrate our wins in a place with no ill will toward us. We settled on The Graduate, a pizza palace with lots of room, pinball machines, and other arcade games of the time. Their pizza was not an award winning culinary treasure, but our players thought it was good, and it came with the option of sausage topping, my all-time absolute favorite.

There comes a time when two foes who seem to be equally matched are destined to meet. It happens all of the time – in boxing when the champion must defend against the number one contender, in football when the two conference champions meet for the ultimate championship, and, of course, in the World Series, when the two league champions meet for the world championship. That same sort of destiny exists at the lower levels of sports and pervades even the softball leagues of the Central Valley. And so it came to pass that the softball championship for the "E" league in Stockton, California was set for a Thursday evening in July of 1973 between Al's Auto Wreckers and Mr. D's Pizza. During the season, Mr. D's Pizza had beaten Al's Auto, but had lost a game to a team that Al's Auto had beaten. Thus, a tiebreaker had to be held to determine the championship.

Al's Auto won the flip. We chose to bat last, which means, in effect, the home team. Some championships, no matter what level, don't turn out as they have been billed, when the expectations do not match the reality. An anticipated boxing war between two fighters turns out to be a one round knockout. A great football game becomes a one-way slaughter.

On the other hand, some events are everything they were expected to be, and more. This game was as good as anticipated, and probably much better. There had been talk in the town that Mr. D's had way too much power for Al's Auto. But the game did not turn into a slugfest. Instead, it was a tense defensive struggle. Shots came ripping off the bats to the fielders on both sides, and great defensive plays were competently, and in some cases, dramatically made. The game went much faster than anyone had been expecting, because most of the innings were 1-2-3 innings, 3 up and 3 down, a testament to the superb defensive plays of both teams.

Going into the last inning, the game was tied at three runs apiece. The top half of the last inning, Mr. D's had runners at first and second with two outs. The runner on second base was the potential tie-breaking run, and being in scoring position, could most likely come home on a single. Knowing this, the short fielder, who usually played as a fourth outfielder, came in to a position of deep shortstop, barely on the outfield grass in left field, as the right-handed batter stepped up at the plate.

This move turned out to be brilliant. The batter hit a clean shot to left field, and the short fielder was in perfect position to pick up the ground ball and in one motion fired it to the catcher guarding the plate (me). I came down with my catcher's mitt, touching the leg of the runner, and in a continuous sweep, raised my glove overhead to show I had held on to the ball. The umpire called the runner out. The tie was preserved, and the side retired.

In the bottom of the last inning, Al's Auto also had runners in scoring position, and also had two outs. Riddle was up at the plate. As coach, I considered him to be the best player to have in this position, under these circumstances. Riddle, I believed, was a pressure player who could come through in the clutch when a hit was needed most.

The packed stands were quiet with wives, friends, and fans of both teams hushed to see if Riddle would once again deliver a game winner in a tense, pressure-packed setting. On the second pitch, Riddle ripped a clean shot to right center field that fell for a hit, and the player from second scored easily to win the game and the championship for Al's Auto.

You would have thought it was the World Series. The Al's Auto players rushed out to the field and swarmed Riddle, hugging and jumping up and down. Suddenly the Boss was out on the field with the team, smiling and cheering. He popped a bottle of champagne, shooting a dramatic cloud of spray over the ecstatic players. He herded the team together for a victory photo. Boss could be a sentimental fool – which was why we loved him.

1973 D League Softball Champions, Stockton, California

**Front Row from left: Rich Goyette, Ray Guadagni,
Nicky Chargin, Pat Riddle, Sam Libicki, George Luke.**

**Back Row from left: Robert "Boss" Chargin, Randy Thomas,
Leonard Talman (partially hidden), John Schick, Joe Flax,
Pete Kelly, Gary Turner (partially hidden), Craig Holmes.**

The celebration did not stop there – at least not for the hardcore players. It was on to The Graduate, where the real party started with the usual pizzas and pitchers of beer. On this occasion, some of the wives and girlfriends tagged along to celebrate, to keep their guys from being out too late, and, if truth be told, to keep them from being corrupted by Riddle. It was just as likely that I could have been a questionable influence, but here again, I seemed to always be the Teflon man. Nothing stuck to me. I was always popular, and no one seemed to believe I would get anyone in trouble. I was too gentle hearted and empathetic.

Don't you believe it, according to Riddle, I was not what I appeared. He said I came on like Little Lord Fauntleroy, but in reality, I was an instigator of trouble and insane chaos, who always seemed to avoid the ultimate blame.

Of course, someone had to be blamed, and that person was usually Riddle. One example will suffice.

After Riddle passed the bar and both of us had been freed from library duty, we were paired in court as misdemeanor deputies assigned to Judge Drivon's court. Judge Drivon, a Frenchman, was a kind man, generally of even temperament. However, he could be pushed to lose his calm demeanor when court did not proceed in an orderly fashion.

On this particular occasion, the calendar was loaded with arraignments, pleas, and traffic cases. Judge Drivon was a methodical processor of cases, and the calendar was going at a ponderous pace. The audience was crammed with defendants, family members, and friends of the defendants. In those times, the attorneys who waited for their particular case to be called either sat in the row of theater chairs behind counsel table or in the empty jury box. Also seated in these chairs were uniformed police and CHP officers who had been subpoenaed to testify at court trials set for that date based on tickets they had issued.

Every seat seemed to be taken on this particular calendar. Every seat, that is, but one. The seat directly in front of me was empty. Riddle and I were in the back row of the jury box behind two uniformed CHP motorcycle officers. The officers had, of course, removed their helmets and gloves. One officer placed his on the floor next to their swivel chairs. The other placed his helmet on the empty chair next to him, directly in front of me.

Judges vary in the speed with which they move their calendars. Some judges are very efficient and move through calendars like a practiced chef slicing and dicing vegetables. Some, on the other hand, are deliberate and slow, carefully working through the tedious procedural requirements of each case. Judge Drivon was the latter.

He listened to and considered every argument put forth by the lawyers and the unrepresented. Some of these arguments were sound, but more commonly, they strained logic, and some were just the immature whining of pissed off people who felt cheated because they got caught. It didn't matter. Judge Drivon dealt with each argument individually and with diplomacy. As a result, his calendars took forever.

A judge who runs the calendar this way is asking for trouble. Long ago, the word had gotten out that Judge Drivon's calendars were unmanageable. This, in turn, encouraged sloth. Lawyers quickly learned that if you weren't completely prepared, just show up and ask for a continuance. The calendar being so crowded anyway, the continuance request was likely to be granted. A wily defense lawyer could continue a case until the cop didn't show up, and then announce he was ready and demand his court trial, which meant the case would have to be dismissed.

If you continued a case like this long enough, something would often change for the better for the defense – a witness's memory faded, a cop retired or was assigned to a new position, a witness would leave town and couldn't be located, or for whatever reason just not show up for court. A continuance rarely, if ever, hurt the defense. In a short time, a judge who runs his calendar this way finds it so jammed with old and new cases, that it would be common to have to work through the lunch hour to complete the morning calendar. This stressed everyone, including Judge Drivon, who constantly seemed to be hopelessly behind and unable to remedy it.

Riddle loved to read, and on this particular morning he was passing the time between cases reading a paperback novel behind the broad shoulders of the motorcycle CHP officer who sat in front of him. I, on the other hand, had no attention span whatsoever. I passed the time looking for mischief.

The CHP officer's helmet caught my eye. My imagination stirred, I pondered the helmet for several minutes. I wondered if there was any possibility that I could take the helmet without the cop noticing, put it on my head, show it to Riddle, and then remove and return the helmet without getting caught. I began to carefully observe the main players in the courtroom. As I observed, I kept one eye on my wristwatch, timing their movements. I knew I couldn't account for everyone, but I wasn't concerned about the general audience members. My attention was focused on the judge, court reporter, clerk, bailiff, and, most importantly, the CHP officer in front of me. I concluded that once a new case was called, the judge would be totally occupied with the people and the papers of that case. The clerk was buried in files from the last several cases and would not have time to look up. The court reporter would pay strict attention to what was being said so that she could record it all, and most of the time she would be reading the lips of whoever was speaking. The main issue would be the cop. I noticed the officer was splitting his attention, looking toward the case being heard at the moment, then turning to talk to the officer to his right. In either event, the officer's head was turned away from me. I was sitting to the left and behind the officer. God knows why I thought it was worth the effort, but I became convinced I could pull it off.

I carefully watched the activities of each of the people in front of me. Suddenly, the moment came – the judge was looking down at his file, the prosecuting attorney checked his notes, and the CHP officer turned to make a whispered remark to his colleague. I quickly leaned forward, grabbed the helmet and put it on my head. I must have looked quite the sight with the helmet and my wrinkled corduroy coat. I quickly jabbed Riddle in the ribs. Riddle looked up from his book, clearly annoyed at being disturbed. It took him a brief moment to register the insane contradiction of helmet and suit accompanying the large grin on my cherubic face.

The helmet was only on my head for about three seconds before I slipped it off and quickly returned it to the seat beside the still-distracted CHP officer. I had intentionally left the general audience out of my strategic calculations, which was just as well because it happened that quite a number of them saw me wearing the helmet. This resulted in a sudden eruption of guffaws and laughter.

The judge's head snapped up and he looked around for the source of the unusual commotion in his courtroom.

He noticed that the attention was mainly focused on the jury box, based on the direction in which everyone was looking. When he saw two lawyers among the law enforcement officers, he was pretty sure he knew who must have caused this commotion. Riddle and I had been the center of previous disturbances in his courtroom. As his piercing gaze settled on us, Judge Drivon observed me with my hands folded in my lap and a very small, Mona Lisa smile on my angelic face. He also observed Riddle doubled over with uncontrollable laughter.

Already stressed from his calendar and not wanting anything else to slow down its already snail-like progression, Judge Drivon had reached the end of his rope. He yelled out, "That's it, Mr. Riddle, I will not warn you again. This is your last warning. The next time it will be contempt of court. Do you understand me?"

Riddle responded to the judge's bellowing by saying in the meekest voice I ever heard from Riddle, he did indeed understand the judge's warning, and that he was sorry, and it would never happen again.

The party at The Graduate Pizza Palace had been underway no longer than an hour before the players who had brought wives and girlfriends left. It was a work night, after all. However, Riddle and I, and a few of the other players who didn't bring along girlfriends, stayed on for serious partying. First, of course, the complete debriefing of the game: the big hits, the best fielding plays, the clutch play, and on and on. Everything about the championship game was analyzed and dissected. The embellishments started that very night, and the stories would continue to grow in the future. Even the opposition was praised and became the best team in Stockton, except for Al's Auto, of course. Nothing elevates your own team better than the quality of your opposition.

As the beer flowed, it came out that some of our players, who were indeed very good jocks, had never won a championship of any kind, at any level, until this one.

That made the win even sweeter and more meaningful, not just for them, but for the rest of us, as well. The party lasted until midnight, when the Graduate closed.

Back at the flat, I broke the wonderful news to Tuna and a new celebration broke out. Tuna, always supportive, seemed genuinely happy for me, even if he had been robbed of a normal evening together. It was another memorable time for the two of us. I did a lot of bragging to Tuna about my contributions to the team's victory. Tuna beamed. We were on top of the world. After a final walk around the neighborhood, Tuna and I finally called it a night around 3 a.m.

CHAPTER TWENTY-EIGHT

Trial Practice

My initial assignment as a research attorney in the public defender law library felt like an eternity. It was actually about four months before I was deemed ready for action and moved onto the four-person misdemeanor team which handled all of the misdemeanor cases for the office. One week after I arrived, the lead misdemeanor deputy ("El Jefe") assigned me my first jury trial. Unfortunately for me, I was assigned the case on Monday and the trial was set for Wednesday. This was not a lot of time for a lawyer to prepare for trial – particularly a lawyer with no trial experience.

Trials have certain stages: jury selection, opening statements, presentation of evidence by each side, closing arguments, and, finally, instructions on the law from the judge. I wasn't just unfamiliar with these stages, I did not even know where to stand in the courtroom. My San Francisco courtroom experience was not helpful here, because that experience dealt with a law and motion calendar, where there were no specified places for the prosecution and defense, nor was there a jury. If only I had the weekend to prepare, but I did not.

The first thing I did was get the file from El Jefe. It contained the police report, which indicated there were two police officers involved. Both had arrived at the crime scene at about the same time. One of the officers provided cover, while the other officer took statements and made the arrest of the suspect.

I went to the jail to talk to my client, who was a heavy-set Native American named Lester Chester McCabe. He was around 50 years old, with one eye missing, covered by a black eye patch. He had been charged under 647(f) of the Penal Code, which was commonly referred to as being "drunk in public." Of course, I noticed that the charge fit the stereotype of Native Americans, who are commonly thought to have alcohol abuse problems. It occurred to me this stereotype might prejudice any jury in front of which Lester appeared.

I researched the code section and studied the "elements" of the charged crime – these were the specific things that had to be proved for someone to be guilty of committing it. Section 647 of the California Penal Code is a misdemeanor which is actually entitled "Disorderly Conduct." It provides, "Every person who commits any of the following acts is guilty of disorderly conduct, a misdemeanor: (f) who is found in any public place under the influence of intoxicating liquor...in a condition that he or she is unable to exercise care for his or her own safety or the safety of others..."

According to the police report, Lester, in the company of two friends, Patrick Elkboy and Jancinto Valle, were rolling a fourth drunk in a sleazy park located just south of the Public Defender's office. When I met with Lester in the dingy gray interview room at the jail, I immediately realized he would not make a good witness. When I asked him to tell me what had happened, he admitted he had been drinking with his two buddies, but he denied being drunk. Then he said he had started shooting dice with a stranger. From a legal and factual point, this would present a problem if Lester testified because gambling with dice was against the law, and Lester would therefore be admitting he was violating the law. Lester went on to say when he ultimately won the dice game, the stranger claimed he didn't have any money. Lester got angry, hit the guy, knocking him down, and then started to wrestle with him on the ground. Lester's buddies, Patrick and Jancinto, helped hold the guy as Lester started to search the person to collect his winnings. It was at this point the officers arrived on the scene.

I decided a second reason Lester would not make a good witness was because of his prior criminal record. A person has a right to choose whether to testify. That is, they have a privilege against self-incrimination. But if a person chooses to testify, the prosecution has the right to "impeach" the witness, which consists of challenging his credibility by bringing up past convictions of crimes of moral turpitude. In Lester's case, he had many prior convictions, the most severe and damaging of which was a murder conviction committed on an Indian reservation. This had occurred some years before but was a conviction the Court would certainly allow into evidence to impeach Lester's credibility, should he choose to take the stand. I knew I could not let that happen. If Lester took the stand, the jury would learn about the prior murder conviction. Even as a novice, I realized they would likely convict him for that reason alone.

It didn't help that Lester talked like a thug. He mumbled and was gruff in manner. There was no way to clean him up. He was short, stout, hairy, ugly, and burly. He did not look like a model citizen. However, without my witness taking the witness stand, what evidence could I offer on Lester's behalf? Perhaps the other witnesses could provide testimony to assist the defense. If either or both Patrick Elkboy or Jancinto Valle described Lester's conduct in a way that justified his actions, there would be no need for Lester to take the stand. That meant I needed to interview them, too. They were both current residents of the county jail because each of them had already pled guilty to the exact charge alleged against my client and were serving sentences of 180 days.

Patrick Elkboy was thin and did not look like he had taken good care of himself. He was only in his 40s but looked like he was in his 60s, with a very wrinkled face from working long days in the San Joaquin sun. He was an alcoholic and the disease had definitely aged him prematurely. While not as rough looking or intimidating as Lester, I didn't think he was going to make a good witness, either. He didn't remember much because he had been drinking so much with Lester and Jancinto. Vague testimony about being blind drunk was not going to be helpful to Lester's case.

Although not as scrawny as Patrick, Jancinto Valle did not make any better impression. He looked like someone who had had a drink or two in his day. Like Lester and Patrick, Jancinto did not remember much about the incident. He, too, had been drinking heavily. Again, this testimony would be damaging to Lester. By the time I finished interviewing these witnesses, I was ready to convict Lester myself.

I had a client who admitted he had been drinking, admitted he gambled, admitted he assaulted and battered another person, and admitted he attempted to rob the victim to get his illegal winnings from gambling. This testimony would not lead a jury to like my client, let alone acquit him. Lester's friends were both too drunk to remember anything. This was not good.

The case had been set for trial because, when Lester saw what his two friends received as a sentence, he decided not to plead guilty. It was not as though Lester believed in his innocence, but the sentences his cohorts received were too stiff to plead guilty to, in his view. While his assessment was rational, it didn't alter the fact that the interviews of these witnesses only produced evidence which would convict, rather than acquit, my client. It appeared to me there was simply no defense. My first jury trial, and I had nothing to talk about. I didn't have much time to prepare, but it looked like even if I had all the time in the world, it wouldn't matter much. And I couldn't settle the case because the prosecution's offer was 180 days in jail, and Lester thought that was too harsh for just getting drunk. I have to admit I also thought it was a lot of jail time for the charged crime of being drunk in public, but what I thought didn't matter.

As I was pondering what seemed like a hopeless situation, it dawned on me that 180 days in jail was the maximum punishment provided by law. Lester might as well take his chance with a jury. Maybe the police officer would not show up, and Lester would win because there would be no evidence against him.

When I went home on Monday after work, I bitched to Tuna about getting a loser of a first case on short notice. Tuna was all sympathy. I felt better. After dinner, I settled on to the couch in the living room and went over the police report again. This being my first trial, I hadn't yet learned when you read something like a police report, it's easy to miss a significant point. You can continue to miss it when you read the report a second or third time. But then on a subsequent reading, you sometimes notice something which can turn the case entirely around, especially if you work to read the report from different points of view. As I sat there on my old couch in my flat on Monday evening, reading the police report to Tuna, that is exactly what happened.

It occurred to me drunk in public was the only charge the district attorney was bringing to court. I didn't know why gambling and robbery had not been charged, but I speculated the district attorney did not wish to file illegal gambling or a felony robbery because, in his view, a couple of drunks playing a low stakes game of dice was not a big deal – the real issue was the people were drunk. Filing felony charges for gambling and robbery upped the stakes considerably and the district attorney must not have thought it was worth the expenditure of taxpayers' money. At least that was my guess. No matter, I began to focus on the fact there was only one charge before the jury – drunk in public.

Turning to Tuna, I said, "Let's see what the police say about our guy, Tuna." I reread the section of the report describing one of the officers giving Lester his Miranda warnings. I explained to Tuna they were warnings an officer must give to a suspect when the criminal process has changed from a purely investigatory stage to an accusatory stage. In other words, once the proceedings have gone from investigating the incident to a custodial situation where the person is no longer free to leave, then, the officer has a duty to give the suspect the familiar warning that if he talks to the officer, his words may be used against him in a court of law.

The usual question for the defense attorney is whether there is any way to prevent any inculpatory statements made by the accused from being introduced into evidence. If the defendant confessed to the crime, but had not been properly "Mirandized," then the confession would be excluded from evidence in court. The usual legal issue is, were the circumstances such that the confession was not voluntary, and thus inadmissible? Did the officer fail to give an adequate Miranda warning? If so, then the confession does not come into evidence at the trial and cannot be used against the suspect.

In this case, the officer had written in his police report that he had properly Mirandized Lester. However, the precise charge in this case was that Lester was so drunk he could not care for his own safety or the safety of others. I found myself wondering, if he had been that drunk, would he have been able to understand the complexities of his constitutional rights? The police report stated in no uncertain terms that Lester not only understood these warnings, but also intelligently waived his rights and agreed to talk to the officer. If Lester was really as drunk as the elements of Penal Code Section 647 (f) require, would he have been capable of understanding his constitutional rights? The police officer was going to testify that Lester did understand his rights, but I now had my doubts.

I didn't want to contest any statement made by my client, but in this case my client's statement did not matter. What did matter were the officer's written statements contained in his written police report confirming Lester understood his constitutional rights. If so, then Lester could not have been that drunk. Lester, therefore, could not be guilty of the charge!

I gleefully thanked Tuna for figuring out our case for the defense. This was not entirely fantastic: if I hadn't read the police report out loud to him, I doubt I would have uncovered the contradiction between Lester understanding his Miranda warnings and the charge of being too drunk to care for himself.

I carefully went back through my emerging strategy with Tuna. First, I shouldn't have any trouble getting my version of the case into the hands of the jury. The deputy district attorney would doubtless start his case by calling the arresting officer, and then establishing that the officer was honest and had followed the book, by giving the suspect the required Miranda Warnings and satisfying himself that my client had understood them. I would cross examine the officer and reaffirm he had done everything correctly. In doing so, I would lock up the fact that the defendant had understood his rights and made an intelligent waiver of them. When the trial reached the place where the defense presents its case, I would point out the defendant could not have been sufficiently drunk to satisfy the elements of the charged crime; it simply wasn't possible to be that drunk and still be able to understand and waive these complex constitutional rights which lawyers have been arguing about for years and years.

I went on to explain to Tuna one of the best features of this strategy was, I would not be in the risky position of having to call the cop a liar. My colleagues had told me juries do not like it when the defense tries to convince the jury that a law enforcement official is dishonest. Here, I would be arguing the officer was completely correct in his conduct and testimony. Lester had indeed understood his rights and intelligently waived them, just as the officer had described in his report. But this meant he couldn't have been drunk under the statute, because a violation was tantamount to being falling down drunk.

And finally, I pointed out to Tuna, the cleverest part of this defense was that it flowed entirely from the prosecution's evidence – I would not need to call Lester, Jancinto, or Patrick.

This, of course, was only theory. Could our defense really be this simple? More importantly, would it work?

CHAPTER TWENTY-NINE

The Jury Trial

I spent Tuesday night on two specific things. I wrote out
my entire cross-examination of the arresting officer,
and I wrote out my closing argument, which I then
presented to Tuna several times. I stayed up late writing
and rewriting the phrasing of my argument until Tuna and
I agreed it was just right.

It was just a few hours later when Wednesday dawned.
I woke up early and exhausted. I had recently bought a
new suit which I decided to wear for my first jury trial,
instead of my brown corduroy sports jacket. It was a very
nice three-piece suit with a vest. I had also gone out and
bought a new pair of shoes on Monday, when I learned I
was getting the jury trial. They were brown loafers and I
thought they looked very professional. I liked loafers,
because I could just jam my feet into them without having
to expend the time and effort bending over to tie them.

As I stumbled around the flat dressing and throwing
some toast, butter, and jam together for a perfunctory
breakfast, Tuna sensed something was up. He got
something of a bum's rush for his walk – I had let him out
earlier than usual and the moment he returned, I let him
in, stepped on to the porch with my briefcase in hand,
slammed the door, and headed off to do battle.

I decided not to walk so I drove to my usual parking
place and went straight to my office on the second floor. I
stopped only to say hi to Judy, the receptionist and one of
my favorite people at the Public Defender's Office. In my

office, I sat at my desk and pointlessly went through my notes. I checked to make sure my file contained everything I needed. I had a fear I might have left something crucial on my desk at home. But, no, my closing argument was in there along with notes for the cross examination, as well as the police reports. I was reassured – slightly.

There was nothing else to do, so I started over to the courthouse. I wanted to stay calm and I didn't want to talk to any of the other deputies at the office. I didn't think it would help my confidence if, in a casual conversation with a colleague, I was told my argument had little chance of success, or if someone gave me some advice which would require last minute research or a change in my trial strategy. It was too late for a different approach. The trial was starting in a few minutes.

I walked purposely by Emma's Café, which was directly across the street from the Courthouse. I stopped there on most mornings. It was my favorite hangout and a few of my favorite deputies were usually there having their morning cup. I loved the owner, Emma, a former women's softball catcher, who still looked like she could double as a bouncer in most bars. There was a slightly younger red-headed waitress, Hilly, who would scream out "coffee time" with a voice that sounded incredibly like a parrot. This was not a casual morning for me. I had my first jury trial and I couldn't be distracted by anything or anyone.

As I climbed the stairs to the courthouse, I suddenly felt like a condemned man walking to the scaffold. Although it was still early, there was already the usual crowd of lawyers and clients talking business. I went around the gathering and made my way to the trial department to which Lester's case had been assigned. There was no one there. This made sense because there was only one case to be heard in that courtroom – my jury trial.

Lester's case had been assigned to Judge Chris Pappas, who had a reputation as a judge whose rulings generally favored the district attorney's office. He believed most defendants were guilty, ascribing to the theory that "where there is smoke there is fire." If the police arrested someone, there must be a reason. It didn't help that, even at this dawning moment in my career, I was convinced most jurors also believed in their heart of hearts that the accused wouldn't be sitting in the courtroom, and the nice officers wouldn't have arrested him, if he weren't guilty of something. As I made my way to the table set aside for the defense, I was thinking once the jury got a look at Lester's one-eyed rough looking mug, any theory of the presumption of innocence would go out the window. Lester was not the picture of innocence. Even I thought he looked guilty.

Judge Pappas was in his 50s, and had greying black hair, beautiful olive skin, impeccable suits, and was always well manicured. He was an imposing figure on and off the bench. He was also an emotional person for a judge and would call it like he saw it. The book on Judge Pappas was that he had little use for defense lawyers, especially criminal defense lawyers and their criminal clients.

Impatient and demanding, he was not consistent, tending to run his court according to how he felt that day. If a lawyer came on strong and it didn't sit right with him, he made the lawyer's life miserable, and worse, the client suffered for it. He ruled more by his visceral reaction to the facts rather than a detailed examination of the law.

For example, when people on skid row came before him, he would talk to them and ask where they lived.

When he heard they were homeless with no means to support themselves, he would often give them a heavy sentence to ensure they had food and shelter for a few months, especially if it was winter. I once watched him with a row of drunks in his courtroom. He asked them all to stand at the same time, and took their guilty pleas first; then, when he learned of their hopeless financial situation, he had them all hold out their hands. When he saw them shaking, he gave them each six months in jail. This was a cruel and unusual jail sentence for being drunk. But people knew Judge Pappas was just trying to give them a place to dry out, get some food, and sleep for several months. He believed he was doing them a favor. In some cases, he was probably right.

Although not apparent in all his rulings, Judge Pappas was a very intelligent person. He had a keen ability to read people and was not usually wrong about his view of them. Even so, lawyers feared his temperament when things didn't go the way he wanted. Most criminal defense lawyers did everything they could to avoid taking their criminal cases in front of him. He gave out heavy sentences. He subscribed to the time honored criminal jurisprudence tradition of "first-class trial, first-class sentence." If you took up the court's time and the state's money by insisting on a trial by jury, you'd better not lose, because if you did, you were going to pay a big price in the form of a much stiffer sentence than had you pled guilty to the case before trial. No judge admitted he poured on extra-long sentences after a defendant exercised his constitutional right to a jury trial, but everyone, including the criminals themselves, knew it happened. Why else would they have an incentive to take a plea bargain? Ironically, in this case, Lester had seen what happened to his friends – they received the maximum sentence of six months' jail for pleading guilty to being drunk. His refusal to plead guilty made sense to Tuna and me: he figured he could not do any worse at jury trial. There was no reason not to take his chances.

The aspect of Judge Pappas' temperament that disturbed the lawyers most was if they filed what he considered to be frivolous motions, or made time-wasting objections, he would rebuke the attorneys by raising his voice and embarrassing them in front of their clients and the jury. More than one lawyer were known to leave Judge Pappas' courtroom ashen faced and shaking. Like a volcano, he gave off warning signs before he erupted. He must have been a terrible poker player because you could see when he was happy, and you could tell, in no uncertain terms, when he was becoming angry. As he moved from impatience to displeasure to anger, his body would slowly gather itself up and, if the lawyer was not tracking Judge Pappas carefully, he might miss the derisive roll of his eyes. When the judge began to lean forward, staring at you and only you – you were in trouble.

The prosecution and the defense lawyers were required to arrive early in the courtroom to meet with Judge Pappas before the jury arrived. This pre-trial meeting was to go over any purely legal issues the case might present and to give the lawyers an opportunity to make motions to exclude or allow specific pieces of evidence. In this case, the only pre-trial motion brought by either side was by me.

The previous evening, as I was developing our defense with Tuna, it had occurred to me it would be extremely helpful if we could prevent the jury from hearing any reference to gambling or robbery. I would need to argue these issues were irrelevant, because Lester was not charged with either of those offenses. If allowed into

Raymond A. Guadagni

evidence, they would be highly prejudicial. This was the first pre-trial motion of my legal career. We were sitting in the judge's chambers. My knees gave a slight tremble as I stood and moved the court to exclude the evidence. The deputy district attorney promptly volleyed back, arguing for the evidence to come in, not as charges, but because factually that was exactly what had been happening when the officer came onto the scene. The jury should know the actual circumstances.

Almost light-headed, I listened as Judge Pappas agreed to allow reference to gambling, robbery (one drunk rolling another drunk) or the fight between Lester and the victim would be highly prejudicial. He went on to rule the officer could explain "in benign terms" what he saw when he approached the scene. This meant we could expect him to testify he saw two guys rolling around on the ground, and he could also describe his observations after he separated them. Then the officer could testify about any drinking symptoms he observed on Lester.

I had just won my first motion – and I felt this was a very fair ruling, as it would let the case be tried on what the charge was, and not on irrelevant, inflammatory circumstances or uncharged crimes.

With no further pre-trial business, the judge stood up and the prosecutor and I quickly rose to our feet. The judge instructed us to leave his chambers by the exit that led into the hallway, rather than the one that led directly into the courtroom. We were to go around and enter the courtroom through the two large doors where all litigants, spectators, and lawyers entered. The judge remained behind so he could pull on his robe.

Still giddy from winning the motion, I suddenly found myself entering the courtroom, which was packed with 45 citizens waiting to be questioned by the judge and attorneys about their qualifications to serve as fair and impartial jurors in this particular case. This stage in a jury trial is called voir dire. I later learned veteran lawyers believed voir dire is the most important part of a jury trial – it can be the moment when the case is won or lost. Getting a strong–minded candidate who is sympathetic to the defense onto a jury can drastically increase the chances of a successful outcome to the trial. Unfortunately, with zero trial experience, this strategic avenue was entirely unknown to me, so I had done almost nothing to prepare for voir dire, other than to skim through a list of common questions posed by defense lawyers to potential jurors.

Once we were all in the courtroom, the judge began by explaining to the jury candidates what type of case was being tried. Then he introduced the parties. First, came the deputy district attorney prosecuting the case and his designated investigator who, in this case, was the arresting police officer. They both stood during their introductions. Next, the judge introduced me as the defense attorney and my client, the defendant.

Up to this very point, everything was going well. I had won the only pre-trial motion and the trial seemed to be starting out on an even keel. So far, so good. But when the judge introduced Lester, he did so by stating his name with his aliases. It made sense for him to let the jury know all the different names Lester had used, so the prospective jurors could determine if they knew the man or had heard of him by any of the names he had used in the past. But as the judge slowly reeled through what turned out to be an enormous list of names, I began to feel he was going too far. It was as if he was trying to make Lester sound like the FBI's most wanted criminal.

"Ladies and gentlemen, the defendant is Lester Chester Buddy McCabe. Please stand, Mr. McCabe. He is also known as Lester McCabe; Chester McCabe; Buddy McCabe," the judge paused for a dramatic deep breath, then continued, "Lester Buddy McCabe; Chester Buddy McCabe; Buddy Lester McCabe, and Buddy Chester McCabe."

My concern over what felt like an inflammatory introduction was made worse by the realization that objecting in front of the jury, or asking for a recess to argue the point, would just make things worse. Even if I persuaded Judge Pappas he should not have done this, the damage was already done. What remedy would there be? Have the judge tell the jury he shouldn't have stated all of those aliases? This would just draw more attention to all of these different names I didn't want mentioned in the first place. I decided not to object. Instead I would move to put it on the record for appeal during a recess in the proceedings, when the jury wasn't present.

The selection process proceeded fairly smoothly after that. The jury was selected and empaneled relatively quickly. By now, I had figured out the prosecutor was a new attorney, and this was his first jury trial as well. Neither of us was prepared for anything like an in-depth grilling of the potential jurors. We both asked benign questions like, "Can you be fair to both sides?" and "Do you have any prejudices against Native Americans?" and "Will you keep an open mind until you have heard all of the evidence from both sides?" – questions that didn't expose real prejudices or biases, since most people like to think they are not prejudiced. Being complete novices, the prosecutor and I both said we were satisfied with the jury and had no other questions for them. Although we didn't realize it then, we had just selected a jury in record time –

about 15 minutes from start to finish. This was a process that in some trials lasts for days. The other juror candidates were excused, and the case was ready to begin.

Next came the opening statement. An opening statement isn't supposed to be an argument by the lawyers, but merely a "big picture" outline of what the lawyer believes the evidence will show the jury. The prosecutor always gives an opening statement, but in asking around the office, I had determined the defense may or may not give an opening statement. The young deputy district attorney opened by telling the jury the evidence would show Lester McCabe was found by the police officer drunk at a park, in the company of two other companions who were also drunk. He went on to say the evidence would show there had been a bottle of whiskey on the ground near the men that was almost fully consumed, that Lester had the smell of alcohol on his breath and seemed to be unsteady on his feet. Finally, the evidence would show Lester admitted to the police officer he had been drinking, but denied he was drunk.

I had come into the courtroom undecided on whether I should give an opening statement, but after hearing this, I decided I should make a very brief statement. I did not want to disclose my main argument – that Lester couldn't have been so drunk if he intelligently waived his constitutional rights – but it did feel like we needed to be heard. So, all I did was remind the jurors that they had just promised to keep an open mind about the case until they had heard from both sides.

"That is all I ask you to do. The evidence, I assure you, will show that Lester was not in violation of the law," I said, speaking from behind the defense table in what I hoped was a calm and compelling tone of voice. "That is, ladies and gentlemen, he was not drunk. He had been drinking, yes, but he was not drunk as defined under the law. Thank you."

This brought the trial to the stage where each side presented its evidence. The prosecution, which had the burden of proof, would go first, which I was sure meant the deputy district attorney would call one of the police officers. The prosecution decided to begin by calling the "cover" officer, who assisted the arresting officer.

The examination of the cover officer started out harmlessly enough, with the prosecutor taking the officer through some preliminary background questions, such as his rank and how long he had been a police officer. Then his questions turned to the preliminary events in the case. Was he on duty that day? Was he in uniform? What was the officer doing when he first observed the defendant? This officer testified he was not the one who actually arrested the defendant. He was the cover officer, backing up the officer, who actually spoke with and arrested the defendant. But though he was only assisting the arresting officer, he did manage to include in his testimony that in his opinion all three of the individuals they had encountered in the park were drunk. He went on to describe the defendant's signs of intoxication, including slurred speech and bloodshot eyes.

While the district attorney was examining this witness, I suddenly noticed the arresting officer rise from the table and start to exit the courtroom. I immediately became concerned. It dawned on me that, although I really needed him available to testify, I had not subpoenaed him as a witness. Maybe the officer was only going to the bathroom, but what if the deputy district attorney had decided not to call him as a witness? After all, the arresting officer's testimony was not actually essential to the prosecution's case. The cover officer's testimony had already gotten the evidence of drunkenness into the record – the only information the arresting officer could add would be Lester's admission that he had been drinking and denial that he was drunk. That might not be worth having the officer stick around for. Then a far worse possibility crossed my mind -the district attorney might have figured out what I had figured out – that the arresting officer was prepared to testify Lester did understand and intelligently gave up his constitutional rights. Had the deputy district attorney realized this would undermine his case? If I could figure it out, then why couldn't he?

I decided I couldn't take the chance. When the arresting officer slipped out the courtroom door, I leapt to my feet and followed him in hot pursuit, leaving my client sitting at the table, the cover officer on the witness stand, a startled judge on the bench, and a bewildered jury in the box. Outside the courtroom, I called out to the officer, who by then was halfway along the hallway. "Officer, are you coming back?"

Surprised, the officer turned and said, "Yeah, sure. I'm just going to the bathroom."

I thanked the officer and turned back to the courtroom. Stepping through the door, I made my way back to my chair at the defense table. As I did so, I realized the room was absolutely still. It was evident Judge Pappas had stopped the proceedings the moment he saw me leave. Then I became aware of his eyes burning down at me from the bench, which for some reason now appeared to be ten feet tall.

Clearly furious, the judge said through clenched teeth, a half second pause between each word, "You cannot leave the courtroom in the middle of the trial, counsel. Do you understand me?"

Looking down at the table, I answered meekly, "Yes, Your Honor. I am very sorry, Your Honor, but I needed the officer in my case and he was leaving."

Judge Pappas retorted, "That is what subpoenas are for. Now sit down."

I was humiliated. Judge Pappas had just dressed me down in front of my client, opposing counsel, and worst of all, the jury. It turned out he was just getting warmed up.

Judge Pappas turned toward the jury and addressed them directly, "You must forgive this attorney. This is his first case and he really doesn't know what he is doing."

My embarrassment was suddenly flooded with indignation. I sprang from my seat and said, "Your Honor, I move for an immediate mistrial. You have put counsel in a bad light, and now my client's right to a fair trial has been undermined."

Steaming mad, Judge Pappas retorted, "It is you, counsel, that has put yourself in a bad light. Motion for mistrial is denied. Sit down. The prosecutor may proceed with his witness." Still looking straight at me, the judge added, "Now that we are all here again."

I didn't realize it at the time, but the situation was actually much worse than I thought. I later learned a lawyer should never make a motion for mistrial in the presence of the jury. This is a "no-no" in trial practice. If the judge denies your request, he is telling the jury he thinks you are wrong. Sensitive exchanges between lawyer and judge like this should always occur in chambers rather than in front of the jury.

The prosecutor soon finished with the first officer. Forcing myself to focus on what was happening instead of what just occurred, I lightly cross-examined the witness. I was able to get him to agree Lester was not falling down drunk. I established bloodshot eyes could be because of pollen or allergies. He testified Lester had not been asked to perform any field sobriety tests, such as the "walk the line" test; or the "finger to nose" test; or the "standing on one leg" test; or the "reciting the alphabet" test. The officer said they never used those tests when arresting a drunk, but only when investigating a drunk driving suspect. I also elicited that the cover officer hadn't talked directly to Lester at all, nor had he taken any statements from him. I finished my cross examination. The prosecutor had no redirect examination.

The prosecutor then called his only other witness – the arresting officer. During direct examination, the arresting officer testified Lester and the other two men were drinking and had all the symptoms of being drunk – even though this officer also testified he had not administered any field sobriety tests. Like the previous officer, he said he only administered field sobriety tests when investigating a drunk driver, and not when he was dealing with a public drunk.

His testimony then returned to the scene in the park, and, almost before I realized what was happening, he testified he had observed Lester going through the pockets of the man on the ground. I realized this violated Judge Pappas' ruling that the robbery should not be allowed into evidence, as it was irrelevant to the charge of being drunk in public and was highly inflammatory. The words were barely out of the officer's mouth when I jumped to my feet and objected. The judge immediately called the attorneys to the bench. When we approached, he said he wanted to see us in chambers. He called a recess and excused the jury.

Once inside the judge's chambers, the judge looked at me and asked me what objection I was making. I said I was moving for a mistrial because of the violation of the in limine ruling. The deputy district attorney disagreed, arguing the judge could just give a curative instruction that the jury should disregard the improper testimony. I responded this would be no remedy at all because the bell had already been rung; the jury now knew my client had committed a robbery, which would prejudice them against him. They might well convict him just because they knew he was guilty of a greater crime of moral turpitude. I went on to argue the remedy suggested by the prosecution was worse than doing nothing. If the judge brought up the robbery again and instructed the jury not to consider it, then the jury would have heard the evidence about the robbery twice. The only proper remedy was to declare a mistrial and start the case over in front of another, untainted, jury.

The judge stared at us for about a minute, this time glaring at the young deputy district attorney instead of me. Finally, he said, "You know, he is probably right" – nodding in my direction – "the only sure remedy would be a mistrial. I should probably grant it. I am not pleased this has happened. However, a mistrial is a severe remedy and I don't think it is completely warranted. I believe the situation can be adequately addressed with an instruction to the jury to disregard the testimony. However, if the defense doesn't want such an instruction then that is his choice."

The words "his choice" hung in the air.

"Motion for mistrial is denied."

I thought this was an unjust ruling and asked the court to reconsider, but to no avail. The judge had made up his mind. The case would proceed.

After the recess, the prosecutor continued without any further problems. The officer explained he decided to arrest the "three Indians" for being drunk in public. His specific basis for arresting Lester was that he was unsteady in his gait, had the strong odor of alcohol, his eyes were watery and bloodshot, he had admitted to drinking, and there had been a whiskey bottle near him on the ground.

The prosecutor then took the arresting officer through the elements of the Miranda Warnings. The officer testified he always carried a card issued by the police department and had been instructed to read the exact contents of the card to any suspect, in a custodial situation, prior to any questioning. The officer said he read through the rights listed on the card and, after each right, he asked Lester if he understood what he was saying. After reading all of these rights, he asked him if, knowing his rights, he wanted to give them up and talk to the officer. The officer testified Lester stated he would be willing to talk to the officer, would waive his right to have a lawyer present, and understood that anything he said could be used against him in a court of law. The officer's testimony could not have been clearer.

The officer then testified Lester admitted he had been drinking with his friends but denied being drunk. Lester told the officer he had shared a bottle with his friends but said he didn't even feel the effects of the alcohol.

The prosecutor concluded his examination by asking the officer if he was sure the defendant had been drunk in public. The officer responded there was no doubt in his mind. With that, the prosecutor stated, "No further questions," and sat down.

Turning to me, the judge said, "The defense may cross examine the witness."

This was the moment I had been waiting for since I was 15 years old and began to think about becoming a trial attorney. For the first time in my career, I was about to cross-examine an investigating police officer. I could feel a fresh surge of adrenaline coursing through my veins. I jumped to my feet and said, "Yes, Your Honor."

I approached the officer sitting in the witness stand. The route I took was around the prosecutor's table, which was closest to the jury. Unfortunately, I did not see the prosecutor's crutches. It seems the young deputy district attorney had broken his ankle in a skiing accident and needed crutches to walk. As he sat at the prosecutor's table, he had placed his crutches on the floor under the table next to his seat. However, one of the crutches protruded from under the table into the path I was taking to approach the witness. My eyes locked on the officer as I stepped quickly toward him, I tripped hard over the crutches, stumbling toward the jury box and the witness stand. In the clumsy process, one of my brand-new loafers flew off my foot, flying through the air and landing with a thud on the courtroom floor, dead center in front of the jury.

Standing momentarily frozen with one stockinged foot in the center of the courtroom, I felt a hot flush wash across my face. The courtroom had once again become silent and still. Looking around, I encountered the intent stares of the judge, the opposing lawyer, the bailiff, the clerk and court reporter, and the twelve jurors – and no one said a word. No one even cracked a smile. They all just sat silently watching me.

I was suddenly desperate to break the ice. "Excuse me, Your Honor, my shoe fell off," I said, smiling as I jammed my foot back into the loosely fitting loafer.

To my discomfiture, another long, still silence ensued. No one, including the judge, to whom the comment was addressed, spoke, chuckled, or even registered a change of expression.

My momentary confidence shattered, I finally succeeded in reaching the witness stand and managed to start my cross-examination. My hope was to carry out the cross-examination in a relaxed and conversational style, rather than an aggressive or confrontational one. It was a style that fit me, and I was pretty sure it would be more effective. My theory was, a witness could be lured into a false sense of comfort and start conversing with the lawyer. Before you know it, the truth might come out.

The examination began in completely safe territory. I had the officer describe the scene and the time of day when he first observed a disturbance. I took him through his actions and decisions while he was dealing with the people in the park. I elicited some benign facts like none of the people were actually drinking when he approached; no one was vomiting; no one fell down in his presence; and no one had any bottles of booze on them while he was there.

Then, I began to set the stage regarding the Miranda warnings. I knew the defense counsel is permitted to ask leading questions of the witness during cross-examination, so that's what I did.

"Was your report accurate?"

"Yes."

"When you gave the defendant his Miranda Warnings, do you believe he understood them?"

"Yes."

"Do you believe the defendant intelligently waived his rights?"

"Yes."

"Did he want a lawyer present with him during your interrogation?"

"No."

"Do you believe that he voluntarily talked to you?"

"Yes."

"So, you don't believe, directly or indirectly, that you coerced the defendant into talking to you against his will?"

"No."

"Would it be fair to say that the defendant was not too drunk to understand and intelligently waive his rights?"

"Yes."

As my cross-examination continued, I began to realize the prosecution had no idea where the defense was heading. The young deputy district attorney sat comfortably at his table, apparently convinced he had a winner of a case that couldn't be lost. The defense was grasping at straws. The deputy didn't seem ruffled at all. He seemed as confident as he was at the beginning of the trial.

When cross-examination concluded, the deputy district attorney asked a few more questions on direct, but nothing about the examination regarding the Miranda Warnings, nor the voluntariness of the statements made by the defendant.

When he was finished, I asked only one question on re-cross-examination: "Has your testimony that you gave this jury on cross examination changed at all, based on the testimony you have just given on redirect testimony by the prosecutor?"

The officer responded it had not. After a glance at the jury, I turned to the judge and said I had no further questions.

The deputy district attorney announced to the judge he had no other witnesses and was resting his case. This meant it was now the defense's turn to present its case. However, by this time I had become convinced my judgment was sound – I could not have Lester take the stand for the obvious reason I did not want the jury to learn about his prior murder conviction. I also had decided not to call Patrick Elkboy or Jancinto Valle as witnesses for the simple reason they would do more harm than good for my client. Their testimony would be they remembered nothing because they were too drunk. That was not going to help.

We would stick with the strategy Tuna and I had developed. No defense was necessary, because the people had not proved their case. I informed the judge the defense would rest without presenting any witnesses. The judge told the jury the court would take a recess, after which the trial would be concluded with closing arguments from the attorneys and legal instructions from the judge.

During the recess, I left my client and went out into the hallway to mentally rehearse, one last time, the closing argument I had passionately presented to Tuna several times the previous evening. I was as ready as I was ever going to be. Before I knew it, the bailiff came out and told everyone to come back in, as court was about to resume. I took my seat at the counsel table and prepared for what would happen now. Because the prosecution has the burden of proof, the deputy district attorney would go first in giving his argument. Then the defense would give our closing argument. And then the prosecutor had one more chance to rebut the defense's closing argument. This seemed grossly unfair to me, because I didn't believe the jurors understood about the rules. The prosecutor got the huge advantage of going first and last. True, the prosecution had the theoretical burden of proof, which meant he had to prove his case (each element of the crime) beyond a reasonable doubt. It was because of this heavy burden that the law gave him two chances to one for the defense in argument. So even if I surprised the prosecutor with my closing argument, he would still have one more chance to rebut my argument.

CHAPTER THIRTY

Closing Argument

A fter the jury was brought back into the courtroom, the judge said, "The jurors are present and in their places. Now we will have closing arguments by the attorneys. First, we will hear from the prosecutor. Sir, you may give your closing argument."

The deputy district attorney rose to his feet and, using his crutches, made his way to the podium, where he began to carefully outline what he believed the evidence showed the jury. He pointed out the defendant had obviously been drinking. The officer had seen all the signs: blood shot, watery eyes, slurred speech, unsteady gait, and the strong odor of alcohol on his breath. He went on to note that even though Lester claimed he wasn't drunk, he did admit to the officer he had been drinking at the park with his friends. The prosecutor argued most drunks don't think they are drunk, but the jury should use their common sense. An older man drinking at the park with his buddies – not eating – but just drinking hard liquor, was drunk. There hadn't been testimony regarding how long they had been drinking, but for Lester to even admit he had been drinking, the odds were that he had been drinking a long time and was very drunk. The prosecutor told the jurors they didn't have to guess at this because the officers were trained observers and knew the law. Both had testified Lester was drunk and that is why they arrested him. The jury should find him guilty as charged.

The prosecutor thanked the jury and took his seat at counsel table. Judge Pappas then looked down at me and nodded. "Defense may give their closing argument."

I gathered my notes and, carefully stepping over the district attorney's crutches, walked around the counsel table to the speaker's podium. I paused for a few seconds, taking a long breath to relax myself as I glanced at my notes one last time. Many thoughts went through my mind. I considered deviating from the script and apologizing for my missteps. I wanted to say, please don't take it out on my client for my mistakes. When I left the courtroom inappropriately, that was not my client's fault. When I tripped over the district attorney's crutches, that was not my client's fault. Please do not convict my client because his attorney is a moron. Yes, this was my first jury trial, please bear with me.

But in the few seconds it took me to have these thoughts, I just as quickly rejected the notion to deviate from my script. I had crafted my written closing argument when I was calm and deliberate. I had taken great care to phrase the concepts I wanted to express as cogently as possible. No, I would not stray from my plan.

I looked up from my notes directly into the eyes of the jury and commenced my closing argument – the one and only chance I would have to convince the jury my client should be acquitted of the charge of being drunk in public. I started by thanking the jurors for their attention to this matter, and for their service as jurors, because the legal system could not survive without people such as themselves willing to serve as jurors.

I then moved to the law. I went through the exact wording of section 647(f) of the Penal Code, which made it illegal to be drunk to the point where a person is unable to exercise care for his own safety or the safety of others, or, because of his intoxicated condition, interferes with or obstructs or prevents the free use of any street, sidewalk, or other public way.

Asking the jury to keep this legal standard in mind, I quickly turned to the facts and asked them to apply the law to the facts, and determine if there had truly been a violation of the code section.

I quickly disposed of the part which refers to obstructing or interfering or preventing the free use of any street, sidewalk or other public way. There had been no such testimony and the district attorney had not argued this part of the code was violated. Then I asked the jury to consider the language in the code section addressing the level of intoxication necessary for there to be a violation of the law. Was Lester so drunk he could not care for his safety or the safety of others? What would that be? I argued this language had to refer to someone who was falling down drunk, so drunk he was virtually helpless, who could not walk or was passed out. He would be, in essence, someone who was drunk out of his mind. That had to be the level of intoxication this code section was talking about. It was not just being under the influence of liquor. It was not a question of a person's ability to operate a motor vehicle being impaired. No, this section contemplated someone who was so drunk he was not able to rationally comprehend what was going on, someone who could not think straight.

I reminded the jury we had all probably known someone in such a condition – maybe someone in our family – whether it was Uncle Henry who drinks way too much or an old friend who was totally dependent on alcohol. Those people are not thinking clearly and are unable to carry on a cogent conversation. They are a mess,

Raymond A. Guadagni

and we have all seen them. That is the kind of drunkenness we are talking about here.

I reminded the jury it is not the defense's job to put on proof of innocence. I told them this was why the defense had not put on a case. The burden was on the prosecution to prove every element of the charged crime beyond a reasonable doubt and to a moral certainty. The prosecution had not met this burden, so it was unnecessary for the defense to even present a case.

I paused for a few seconds to let this sink in, and then went on, "Nevertheless, even though it isn't required under the circumstances, I am prepared to prove my client was completely innocent of the crime charged."

After quickly pointing out the evidence showing that Lester was not passed out or falling down drunk, I quickly moved to the heart of my argument – the interrogation of Lester by the officer. I began with the Miranda warnings – the important Constitutional rights of which a suspect in a custodial interrogation must be advised. But more than just advising the suspect of the rights, the warnings are ineffectual unless the suspect is competent to understand them. If the suspect is not able to understand his rights intelligently (for example, if he were too drunk to do so), then his subsequent statements would not be voluntary, and therefore could not come into evidence.

I had finally reached the point of no return. Looking intently at the jurors, I said, "But that is not what happened here. The uncontroverted testimony of the arresting officer showed Lester understood his rights, intelligently gave them up, and intelligently agreed to talk with the officer. Lester made an informed decision to talk. The officer, the only witness giving evidence regarding the interrogation, was being completely honest with you. He

242

told it like it is. He testified under oath that Lester was paying attention to him and rationally understood what the officer said, intelligently gave up his rights, and agreed to talk to the officer voluntarily."

I tried to hammer this home: "If Lester could understand these complex Constitutional rights, and intelligently give them up, and voluntarily agree to talk to the officer, then he could not have been so drunk that he could not exercise care for his safety or the safety of others. This means he was not guilty of this offense."

I thanked the jury for their service, returned to my place at counsel table, and sat down.

The prosecutor now had one last opportunity to present a rebuttal argument. It was clear he had been caught off guard. He slowly rose to his feet, turned to the jury and then simply repeated his argument by asserting the officers were the only witnesses, they said Lester was drunk, and therefore Lester was drunk. He also thanked the jury, and, with that, sat down.

The judge moved immediately to the next phase of the proceedings, charging the jury with the legal instructions of the case. He began by informing them the required standard of proof in criminal cases is proof beyond a reasonable doubt. He told them of the presumption of innocence that benefits a defendant. He also went over the elements of the charged crime. He read them section 647(f) of the penal code. He gave them general instructions about picking a foreperson and how to conduct their deliberations. Then the judge turned to the bailiff and asked him to escort the jury to the room where their deliberations would occur.

As I sat next to my client watching the jurors file out, I realized the entire trial, from picking a jury to final legal instructions by the judge, had taken only two hours. I wondered if that was a record. But what I really wondered was how long the jury would deliberate – and whether justice would be done.

CHAPTER THIRTY-ONE

The Verdict

W e did not have to wait very long. When the jury left, the judge declared a recess. I said, "Goodbye for now," to my client, who would be taken back to a holding cell to await further developments, and walked slowly back to the office, thinking over the blur of the trial. As I stepped into the reception area, I was met by the receptionist, Judy, who had been waiting for me. The court clerk had called to say that I was to return to court immediately.

I couldn't believe it. I looked at my watch – it had only been twenty minutes. Was this even enough time for the jurors to elect a foreperson, let alone decide the case? Was this good or bad? I knew from discussions with the experienced trial attorneys around the office longer deliberations tended to favor the defendant because it meant at least one of the jurors wasn't ready to convict. In this case, however, it must mean the jury either didn't accept my argument at all or they believed it totally.

Then I realized the jury might not have reached a verdict at all. They might just have a question. Maybe they wanted the court reporter to read back some of the officers' testimony. As I crossed the street to the court-house, I realized Judy didn't say the jury reached a verdict. She only said I was needed back at the courtroom immediately. I relaxed a little. The jury probably had not reached a verdict yet.

When I stepped into the courtroom, the prosecutor was already seated at his table, but the jury was not present nor was the judge. I asked the prosecutor if he knew what was going on? He looked up from his counsel table with a relaxed smile and said, "They've got a verdict, can you believe it?"

I felt a sudden tightening in my stomach. A door opened, and the bailiff led my client into the courtroom. I slowly sank into my chair. There was nothing to do but wait.

Within a few minutes Judge Pappas entered the courtroom. He looked down at the young lawyers and told us he wanted to go over a couple of things before he brought back the jury. First, he informed us the jury did not have a question. Rather, the jury had indeed reached a verdict.

I was having difficulty tracking the judge's additional remarks. The jury had reached a verdict. What could this mean? They must have convicted Lester. They couldn't have understood my argument. They dismissed my legal theory of why Lester was not guilty and maybe even laughed at it. This was an American Indian and everyone knew they love their firewater. Those racist bastards, I thought. The jury probably bought into the district attorney's succinct argument that the police officers were highly trained professionals who said Lester was drunk, so he was drunk. It wasn't rocket science.

I had lost my first case. I tried to comfort myself by deciding I would be back, and next time I would have a better case with more time to prepare. This had been a case no one in the office wanted to waste his time on, which was why my supervisor had given it to me. The more experienced lawyers knew the case was a loser, dead on arrival, a convicted murderer drunk and fighting in a public park.

These comforting words running through my mind did not really comfort me at all. I knew most cases at a public defender's office were losers. I flashed back on one of the questions I had been asked when I had interviewed for the job: "Do you mind losing a lot?"

I found myself wondering if the trial would have gone better if there had been more time to prepare. I only had time to develop the Miranda-warning argument. There were so many other aspects of the trial I should have been better prepared for: jury selection, jury instructions, cross-examination possibilities, subpoenaing the arresting officer. But then I realized this was probably just typical of the steady diet of cases I would see as an attorney at the public defender's office. Well, I thought, at least it was good trial experience.

Judge Pappas finally finished his comments to us – which I wouldn't have been able to repeat if my life depended on it – and, looking around the courtroom, announced he was going to bring back the jury. Returning his attention to the lawyers before the bench, he advised if either of us wanted the jury polled, we should ask him after the verdict had been read aloud by the clerk. He was looking right at me when he said this, which meant the judge himself must have thought the defense had lost. Polling a jury involved the judge asking each juror individually what his or her vote was, in order to confirm the votes matched the verdict of the entire jury. In a criminal case the verdict must be unanimous. All twelve jurors must agree on guilt or innocence.

I had heard from trial lawyers that sometimes a particular juror might be pressured into voting in a way the juror actually wasn't comfortable with. By polling the jury, that juror might then say it was not truly his or her intended verdict. This could result in the jury being sent back to deliberate further or it could result in a mistrial. In any event, only the loser would care about polling the jury. I knew I would have to ask for the jury to be polled, but, in my heart, I did not want to. After all, in a twenty-minute verdict, it didn't seem likely there could have been time for a juror to be coerced into rendering a verdict against his or her will. Polling the jury would only confirm that each and every juror thought the defense case sucked.

I had a headache from the tension of the morning. Now I felt sick to my stomach, as well. Maybe litigation wasn't for me.

Judge Pappas looked at the attorneys one last time, and said unless either of us had questions, he was going to have the jury brought into the courtroom to render their verdict. Both the deputy district attorney and I indicated we had no questions. With that, he nodded to the bailiff, who left the courtroom.

"Remain seated," the bailiff boomed as he stomped back in with the jurors trailing behind.

The courtroom came to silent attention as the jurors took their seats and looked toward the bench.

Judge Pappas swiveled toward the jury and said, "I understand the jury has reached a verdict."

"We have, Your Honor," said a thinly built, slightly balding older man rising hesitantly from his chair in the jury box.

The judge glanced down at the jury list in front of him, where his clerk had given him a typewritten chart of the names and locations of each member of the jury. "Are you the foreman, Mr. Wagner?" asked Judge Pappas.

"I am, Your Honor."

"Have you filled in, signed, and dated the verdict form?" asked Judge Pappas.

"Yes, Your Honor."

"And is the verdict unanimous?" asked the judge.

"Yes, Your Honor."

"Then please hand it to the bailiff."

The bailiff took the form and gave it to the judge, who looked over the verdict carefully, appearing to check the date and signature, as well as the final verdict. The judge then handed it back to the bailiff, who had remained at the front of the bench. The judge directed the bailiff to give the verdict to the clerk.

Looking down at the defendant, Judge Pappas said in an unusually formal tone, "Mr. McCabe, please stand and face the jury." Then the judge turned to the clerk. "Madame Clerk, please read the verdict of the jury."

There wasn't a sound in the courtroom as the clerk unfolded the verdict, scanned it, raised her head and looked directly at me. After what seemed an eternity, she cleared her throat and read, "We the people in the above entitled cause, find the defendant, Lester Chester McCabe, not guilty."

The courtroom remained absolutely silent for several seconds. There weren't many people in the audience – Lester had no relatives present and his two friends were both in jail. Several deputy district attorneys and deputy public defenders had come to hear the verdict, but they all sat quiet, perhaps like me, not believing what they had just heard.

The silence was broken when Lester, raising a closed fist into the air in a sign of triumph, turned to me with a broad grin and said in a loud and distinct voice, "One down, one to go."

I was pondering this unexpected remark as the deputy district attorney and I started to rise in our seats and turn toward our respective colleagues. This prompted Judge Pappas to slam his gavel down on the bench and bellow, "Order in the court, we are not finished yet." We both plunged back into our seats. After a meaningful stare, the judge asked if either of us wished to poll the jury. I responded first by saying, "No, Your Honor."

However, the deputy district attorney indicated he did want the jury polled. Accordingly, Judge Pappas asked each individual juror if the verdict of "not guilty" was, in fact, their individual verdict. Each juror said it was.

With the polling of the jury completed, Judge Pappas ordered the verdict recorded and then addressed the jury, explaining they were now free to discuss or not discuss this case with anyone. He told them it is common for the lawyers or their representatives to want to talk to the jury after the case is over to get their opinions on what they thought about the case, and what evidence they found most impressive or persuasive. He also told the jury they had the absolute right to not talk to anyone about the case. He said if anyone persisted in trying to talk after a juror had made clear he or she did not wish to discuss the case, the juror should advise the judge, who would treat it as a violation of a court order and subject the offender to monetary sanctions.

With that final instruction, Judge Pappas discharged the jurors and thanked them for their time and efforts.

After the jury left the courtroom, Judge Pappas turned back to the attorneys and said, "That concludes this matter, gentlemen. Are there any final questions?"

The deputy district attorney and I each said no. The judge rapped the bench with his gavel. "Court is adjourned," he said, rising and turning toward his chambers.

I turned to my client and extended my hand. Lester turned his rotund body toward me, locked his one good eye on mine, shook my hand, and said, "Thank you."

Simple words, but they meant the world to me. I shook hands with the deputy district attorney, who was gracious in defeat. Then I quickly left the courtroom. I wanted to talk to the jurors before they left the building.

By the time I got out of the courtroom, most of the jurors were down the hall proceeding to the elevator. I walked briskly to catch up with them. The first person I reached was an elderly lady who had sat in the first row of the jury box. I asked her if she would mind talking to me, explaining it was my first jury trial, and I would really appreciate some feedback. The lady graciously said she would be happy to talk.

This conversation with a juror from my very first jury trial taught me a lesson I never forgot. Jurors don't always decide cases in accordance with the law or the judge's instructions. This kind elderly lady explained the jurors could tell both the district attorney and the defense attorney were young and inexperienced. The jury really wanted both young lawyers to win their cases, but they knew this was impossible, so they would have to end up favoring one side or the other. It was clear I felt passionate about my client. At one point she had thought I was going to cry and this affected her. She started to pull for me to win my first case. I found myself thinking this was not a legal standard that should be considered by a jury. The judge had specifically instructed the jurors not to let sympathy for or against a party play into their decision at all.

I asked the kind lady if she or anyone else on the jury had noticed when my shoe flew off and landed right in front of the jury. I couldn't understand how no one saw this or said anything. She smiled and said, "Oh, we all noticed. We thought it was just precious."

Great, I thought to myself – make sure you endear yourself to the jury by tripping or falling or starting to cry. I had been looking for a useful takeaway – but for future cases, especially as the years went by, I couldn't rely on being young, precious and inexperienced.

I thanked the lady and succeeded in catching a few other jurors before they left the courthouse. They reiterated some of the same thoughts of the elderly lady. They added the jury considered the significance (or, in this case, lack of significance) of the alleged crime and the harm (or lack of harm) to the public, and just didn't feel this case was a big deal. Despite my conviction I had come up with the perfect legal defense to drunk in public, it turned out the jury based its decision on the broadest equities of the case: the fact that it was just a misdemeanor charge of a person drinking too much, no one was driving a motor vehicle, and no one was injured or harmed. Further, it had helped that the jury felt sorry for me, the young defense attorney, who, in his first case, lost his shoe in front of the jury by tripping over the district attorney's crutch.

I also learned the personality of the attorney was important. A jury trial may not be a popularity contest, but it was clearly important for the jury to like and trust the attorney, which will spill over to the attorney's client, thus benefitting the client. The bottom line was, juries –

generally not trained in the law – may decide things based on what they think is fair, as opposed to what is legal.

It would take me a couple of days to fully understand Lester's perplexing remark at the end of trial. It turned out, unbeknownst to me, Lester had another pending charge going to trial on a different date at a different location. It was a felony charge for being an ex-felon in possession of a firearm. A convicted felon is not allowed to possess firearms. I did not represent Lester on this charge because I was a new attorney and did not handle felony matters. Felonies are major crimes and they carry state prison sentences, not local county jail time. These types of cases are reserved for experienced trial attorneys. I eventually looked up Lester's other case out of curiosity, wondering what defense Lester may have in that case. In reading the investigator's report and interview with Lester, it appeared Lester's defense was going to be problematic. Lester had told the investigator, "I only fired one shot."

This seemed more like a confession to the charge of "ex-convict in possession of a firearm" than a defense. I was happy I didn't represent Lester on this charge. The felony deputy public defender was probably not going to be happy with me for getting Lester off on the drunk in public charge, because now Lester would probably not plead guilty to the felony gun charge. He would figure, why not demand his Constitutional right to a jury trial? That was his right, and it had worked out well – this time.

CHAPTER THIRTY-TWO

The Buy

ack at the office on the day of the trial, it was time to
celebrate. There was a long, time-honored tradition
of the winner of a jury trial buying his colleagues beer. It
was affectionately called "the buy." This ritual was
infrequently observed, because public defenders rarely
won their trials. This was not because they were not quality
lawyers, but because their cases were usually losers. A
lawyer can only do so much. He or she is restricted by the
facts of the case, and the facts of many of the cases for
criminal defense attorneys were less than promising.

I hadn't expected to win, so I hadn't thought ahead to
be sure I had the money to make "the buy." Fortunately, I
discovered I had $30.00 in my wallet. There were twelve
lawyers employed at the Public Defender's office. I had to
cross my fingers the money would purchase enough
pitchers of beer to take care of my obligation. The rare
beer drinking celebrations were always held at
Xochimilco's, the Mexican restaurant two doors down
from our office. This place was not an upscale joint, and
beer was served in big pitchers for $5.00 each. This meant
my modest $30.00 fund should be enough to pay for
about 60 beers.

With a buy in the offing, the lawyers packed it in early
and we found ourselves filing into the dimly lit restaurant,
pungent with the smell of beer and grease, a little after
four in the afternoon. As we dropped onto the hard
wooden chairs, several deputies were trying to remember

how long it had been since the last buy – they decided it was at least six months. This sounded about right to me – there had only been one buy since I had arrived at the office. The beer began arriving and one of the senior deputies rose and proposed a toast to me, as the winning lawyer. Everyone took a deep pull on their beer. I basked.

There were a number of reasons the lawyers were happy on the occasion of these buys. First, the lawyers were all about the same age with similar backgrounds. They worked closely together and many of them socialized together. For the most part, everyone liked each other and was genuinely happy for their winning colleague. Further, everyone likes free beer and they were glad to celebrate when someone else was buying. For me, I got to describe the case and how I thought it was won. I didn't have to offer to talk about the case. They asked me to. They demanded it. They knew the local opposition and wanted to know which deputy district attorney I had been up against and what effect it had when he heard the verdict. I also owned up to my post-trial conversations with the jurors and their take on the evidence and how they actually reached their verdict. It was fun being the focus of attention, especially when it was my first jury trial. I finally felt like I was one of the boys.

When a deputy wins a trial, the Boss would usually come by at some point to congratulate the winning lawyer, join the party, and partake in the celebration. True to tradition, Boss did drop by my party. He slapped me on the back and made a speech about how these wins were hard to come by and so important to the balance of justice in the county. Boss waxed eloquent, asserting that poverty was a root cause of crime, and we public defenders must be on the side of the poor and downtrodden until they had the same opportunities to succeed as the rest of society. Boss went on to say his office had to keep the police and prosecution from running roughshod over indigent citizens and these occasional wins were key to this mission. These inspirational speeches never failed to bring cheers from both the young and veteran lawyers gathered at the restaurant, most of whom shared the Boss's opinion. Of course, the volume of cheers was in large part dependent on the degree of inebriation of the public defenders in attendance.

All of the free beer, plus a few additional pitchers, had been consumed by the time the celebration wound down. It was around 7:00 p.m. when the last of us – Riddle, me, and couple of the other deputies with whom I was especially close – finally filed out into the warm dusk. I stopped by the office to pick up my things and then began to make my way home, still high from the rush I had felt the moment the verdict had been announced.

Arriving home, I let myself into the flat. Sensing my excitement, Tuna came running and we suddenly found ourselves jumping up and down, Tuna in my arms licking my face, clearly as ecstatic as I was.

We went upstairs and, settling in, I began explaining every detail of the trial to Tuna. He seemed receptive to hearing the blow by blow, and didn't mind when I repeated another short version of the trial on the phone to my mother. At last, it was time for dinner. Tuna did not get human food unless the occasion merited an exception to the rule. What occasion would be more important at this point in my life than winning my first jury trial? I baked a ham and we both settled down to a ham dinner (and all the trimmings, which in this case consisted of pineapple slices on top of the ham). Kicking back, we ate in front of the television where we watched whatever happened to be on – it didn't really matter that evening. What could be better than a man and his best friend celebrating and being together? If a human doesn't have another human to share life with, then there is nothing better than being with your beloved dog.

CHAPTER THIRTY-THREE

Another Dognap?

Life went back to normal very quickly. It was apparent most of the other lawyers in the office didn't give my first trial victory any further thought. In fact, none of the lawyers ever mentioned it again. One of the more artistic secretaries drew a picture of me in my new three-piece suit with one shoe missing; the story had spread around the office like wildfire and did come up from time to time when someone wanted to needle me. Otherwise, it was as if the trial had never occurred.

One nice thing happened right after the trial, but I am not sure it was connected. The wife of one of the other deputies was a true artist. She painted a beautiful picture of Tuna trotting along a woodsy trail in a forest setting. It was a great likeness, and the landscape was reminiscent of Mt. Veeder Road in the western mountains of Napa. It was a lovely painting, which I still have. I don't know why she did this for me. She may have overheard me saying I wished I could have Tuna with me at work. I decided to display this beautiful painting by putting it in a window frame.

I dragged Riddle shopping. We went to lumber yards, junkyards, garage sales, and thrift shops, until we found an old beat-up wooden frame. I mounted the masterpiece and hung it in my office. Now I had the window I had always wanted – which was quite an accomplishment, since my office had no exterior walls, and hence, no windows. I could look at the outside world; and when I did, I would always see Tuna prancing around in a forest setting.

For the next several months, I continued to be assigned a constant stream of misdemeanor cases. I was able to settle most of these in a reasonable way for my clients. However, there were a couple of cases where I wasn't able to obtain reasonable plea bargains, with the result that both clients opted for jury trials. I got very lucky and went on a short win streak, although by public defender standards, it was a sizzling hot streak of which to be proud. I won both jury trials, which made three jury trial victories in a row. And they were my first three trials. This was almost unheard of at the public defender's office. My beer costs were mounting, and my reputation was growing. Boss told me if I kept this up, they would be opening the doors to the jail and letting everyone out. Tuna was of course there to welcome me home after each of these trials, delighted with our victories – and our celebratory dinners.

On a dreary overcast Saturday morning one weekend, I stood on the porch waiting for Tuna to come back from his morning run. It had been more than an hour and I was beginning to get worried. Tuna would not run away. I knew that. The only protracted time he had ever been away from me was the time in San Francisco when he had been dognapped by the twelve-year-old girl and kept inside her house for three and a half months. I decided Tuna's absence once again could not be volitional. Something must have happened.

My imagination started to churn. Just like before, I began to worry he had been injured or killed by a motorist, or had been picked up by the pound, or was dognapped again. What were the odds of that? I called my buddy Riddle and told him my fears. Riddle was not a fan of Tuna. He didn't like Tuna's manners, because Tuna was always jumping on him or sometimes crudely mounting his leg. But he was a reliable friend. He knew I loved Tuna, and while he responded to me like he didn't care (I think his exact words were, "Tuna is missing? Great, you are better off without that flea-bag mutt!"), he immediately drove over to my house to help me search for him. Riddle told me not to worry, we would find him. Riddle was the manifestation of optimism and confidence.

Piling into my old Volkswagen station wagon that I had obtained through my dad's wrecking yard, we drove around and around the area of Stockton where I lived. We had been slowly driving through the neighborhood for over an hour shouting out of our respective windows, when Riddle spotted Tuna trotting down a sidewalk. He looked like he had been in a fight, out of sorts and disheveled.

I quickly pulled to the curb and Riddle threw open his door, calling to Tuna to jump in. Tuna turned to us with a look of surprise, which turned to relief and delight as he ran over and jumped into Riddle's lap and gave him a lick on one cheek. As I pulled away from the curb heading for home, my sense of gratitude and joy at finding Tuna was suddenly swept away by a horrible stench. Tuna smelled to high heaven. My hand leapt to the window handle, which I desperately cranked down, thrusting my head out gasping for air.

Riddle was less fortunate, pinned in his seat by the wiggling dog in his lap. In a single motion, the burly Riddle threw Tuna over his shoulder into the back seat. He then quickly began cranking his passenger side window open, so he too could get some relief. I started to gag, which did not help the chaotic situation. Riddle was loudly cursing, and I was retching with my head hung outside my driver's side window. Tuna, always turned on by loud noise, made a move to jump back to the front seat where the entire hubbub was occurring, but sensing he might be killed by Riddle if he attempted a return, he abruptly settled into the back seat.

As soon as we got home, Riddle took off, still cursing under his breath. I took the stinking, foul-smelling Tuna into my apartment for an immediate bath. I continued to gag as I bathed my dog. I repeated the shampoo treatment twice until I was positive he was clean. I dried him off and then went outside to clean the car.

Riddle and I were never sure what had happened to Tuna. Our best guess continued to be he had lost another fight. Tuna was more of a lover than a fighter. Of course, I forgave him. He probably hadn't had much choice in whatever happened. I am pretty sure Tuna did not voluntarily dive into a vat of shit. Thankfully, Tuna never got into anything remotely like that situation again. This was fortunate because my stomach could not have taken it.

CHAPTER THIRTY-FOUR

Matchmaker Tuna

Soon Tuna would do the most altruistic thing a dog can do for his master. One might even say Tuna acted against his own best interests. He brought a new person into my life. This meant, of course, I might be spending more time with this person than with Tuna, and certainly Tuna would have to share me with another human. Still, Tuna undertook to bring this person into my life.

It was the fall of 1973. I was 26 years old and one of two bachelors in my office. Things were good. I had lots of friends at the office, and my best buddy, Riddle, continued to think I was the funniest person he ever met. Things were going well socially, and, of course, I had my pal, Tuna, for great companionship. By now, Tuna was the longest relationship of my life outside of family. While I was finally deeply happy in my life, I don't think I realized how ready I was to have a steady relationship with a woman. Tuna took care of that.

Her name was Ann. She lived in the flat below Tuna and me, but we hadn't met, as she had only recently moved in. One October morning, I had to postpone exercising Tuna to go to an early eye appointment. The appointment was at 6:45 in the morning because it was a workday, and I had to be at work by 8:00 a.m. This required me getting up very early to get to my appointment. Upon my return to the flat, I took Tuna outside for his exercise, starting as usual on his leash. After a short time, I would take Tuna off of his leash and let him run around.

On this particular occasion it was still early, and very cold outside. I was wearing a suit and a trench coat. The eye doctor had dilated my eyes, so I was also sporting those funny looking cardboard dark glasses. I must have looked like an FBI or CIA agent, or, more probable given the area where I lived, a narcotics officer. After a time, I let Tuna off his leash so he could run about freely.

It happened that at this very moment, an attractive brown-haired young woman stepped out of her flat to empty her garbage. She was in her bathrobe, lifting the top off the garbage can, paying no attention to the man and his dog some 100 feet away.

Tuna and I both seemed to sense Ann's innate sexual attractiveness, but it was Tuna who made the first move, running over to her, and, without barking any social amenities or commencing any foreplay, jumped up and started humping her leg.

As soon as I realized what was happening, I hurried towards them with the purpose of rescuing the young woman from Tuna's sexual assault. Still wearing the awkward and unflattering cardboard sunglasses, I stumbled through a flower bed and across a cement pathway, determined to rescue her from this outrage.

Upon my arrival, Tuna was really getting down to business, so I had to act quickly. I grabbed Tuna around the chest and pulled, but he had clamped onto Ann like a Gila monster. Summoning extra muscle, I ripped Tuna off Ann's leg.

Undeterred, he continued the humping motion as he hung there in my arms. With a sheepish grin, I set Tuna down on the ground, which had the effect of finally making him become still. Eyes bright, he stood there looking up at Ann with a friendly expression as I hastily snapped his leash back into place. Then I turned to this lovely young woman, standing there in her bathrobe, still holding the garbage can lid in one hand. I introduced myself and apologized profusely for Tuna's conduct. Ann accepted my apology. She said she knew who I was from our landlady but had thought, from her description, that I would be much older. She introduced herself and thanked me for saving her. She assured me she had no injuries. She had already turned and started toward her apartment when I found myself asking if I could take her out for coffee to make up for the chaos she had just been through. She stopped, looked back, and in a calm, soft voice, said, "That would be nice."

On our first date we went to a local restaurant called Fat City, named after a book and movie of that name about the town of Stockton. It was a modest place, but sort of hip for Stockton in 1973. After dinner, we went to a movie called *Where's Poppa*, a comedy starring George Segal and Ruth Gordon. This date may have been fairly tame, but it was a thoroughly enjoyable time for both Ann and me. We were comfortable with each other. We both laughed a lot. From there, our romance took off. Of course, the traumatic beginning of the relationship between Ann and Tuna had to be overcome, and it is not clear if Ann ever fully trusted Tuna's subsequent amorous flirtations. However, she came to see his better side and understood he brought me happiness. They subtly vied for my attention, and, in the end, though Ann won my heart, my unconditional love for Tuna never waned.

Ann was only twenty years old when we met, as opposed to my advanced age of twenty-six. She was in her senior year of college at the University of the Pacific in Stockton. She lived with her best friend, Kathy, who also was a student at UOP. Ann was the second of four daughters to Chuck and Bev Berkstresser, who lived in Sacramento, California.

CHAPTER THIRTY-FIVE

Another Move

A nn, Tuna, and I quickly became an item. You wouldn't see me without Ann, and usually Tuna was with us, too. We went on walks together, and had many adventures Tuna could also enjoy, like picnics at a park or hikes in the foothills surrounding the outskirts of the city. Ann had joined our family, to the point we decided to live together.

The flat was not the best situation for Tuna, because he had no back yard in which to roam. With me working full time, it would have been better if he weren't so cooped up. With both Tuna and Ann in mind, I found a small two-bedroom home to rent, at what seemed like the ridiculously reasonable rent of $85.00 per month. Even my second story flat, which I thought was inexpensive, was $110.00 per month. This small house, located on East Castle Street in Stockton, had a roomy back yard and a detached garage providing storage room.

The ridiculously reasonable rent did not seem so ridiculously reasonable when we realized we had moved in with another family – a family of rats. Nevertheless, an entire house (ok, shanty) for only $85.00 per month was the best deal in town. It was here that life for the three of us really started in earnest.

The old house was a very small two-bedroom home with one bathroom and a kitchen. There are two-bedroom houses and two-bedroom houses, but at 650 square feet, this was one tiny two-bedroom house. It was so small, there was a place in the middle of the house where you could stand and see every room and corner of the place. The floors were linoleum throughout. The only difference between this house and a monkey cage was a drain on the floor. The yard was roomy, though, and allowed Tuna plenty of space to roam without the danger of the streets and highways. Tuna was a born excavator, and immediately started digging his way to the freedom which called him from the other side of the fence that confined him. Most of the time, however, Tuna was an inside dog, because most of the time, inside is where I spent my time.

In and around Castle Street, there were a variety of neighborhoods that made walks interesting and enjoyable. Only a few blocks away the neighborhood gave way to an affluent area laden with brick and stone mansions, surrounded by beautifully maintained landscapes. These magnificent homes were gorgeously immense, each home custom built and unique. Each provided an aesthetic architectural work of art for anyone taking a stroll to study, examine, or just plain enjoy. Ann, Tuna and I routinely went on walks in this plush neighborhood. Ann and I found ourselves fantasizing about living in a place like one of those homes. We started thinking about a future together. We enjoyed each other's company, and at this point in our relationship, thinking of our future began to come very naturally.

There were other areas surrounding the Castle Street home, including a neighborhood cluster of shops, cafes, and bakeries. These little businesses were easy to walk to and fun to explore. There was a movie theatre close by, and it turned out Ann and I were both movie fans. The little home and its surrounding neighborhood, plus little shops and businesses, created a very comfortable setting for our newly formed family.

Soon, our family expanded. Ann and I decided to get a kitten. Of course, Ann had concerns about how Tuna would take to a little kitten, but I assured her that not only would a kitty be unharmed by Tuna, it would give Tuna a companion. With the arrival of Ann, Tuna did not have my full attention anymore. A kitty would help the situation.

Welcome, Bruno — a jet black kitten we got from a member of the secretarial pool at the Public Defender's Office. I brought the kitten home on a Saturday afternoon. Ann was waiting with Tuna in the back yard. I brought the kitten out to meet Tuna. The moment Tuna saw the kitten he seemed surprised and curious. He got very close and started to sniff the kitten. Bruno immediately hissed, and Tuna backed off. We put the kitten down on the lawn and remained close to it. Tuna was no longer paying attention to Bruno.

Perhaps it never crossed Tuna's mind Bruno would be staying. Over the next several days, Ann and I both watched over the interplay between Tuna and Bruno quite closely. We noticed when we peeked from outside a room, all Tuna did when he thought he was alone with the kitten was sniff him and even licked him a couple of times. We still monitored them carefully.

The plan of all living in harmony was working well. When Ann or I let Tuna and Bruno outside in the back yard to play and do their business, they seemed to play appropriately or, at least, exist without Tuna attacking the young kitty. Of course, Tuna would explore and sniff Bruno, and the little kitten would seem distressed at times, or would start shaking its tail which, we know, in kitten language is not a sign of happiness. But Ann or I were there to make sure the situation never grew in intensity or danger to Bruno.

After another month, Ann began to feel comfortable enough with the two of them that we didn't feel it was necessary to stay at their sides outside to ensure no trouble ensued. Our mode of operation changed from staying outside in the backyard with our pets in some supervisorial capacity, to merely letting them outside. Ann and I believed this change worked well. Still, within a few days after this change, Bruno disappeared and was never seen again. Was this just coincidence, or did Tuna drive Bruno from the home? We never learned the answer to this question.

The next pet brought in for Tuna's perusal, and to give him enjoyable companionship, was Omar. Omar was another kitten. He was cute, with a white coat and very fluffy fur. Omar came from another friend, whose cat had just given birth to a lovely litter of kittens. Not knowing what really happened to Bruno, and not really knowing if Tuna was complicit in Bruno's disappearance, Ann and I decided to really take it slowly. We brought Omar into the house and called Tuna over to see Omar while I held the kitty in my arms. Tuna sniffed the baby, and didn't seem to be alarmed or upset, nor did it appear his predator instinct was stirred. Of course, this was only the first day, but we had high hopes for peaceful harmony.

The same pattern followed with Tuna and Omar as it had with Tuna and Bruno. They were supervised by Ann and me, and never left alone when they were together. There were no signs of any problems, except Tuna played a little rough with such a young kitten. The rough play, however, didn't appear out of the ordinary. It just seemed what play might be like between a six-year-old dog and an eight-week-old kitten.

Omar had been with us for a month when one Saturday afternoon we let Tuna outside to play, after Omar had already been outside for about half an hour. Tuna made a beeline right at Omar. Omar, who was on the backyard lawn, looked up and saw what must have appeared to be a gigantic monster coming toward him.

There is a crude old saying describing fear: "He scared the shit out of me." Well, Omar was so scared by the sight of a behemoth dog bounding at a high rate of speed straight at him, that he had a bowel movement on the spot. I yelled for Tuna to stop and ran him down to make sure he didn't hurt Omar. It was not clear whether Tuna meant any harm or just wanted to play, but what was clear was Omar was traumatized.

Omar survived for a shorter period of time than Bruno. Omar lasted less than two months and then – gone; vanished. Again, no one knew for sure why Omar disappeared, but for Ann and me, who each had several cats growing up in our respective households, we couldn't understand how this could happen twice in such a short time. We both speculated on what may have happened. Was there a serial baby kitten killer around the Castle Street neighborhood? Was there some weed poisoning around Castle Street homes which each of the kittens consumed to their detriment? Or, perhaps Tuna was just too old a dog (even at the relatively youthful age of six years) to put up with little kittens. Maybe we were wrong to expect a successful socialization of the cat and dog relationship under these circumstances.

No one ever found any signs of a serial kitten killer, nor did anyone ever see deceased kittens lying around gardens that had been sprayed with weed killers. Of course, no one ever saw Tuna chase the kittens away, nor did anyone observe the kittens flee from fright at the sight of Tuna. Anything was possible. But one thing was certain, Tuna's household would not be trying to assimilate any more pets into their home for his companionship. Ann and I received this message loud and clear.

CHAPTER THIRTY-SIX

Going Home

With the exception of the kitten situation, things were going great for Tuna, Ann, and me. Things went so well that one day, Ann popped the question of a permanent relationship. It is true the man traditionally asks the question, but, as things worked out, Ann knew I loved her and she knew she loved me, so she decided to do the asking. I was delighted, and answered in the affirmative, without hesitation. We immediately agreed on a wedding date in early November, some 3 months away. The first person we told was Tuna. His reaction was to run around the house at full speed. He only did this when he was happy and wanted to play. He was celebrating the permanency of our family. We then called our families – my parents in Napa and Ann's parents in Sacramento. Everyone was delighted, and wedding plans began immediately.

Meanwhile, I had been talking for some time about long-range plans relating to my career. I have always planned for both the short term and the long term. Short term, in Stockton, my plan was to have as much fun as possible -- before Ann, that mainly meant with my best buddy, Pat Riddle. The short-term plan also called for getting as much legal experience as possible before moving back to my hometown in Napa – which, of course, was my long-range plan. Professionally, I had to pay my dues and learn the ropes, getting as many jury trials under my belt as possible.

Now that Ann had come into the picture, my attention began to focus on the long-range plan. Going to Napa was now foremost on my mind. I had about a dozen jury trials under my belt and realized I was ready to go. Unless we were going to stay in Stockton for the rest of our lives, I decided the sooner we left, the sooner we could start over. As I thought this through, I had a rising sense of urgency on the professional side. When we got to Napa, I would have to start from scratch, setting up a law practice, attracting clients, and developing contacts in a different county. I wouldn't have anyone who could assist me – all I would have is my roots from growing up in the town. Yes, I thought – it was time to get at it.

My hope was Riddle would want to join me, as well as another friend I had made at the office named Louis Zolton Gasper, whom we called Lou. Lou had a towering intellect and was quite possibly the most articulate person I had ever met. I remember Lou cross-examining a particular witness who was very hostile to Lou's client. She remembered all the negative things to be said about Lou's client, but none of the positives. It gradually became apparent to everyone in the courtroom she was not going to give an inch. Toward the end of his lengthy cross-examination, Lou asked one more question. As she had on several previous occasions, the witness declared she did not recollect the event.

Casting his penetrating gaze at the judge, Lou stated in a loud and booming voice, "Mrs. Smith, once again, I see your memory fails with abrupt convenience."

Of course, there was an objection because it was not a question, and was argumentative to boot, and, of course, the judge sustained the objection, but the point had been eloquently made: this witness was completely biased and could not be believed. With a long line of simple questioning and one well-timed surgical thrust, Lou had destroyed the witness's credibility.

When I approached Lou about the prospect of starting our own law firm in Napa, he was excited and ready for the move. Lou had a chronic disease affecting his autoimmune system and was having difficulty passing the county health requirements for insurance purposes. In fact, he had only been allowed to work at the office because he had signed a waiver releasing the County of San Joaquin from responsibility to provide him with health insurance. As this appalling red tape continued to build from the county, Lou had gradually become convinced his employment future at the Public Defender's office was limited at best. Besides, Lou had gone to law school at the University of San Francisco, and the prospect of a practice in Napa was a lot more appealing and attractive than practicing in the Central Valley. Lou's wife Nancy was also thrilled at the prospect of a move to Napa.

As for Riddle, he initially needed no convincing to move to Napa. However, as the date was approaching, Riddle was becoming serious about a woman. In fact, he became engaged. Her name was Katherine. It seems Katherine was a Central Valley girl who did not want to move. And, as is so often the case with people in love, where one goes the other follows. Or in this case, where one stays the other stays, too.

It was a devastating blow when Riddle finally told me he would not be coming to Napa.

It was a sunny Saturday morning in September and Ann and I had just finished breakfast when Riddle knocked on our front door. He was not his usual happy-go-lucky self. He sat at our kitchen table and spoke in a soft voice with his head bowed. Eventually he looked up and staring into my eyes said he was not coming to Napa. He said it was because Katherine was not ready to move at this time. She was still in college, her family was living here, and he just couldn't move without her. He said they might be able to move to Napa in a couple of years, once Katherine completed college. He could join our firm at that time. He said he was still interested in practicing with Lou and me. I told Riddle I had to speak to Lou but, as for me, we needed Riddle now not later. Riddle offered to send money on a monthly basis until he could join us. I told him we weren't interested in his money. We needed his personal presence. Riddle said he couldn't do that and the conversation was over. We shook hands and he left. I felt sick. In addition to my disappointment and sadness, I wasn't sure we could succeed without him.

Riddle had been central to my professional plans for a successful law firm. Riddle was the complete package as a lawyer: smart, fearless, handsome, and very personable. He was going to be a success, no matter what field of law he entered. We were a match made in heaven. I knew Napa, and Riddle was going to take it by storm.

But Riddle and Napa were not meant to be. I was left to start my practice on my own with no hotshot lawyer to wow the clients. Lou was great, but he was not the born rainmaker Riddle was. Riddle would impress you with his legal acumen, and he would charm you with his personality. He was so sure of himself you naturally believed him. He exuded confidence. He was a born leader and people followed him. With Riddle in the mix, I was convinced our firm would have a substantial following within a year or two. Without him, it was another story. I believed success would happen, but I knew it would not happen quickly. It would take a lot more time.

Annie and I married in Stockton on November 2, 1974. Attending were a mixture of my friends and Ann's and, of course, our relatives. As to friends, mine were mostly divided between Stockton friends (primarily my office colleagues) and Napa friends. San Joaquin County Judge William Giffen performed the small but lovely evening ceremony. Some of my law school friends were also there. Mike Low, Bob Trevorrow, and their music group played their arrangement of the Beatles song, "In My Life" as Ann came down the aisle. She was beautiful. It was one of the happiest days of my life. Years later, when our daughters married, they each selected the same song to be played as I walked them down the aisle.

I had prepared Tuna for the permanency of my relationship with Ann, but I doubt he appreciated the full implications of "permanent." He had spent time with other female companions in years past, but never one who stayed for so long. Little did he know within a few years our family would grow. Tuna had become accustomed to Ann from Castle Street, and as far as I could tell it didn't seem like a big deal to him. I suspect it was something of a surprise for Tuna when Ann and I went on a vacation for a couple of weeks after the wedding and he discovered himself once more staying with my parents in Napa during that period of time. But I wasn't worried – Tuna had lived with my parents off and on as I had gone through various transitions in college and graduate school, so I knew he would be well taken care of and relatively content.

As soon as Ann and I returned from our honeymoon things began to happen fast. We decided it was time to get the ball rolling on the move to Napa. Lou and Nancy completely agreed with us. Our first trip would be to find office space in Napa before we terminated our employment in Stockton.

My father and I had had our differences while I was growing up in Napa, but I have to give him credit for putting a lot of energy into helping us find a law office. Big Al got wind of a very large room for rent in the old Plaza Hotel. The dilapidated building had two great advantages: first, it was located directly across the street from the front entrance to the historic Napa Superior Courthouse. You could not have a better location. Better digs, yes, but better location – no way. Second, the rent was only $110.00 per month, which was ridiculously low for commercial space in Napa in 1975. Further, there were almost no utility expenses. The main source of heat was from steam radiator heat that heated the entire hotel. The room itself was very large, with ample space to divide into offices. My father called in some favors from friends – a carpenter built the room dividers and a painter painted the entire premises. The place went from looking like a dump to looking like a palace (I am not sure I would pass a polygraph based on that statement). We had new carpeting installed (again, from some people we knew who gave us a great discount). Soon, the place was ready to open.

I contacted some friends I still knew who worked at the local newspaper, and we were allowed to have an article about the new law firm in town, with interviews and pictures. This widespread announcement for our practice amounted to free publicity, a genuine boon to a new business.

Lou was the first to give notice to Boss. He moved to Napa in December 1974 and opened our doors in the first week of January 1975. Everyone was sad to see Lou leave the office. He was very popular and respected with our colleagues. Lou was determined to make our plans work.

He and Nancy had made several trips to Napa from Stockton to look for a home to purchase. They found one in Browns Valley in west Napa. When Lou and Nancy closed escrow, it felt like a big step. The transition to Napa was happening.

I followed on Lou's heels, giving notice to Boss, but agreeing to work through the end of January 1975. Going into Boss's office to have the talk was difficult for me. I was so grateful he had given me the job and for his kindness and support for me as a new lawyer. He was gracious and wished me the best. He even said if I was going to go into private practice, then I should do it sooner than later. He told me to stay in touch because I was one of his boys.

Now it was official. I had quit my job. I would be joining Lou on February 1, 1975 in Napa.

Through the fall and winter as we were gearing up for the move, Ann and I had also made several weekend trips to Napa to look for a place to live. We wanted to purchase a home. I had lived a frugal bachelor's life in Stockton and had saved money from working. Together with my accumulated San Joaquin County retirement funds, we had enough for a down payment.

We both wanted to have a peaceful place in the country. We were determined to have a serene life in a beautiful setting. After several weeks we found a place that was beautiful, and, more important, in our price range.

Mt. Veeder Road was located in the western hills of Napa County. The geography was mountainous, thickly populated with redwood trees, and visually beautiful all around. The place that caught our eye had a large redwood house which was extremely spacious. There was an outbuilding that had been used by the previous owner as her art studio. The house and studio were located on five acres of lovely, wooded, hilly mountainside. We went in knowing it would require lots of work to maintain the property. There was a pasture where I could plant a large vegetable garden. Of course, it would need a rototiller for preparation. There was poison oak on much of the property that would need to be dealt with. I had grown up in Napa, but the truth was, I was a townie – I didn't really know a lot about the rural mountains west of town. So, while Ann and I understood the place would require a lot of work, we really didn't have a clue what we were biting off.

For example, there were a lot of wild animals in these western mountains, including mountain lions, deer, raccoons, and snakes. I hated snakes.

There was, however, one thing there wasn't much of, and that was water. The entire area was water deficient. One landowner might have a well with adequate water, but his neighbor might have none. We were that neighbor. We had no water. There was a dried-up well, and a storage tank for all the water it wasn't producing. Our more fortunate next-door neighbor had an active spring on his place and was kind enough to let us draw a small amount of water from it. This was accomplished by a little, gravity fed, flexible plastic tube extending from the neighbor's spring up the hill down to our storage tank and then, on the good days, on into our house. We had to be so careful about our usage of water. It was something we did our best to look past, because of the beauty of the setting. This was a mistake. Squirrels, coyotes and other animals were constantly biting into the soft tubing, with the result that we were constantly traipsing up and down the hillside, plumber clamps in hand, hunting for the leaks.

The water deficiency inconvenience was multiplied by how the leaks were discovered. Picture yourself in the shower getting ready for work. Just after you have lathered yourself with soap, or your hair with shampoo, the water suddenly and completely stops. The next thing you knew, you're hiking around in your bathrobe out on your hillside acreage, with the plumber clamps in your robe pocket, holding the gravity system water hose in the air above the country wildflowers and weeds (and maybe poison oak) in the hopes of spotting the leak. Sooner or later, you discover the location of the leak and repair it, so that you can get back to your shower, and possibly get to work on time. Not a great way to start the morning.

Overlooking the water problems on this property was a mistake. It was also not prudent to move to such a remote location while starting a law practice. My fledging practice was already consuming an enormous amount of time. Besides the actual practice of law, there was the rainmaking, as well as the attendance at bar association meetings, service clubs, and charitable organization boards that had to be joined for purposes of service, and for the ancillary reason of meeting people and making connections with them. On weekends, I either worked at the office, or, if I got to stay home, I was too tired to rototill, spray poison oak, and put in the countless needed hours of general cleanup work. The timing could not have been worse. Further, Ann was in the same bind – she needed to work so we had a paycheck coming in. While my practice was getting started, it barely covered the overhead in the early months. This all meant neither of us could put the necessary time into our property to make it livable and keep it that way.

Unfortunately, water wasn't our only problem in the department of basic necessities. The old house was on propane heat, which was expensive. Since we had little income, we could only use the heater when we were freezing. To be even moderately comfortable the rest of the time, I needed to be chopping wood, so the fireplaces could be used. Chopping wood took time and skill, both of which I lacked.

What's more, the waterline wasn't the only thing that broke. It seemed like something gave out, snapped, leaked, sagged, or collapsed every day. And I didn't have a handyman bone in my body. I was as handy as a pig with knitting needles. Ann was way better at fixing things than I was. I got frustrated easily and had no confidence. When it came to homestead, there was a lot of quit in me.

What about Tuna's acclimation to this setting? Well, that is a more difficult question to answer. On the positive side, Tuna really liked having room to roam. I am not sure of the negatives, but I can speculate. For instance, I think perhaps Tuna had never, ever experienced the kind of animals he encountered on Mt. Veeder. I never actually saw him get into it with another animal, but I did observe what appeared to be the results of an encounter with one.

One morning after I had gotten up and dressed, I let Tuna out to roam. After breakfast, I decided to go out and see what he was doing. I went out on the deck but didn't see him. I went down to the big flat field where we had our vegetable garden. I immediately saw things weren't right.

The artichoke plants were all trampled and disheveled, like someone or something had smashed them. Other plants looked like they had either been eaten or trampled on as well. I was bewildered, but even more, I was concerned about Tuna. Had he been run off by wild animals or, worse, had he been injured? Tuna had never shown much judgment in deciding whether or not to fight. The phrases, "Discretion is the better part of valor," or "Run away so you can fight another day," had no meaning to Tuna. He was the alpha dog, so he always chose to fight. The problem was he was not a good fighter. As best as I could tell, he had lost almost every one of his fights up to the point when we moved to Mt. Veeder Rd. I was suddenly very worried about his wellbeing.

If the plants looked disheveled, you should have seen Tuna when he surfaced. I was still down at the garden perusing the damage when I heard some noise coming from the brush a couple of hundred yards up the hill. As I studied the woods, Tuna emerged, slowly making his way down toward the garden where I was standing. He was noticeably limping and walking, not running as was his usual mode. I called out to him, encouraging him to come running, or at least trotting. No such results. Tuna had heard me and clearly saw me, but was unwilling or unable to move any faster than his slow tentative steps. For Tuna, this was a snail's pace.

When Tuna finally reached me, the first thing I did was inspect him for wounds. He seemed to have a limp, and his coat looked like he had been drenched in mud, with his fur all matted and chaotic. His entire coat had one big bed-head look to it. I continued to slowly work my hands over his torso and carefully down each leg, probing for sensitive spots or blood. To my surprise and delight, Tuna seemed to be unhurt. I found no bite marks, nor did anything seem to be broken. He had no abrasions or lacerations of any kind. But he sure looked like he had been in a war. As I talked to him calmly, it was clear he was happy to see me. He started wagging his tail. It was such a relief to see him uninjured.

We never did figure out what caused the trampling of the garden, nor the identity of Tuna's assailant. Whatever happened didn't seem to deter Tuna from running around the mountainside, or from enjoying the spacious surroundings perfect for a dog who likes to exercise and run. Mt. Veeder was still a perfect setting for Tuna. The same could not be said for Tuna's human caretakers.

We only lasted on Mt. Veeder Road for nine months. The additional burdens of country living were just not working out for us. We decided to move. It was a move, I might add, we never regretted, given the water issues, the vast amount of time needed for chores, including lots of wood chopping, and the expenses of propane and electricity. It all made the decision easy. Even our bountiful vegetable garden didn't work out. Tending to a garden as big as the one we planted was a full-time job in and of itself. It was beautiful and productive, but oh, so time consuming. We knew things just were not working out up in the mountains. We decided to sell and cut our losses.

We placed the Mt. Veeder home on the market with a realtor. Ann and I started looking around Napa for more suitable housing for our current needs. We finally settled on a house on Shetler Avenue in South Napa – a ranch style home we both really liked. It had two bedrooms which was enough for us. A major reason for selecting this home was because it sat on a half-acre. It had plenty of room for Tuna to explore, excavate and exercise. It was, of course, more than enough yard for me to neglect. For Tuna, this home was fine. We liked the house too, and we all were happy there because we were in town, close to our jobs, and not in an isolated forest setting with no water.

Chapter Thirty-seven

A Fight Tuna Wins

We lived on Shetler Avenue for about three years. As we settled in, Ann and I began talking about starting a family. When we decided to have a child, we realized we would need to make some changes to the house. Because it had only two bedrooms, we decided to add another bedroom.

Meanwhile, my law practice was growing, and Lou and I had taken in another lawyer, Joe Flax. Joe was the friend who had told me about the Stockton job opening. In Napa, he had been a high school sports hero, with more letters than any other athlete in the history of the school at the time he graduated. He lettered in football, basketball, and tennis every year of his eligibility.

For me, things were progressing pretty well, both in my business and in my home life. Ann had quit her part time job at the bank and found full time employment at the Napa County Health and Human Services Agency as an eligibility worker for public assistance. This job had good benefits and provided the steady paycheck we needed while my practice grew. At home, Ann and I worked diligently on becoming pregnant.

There was one very unfortunate incident, however, that detracted from this rosy picture of a tranquil life. The incident involved Tuna, who was mostly responsible for it, except for a tiny fraction which may have been attributable to me.

Ann and I usually began our weekends by sleeping in, and then taking Tuna for a walk around the neighborhood. On this particular morning, we had gotten up unusually early for a Saturday morning, and headed out for our walk with Tuna on his leash. We had all enjoyed a brisk stroll along the western side of town and were almost back at the house when I unleashed Tuna to have one last bit of run before going into the house. The house was on a long narrow side street which was not heavily trafficked. It was a safe place for Tuna to run around and smell the plants and weeds along the road, and, of course, pee on them as well. Almost immediately upon releasing Tuna, I spotted a tiny dog about three quarters of a block away. It happened our next-door neighbor owned a tiny dog, but I wasn't able to tell if this was that dog. It wasn't even near its own house. After a couple of more steps toward the dog, both Ann and I recognized it as our neighbor's little Chihuahua, which had been a nuisance to us ever since we had moved into our house. This little dog would take his morning bowel movements on our front lawn. Further, he constantly barked at us every time we came outside our house. It's not as if this little dog played favorites and barked at only us. He was an equal opportunity yapper who barked at anything that moved. He was a little wisp of a dog who wasn't big enough to terrorize anyone, but how he tried. He snarled at squirrels, yapped at delivery guys (pizza delivery, UPS, you name it) and loved charging after little children on tricycles and older kids on bicycles. He was a royal pain to us mainly, however, because our lawn was his toilet, and he yapped at us more than anyone because of our convenient location. It was a bark that drove us crazy. To say "bark" does not adequately describe the inflection, volume, and pitch of this constantly grating yapping. A few seconds of this racket caused my blood pressure to skyrocket, resulting in a dizzying, buzzing sound in my head that could drive an otherwise sane person (me) to the verge of insanity with homicidal thoughts and intentions.

Being annoyed and hateful is one thing. Acting on that annoyance and hate is quite another. Ann and I never had any intention of doing the dog any harm. Really. In fact, Ann and I blamed the neighbors. They should have controlled their dog, rather than letting him out every morning to use our front lawn as a toilet.

Upon being unleashed, Tuna bolted as he usually did when released. The fact he was dashing toward the neighbor's dog didn't alarm me at first, because he was so far away. Under my breath I said, "Sic him, Tuna."

I had never used "sic him" as a command with Tuna. On this occasion, the words had slipped out as a joke between me and Ann, a salute to our feelings about the annoying little dog. If there had been the slightest possibility Tuna would pick a fight when ordered to do so, I would never have uttered the words, because Tuna had lost every fight he had ever been in.

But Tuna obeyed the command. It was as if Tuna knew how much this little runt annoyed me, so decided to assert his dominance over this little twerp of a canine. Tuna covered the half block in record time. He was barking like a maniac as he closed in on the rat-dog. The little rat-dog just froze as Tuna bowled into him, knocking him to the ground. Then, Tuna grabbed the little dog in his teeth as if he were a chew toy and commenced shaking the rat-dog from side to side, in what appeared to be a death grip.

Ann and I were horrified. I ran as fast as I could to the two combatants (actually, the perpetrator and the victim), and started to pry the rat-dog from Tuna's mouth, all the time commanding Tuna to let the little dog go. I was finally able to extract him from Tuna's slavering mouth, and the little dog dropped to the ground, stiff as a board. It was almost as if he was no longer a real dog, but a toy dog made out of cardboard. I entertained the desperate hope it was the dog's way of playing dead, so the big dog would stop trying to kill him. I held Tuna until Ann could get to us and leash him up. I asked Ann to put Tuna in the house, while I tended to the little dog.

The problem was he appeared to be dead. I picked him up and he was still stiff as a board. I figured he was literally scared to death by the much larger dog and the trauma of the violent attack. I found myself talking to him and trying to coax him back to life, but with no apparent success. Finally, I decided the only thing I could do was to take him next door to our neighbors and explain the situation. This was not a conversation I was looking forward to. As I carried the lifeless little form across the lawn where he had just that morning defecated, I ran through the possibilities in my head. "Hello, we are your neighbors next door, and my dog killed your dog. Sorry." Would they be angry? Would they sue? Would they hit me? Would they demand Tuna be put down?

To complicate matters, I didn't have a relationship with these neighbors, and what I knew about them was not good. I recognized their last name from court calendars in the criminal department. If the male member of this household was the same Leo Bartelt mentioned in various court documents pertaining to assault with a deadly weapon, lewd conduct, and drunk in public, a productive conversation with him would be unlikely. He was a violent sexual deviant, with alcohol problems. But Tuna seemed to have killed his little dog. I was stuck.

Having decided to come clean, despite the possibility I was about to meet the Leo Bartelt with a nasty criminal record, I needed to get this unpleasant confrontation over with. Desperately hoping I could somehow avoid getting beat up or starting a feud, I approached the neighbors' house. When I was about two feet from the doorbell, a miracle happened. To my shock, the completely still, dormant, little dog sprang to life in my arms. I quickly put the little doggie down and began talking to him and petting him. I had previously checked his tummy and back. Except for ruffled, saliva-wet fur, there were no wounds, no blood, no puncture marks. Suddenly the little dog was fine. At least that was my best medical opinion.

Seeing is believing, and with the dog standing on all four legs and walking around, albeit slowly, I decided there was no longer any need to confess to the neighbors what had happened. Their little dog had no visible injuries at all. Why make a big deal out of it? I left the dog on the porch, turned and walked back to my house without ringing the doorbell.

Three or four days later, our doorbell rang. Ann answered the door, and there stood a young girl. She introduced herself as our next-door neighbor. She could not have been more than eight years old. We did not know her or even recognize her by sight, but she was by herself, and presumably had walked next door from her house. She inquired if we knew anything about her dog. We both said that we had, of course, seen a little dog on our front lawn almost every morning and that it barked a lot. We both declined to use our usual description of "rat-dog" in talking about the small canine. We asked the young girl if this was her dog. She said yes and proceeded to tell us she was asking around to see if anyone had noticed anything about her dog that was unusual. I asked if the dog had run away or was missing. Her answer was as direct as if she had shot us with an arrow. Her little dog had died, and she wanted to know why.

She said it had not been hit by a car, nor were there any signs of mistreatment or injury to it. It just died. She said it had been a dog of high pedigree, a purebred toy poodle. She said her parents had papers to prove this. Any inclination I had to relieve the little girl of the mystery of her doggy's death ended with her representations (presumably furnished to her by her parents) this was a high-priced dog. It would be just like these shady parents to press their little daughter into sleuthing around the neighborhood in a not-so-subtle attempt to solve the mystery. Their dog's lineage and ancestors, I told myself, were probably no purer than Tuna's ancestors and his Heinz 57 background.

After the dog interaction a few days earlier, I had done some research at the court and learned the father of this girl was indeed a criminal of long standing. Both parents were of little financial means. It seemed impossible they would have been able to afford an expensive purebred dog. It would not be beyond them, however, to scam some person into believing they owned an expensive dog who was irreplaceable to their family (despite the evidence the dog was not watched or conscientiously cared for by these dog owners). Nevertheless, they would doubtless take the position there was no way to replace this dog even with another dog. Alas, they would lament, the only possible, reasonable way to compensate our family for the loss of our dog would be with money, as inadequate a remedy as that would be.

These thoughts were racing around in my head as I stood at the front door listening to the little girl inquire about who may have injured her dog. My fevered thought process led me to the conclusion divulging anything would bring trouble to my family and create a long-lasting problem with neighbors who were not people with whom I wanted to become embroiled in a feud. I claimed ignorance, even though the culprit was lying at my feet, resting not more than two feet from this inquiring little girl.

On reflection, this was a thoroughly regrettable and unpleasant experience on so many levels. It's true the little girl's father was despicable. The little dog was undoubtedly an annoyance. But it was undeserving of its fate. I should have told the truth. I continue to feel guilt and shame about the incident to this day.

We never again let Tuna off his leash when he wasn't in our backyard or in the field down the street.

CHAPTER THIRTY-EIGHT

Our Family Expands

I t was not long after the dog incident that Ann became pregnant. We were thrilled. Once again dipping into the deep pool of my father's friends in the construction trades, we managed to remodel our house to add a third bedroom. We were ready to welcome our new arrival.

On January 22, 1978, at 3:46 p.m., Ann and I were blessed with a daughter, Julia Christine Guadagni. She was 7 pounds 10 ounces, 20 inches long, and Ann and I thought she was the most beautiful baby either of us had ever seen. We were filled with grateful emotions of love and joy – and a sense of anticipation. We knew this addition to the family would change our lives.

We brought our Julia home to the Shetler Avenue house, where we had set up her bedroom down the hall from ours. One of the first evenings home, Ann tried to steal a little sleep while I kept Julia in my arms and watched a movie. I still remember – the name of the movie was *Children of the Corn*. It was a horror movie, and within a year or two it would not have been appropriate for Julia to watch, but it was okay now. She was a tiny baby who slept the entire time. Sitting with her cradled in my arms peacefully sleeping, with Tuna by my side on the floor taking a snooze, and knowing my beautiful bride was nearby in the bedroom getting some much-needed rest, produced a feeling so wonderful it is beyond the reach of words. I count the memory as one of the happiest of my life.

Even though our family had now expanded, life for Tuna went on as usual. One child was very manageable with two adults, so Tuna still got plenty of attention and was still allowed to be a house dog. The status quo, however, might not last if the family expanded. Only time would tell.

CHAPTER THIRTY-NINE

An Incident Tuna Did Not Cause

Very shortly after Julia's birth, Ann and I decided to move again. This time the decision was based on location. Most Realtors will tell you the most important factors influencing the market value of real estate are location, location, and location. The maxim was ringing true for us. Our wonderful house was in the southern part of the city near the Napa State Hospital, which housed the mentally ill, including some criminally insane people who were there for being dangerous to society. Additionally, the southern part of town was near Soscol Avenue, where most of the automotive industry was located, from mechanical repair shops and body repair shops, to new and used car lots. This type of industry was not helpful in raising real estate values. Finally, the south part of Napa was not as desirable geographically, as it was a windier part of the city, and closer to a run-down area known as American Canyon, which bordered the city of Vallejo and contained old, mostly dilapidated, houses. American Canyon was also where the city dump was located. The farther away a house was from American Canyon, the better for resale purposes.

By this time, I had renewed my friendship with Wayne Davidson, with whom I had grown up during my school years in Napa. Wayne had become a real estate agent. If I had connected with him professionally before relocating to Napa, he doubtless would have steered us away from

Raymond A. Guadagni

both the Mt. Veeder property and the Shetler Avenue home.

Wayne had been one year ahead of me at Napa High. He was a very popular kid, active in student government, and a star baseball and football player. In those days we had what were called "senior superlatives," when the students of the senior class voted to award titles such as "most popular," "most likely to succeed," and "best personality" to their classmates. Wayne was voted "best looking."

In those days, a senior would never associate with underclassmen. This was just the way things were. Today, it's gratifying to see kids of different ages and classes mix with each other. It is not uncommon to see freshmen and juniors be friends, or even a senior and a freshman. No one seems to think this odd any more. But, not in the 50s and early 60s. Wayne was ahead of his time. He DID associate with underclassmen, and even though the association was forbidden, Wayne was popular enough to get away with it and not be ostracized for his conduct. This was one reason I looked up to Wayne. He had never been a person to think he was better than you. It was almost as if he considered his good looks and great sports abilities as just gifts he had been born with, not reasons to feel he was better than anyone else. This was a remarkably mature view for a teenager who was idolized by boys and girls alike. These qualities stayed with him throughout his adulthood, and as adults we became best of friends.

Wayne and I had reconnected when Ann and I came to Napa and it wasn't long before he and I began to play poker regularly. It was at one of these guys' only poker parties when I mentioned my concerns about the resale value of the Shetler house. Wayne thought for a moment and responded he knew of a place we might like, and he

296

was sure he could get it at the right price. It developed the house was owned by Wayne's real estate partner, Richard Bennett, and Wayne knew exactly what Richard was looking to get from a buyer. As the poker game progressed and we sipped cold beers, Wayne described the house to me. He was right – it sounded attractive. It was located in North Napa – the other side of town – in a relatively new subdivision called The Vineyards. There were four bedrooms, two bathrooms, and the living room had a cathedral ceiling!

Wayne took Ann and me to see the house the next day. We both liked the location and the style. The price was reasonable, and the small back yard would be easier to care for than either of our two previous properties had been.

Ann and I made an offer, and it was accepted. For the third time in three years we moved to a new house.

Located on Cabernet Court in North Napa, our new house had a nice master bedroom, with Julia's bedroom right next to us. There were two more bedrooms which we earmarked for another child's room and an office. While the back yard was very small, it was enough for Tuna, who continued to mostly be an inside dog. The home was only a block from a community park, where the Vineyard subdivision residents took their dogs to walk and their kids to play. The park was a place Tuna and I came to know well, because he ran and explored there quite often. Our family also used the area with friends for volleyball games, touch football and softball, and, of course, picnics.

Ann, Julia, Tuna, and I settled into our new life at Cabernet Court. We were comfortable and happy there. In fact, the first Cabernet years were remarkably smooth – with the notable exception of one incident. It had nothing to do with the home or its location, or the neighbors or other pets or animals. It was an incident in which Tuna really stood out – this time in a very good way. He had always been an extremely loyal companion to me, whether I was right or wrong in a particular situation. In the particular situation I'm referring to, Tuna exhibited this extreme loyalty – and I was particularly wrong.

In the summer of 1978, I was once again playing softball for a team called Al's Auto Wreckers, only this team was located in Napa and not Stockton. We had a very good team in Napa, on a par with the old Stockton team. I had started it up as soon as Ann and I moved to town, and we had already won several championships in Napa, which was quite an achievement, because the Napa league was very competitive.

Our team members became close as we played together, and quickly fell into a custom which we honored as if it was a command from heaven above. Win or lose, we would always go to Sam's Pizza Place after each game. At Sam's, we would energetically discuss the evening's game, the great plays or bad plays, and the good or bad calls made by the umpire. We never practiced before a game, but we always broke the action down in minute detail afterward at Sam's. These conversations occurred over multiple pitchers of beer and several extra-large pizzas. Our team favorite was a combination pizza with an emphasis on sausage topping. Most of the time, we would eat and drink for an hour or two and then go home. Games were always on Thursday evenings, and we all had to work the next day. Game times ranged from early evening to late evening, with the latest games starting at 9:00 p.m., which felt very late for a weeknight softball game at Kennedy Park. Kennedy Park was located in the southern part of town where the wind blew strong.

Usually it was very cold at the late games, even in the summer.

On this summer evening, Al's Auto played a late 9:00 p.m. game. We were up against our nemesis, the previous year's defending champions, ACE Hardware. ACE had full uniforms as opposed to just jerseys like the rest of the teams. They were well-disciplined, and unlike us, they even practiced during the week. Our two teams were perennial contenders and the championship usually went to one of us. This was a close game. We beat them by scoring the winning run in the bottom of the last inning. Al's Auto went to Sam's in a celebratory mood that evening.

By midnight, most of the players had wisely gone home, but a few of us diehards still lingered over our beers. Specifically, there were four of us left – my dear friend and law partner, Joe Flax, who, in those days, really enjoyed his beer. There was also Jeff Cox, a Napa County probation officer who later became the chief. Jeff, at this time in his life, also really enjoyed beer. There was Don McConnell, a superb athlete and a friend from middle school, who continued to lounge comfortably at the Formica table. Though I was usually a light hitter when it came to the consumption of alcohol, this evening I had had more than my usual.

We all shared a long-standing interest in sports of all stripes, and it happened one of the leading sports news stories at the time involved the owner of the Oakland Athletics, who was attempting to sell his baseball team for an asking price of $12,000,000. We had each been following the story in the local Bay Area sports pages and it was the topic of our conversation that fateful evening. We were all fascinated that a major league baseball team was for sale within 50 miles of where we were sitting. We ordered another pitcher of beer. As it disappeared, we found ourselves talking about buying the team – and the idea felt very reasonable. We had one minor problem to resolve, but otherwise it was full steam ahead. The problem, of course, was how we could raise millions of dollars to make the purchase. After much discussion, we decided the logical solution would be to put together an investment group.

As a first step, we would pool our resources. In the course of a candid, well-lubricated, exploration of our net worth, we realized we would still be coming up considerably short. If we had been sober, it's just possible we would have realized this instantly, and more detailed attempts to make this dream come true would have ended without further deliberation. However, we were not sober, so we continued to cogitate how to raise the money.

I boldly announced I was sure my father Big Al would love to be in on purchasing a professional baseball team. I offered on his behalf to pledge his wrecking yard, real estate and all, to the financial pot. Joe and I owned our law office building by now, so we of course pledged that. Don McConnell, who worked at Basalt Rock, a subsidiary of Dillingham Corporation, pledged his entire stock and retirement fund to the venture. Jeff Cox did not exactly have any money, but he was part of law enforcement by virtue of being a probation officer, and as such, pledged his vast powers as a public official. Less than another pitcher of beer later, we all pledged our personal residences as well, though most of us had little or no equity in our homes. Scrawling on a paper napkin, we came up with a quick estimate of the money we knew we could raise. In our glowing enthusiasm, we forgot the difference between gross and net. As a result, we totaled up a wildly overstated amount, happily disregarding the mortgages which obliterated the equity in all of the real estate now in the pot.

Even with this significant enhancement of our resources, we still came up quite short on funds. Undeterred, I suggested we concentrate on coming up with financing for the project. I proposed we put together $100,000.00, and then have Charles O. Finley carry the balance for one year with a balloon payment. This meant our offer would consist of a $100,000 down payment, with the balance of $11,900,000 all due and payable in one year. I had written the two figures down on another napkin to be sure my friends would clearly understand my proposal. I looked around the table, proud of my creative solution. My compadres were simply delighted.

In our enthusiasm, we quickly decided it was unnecessary to engage in further investigation. We agreed there was no need to look at the books or the assets or liabilities or the payroll or contracts of the ball players. With a final glance at one another over the sea of empty beer pitchers, we decided to make the offer.

Time was of the essence. Other investment groups had to be out there putting their best offers together at the very same time we were developing our own. It was just past two in the morning when we quickly drafted a telegram to Charles O. Finley's office in Chicago, Illinois. While the rest of us were hammering out the wording of our terse offer, Jeff Cox used the pizza parlor's pay phone to call the sports department at the San Francisco Chronicle. After making a vague but ominous reference to his awesome status as a Napa County Probation Officer, Jeff somehow succeeded in obtaining Mr. Finley's office address in Chicago.

The telegram to Mr. Finley set out a "concrete offer" to purchase the A's. We used the word "concrete" in deference to Don McConnell's employment at Basalt Rock, which specialized in concrete – Don, or the alcohol consumed by Don, insisted we use the actual word in the offer. When we were done writing the telegram, some of us were surprised to discover we were actually offering to pay $15,000,000 for the team. This was $3,000,000 more than Mr. Finley was asking. I recall questioning this sum, but the response I received was twofold: first, it was a nice round number and sounded good; and, second, it would be attractive to Mr. Finley, because it was more than he was asking. My arguments against the additional three million dollars fell on deaf ears.

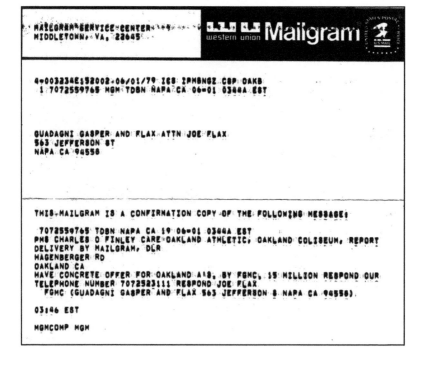

The total price was set forth in our telegram, but we decided against setting out the specific terms of the deal – which, because of the higher offer price, now called for a balloon payment of $14,900,000. We asked Mr. Finley to call us, listed my law partner Joe Flax as the designated spokesman for the group, and gave him the phone number to our law office.

I arrived home at about 2:30 in the morning. I was still in a state of inebriation, and my gait was less than steady. When I staggered through the front door, the house was dark, making the furniture and me a dangerous combination. Sure enough, I stumbled into the clothes closet door in the bedroom. The crashing sound woke both Ann and baby Julia. This was not a good start, but when she jumped out of bed and flicked on the lamp, I made up for it by happily announcing that our future was set. I reminded her how she was always after me to "bring home the bacon." With this investment, I enthusiastically assured her, I was going to be bringing home the entire butcher shop.

Ann is, by nature, a very even and thoughtful person. One of the things I love about her is her calm strength. Unfortunately, on this occasion I had disturbed our little girl, awakened Ann, was drunk, and had jubilantly informed her I had invested everything we owned in an impossible scheme to buy a baseball team. My reliance on Ann's well of calmness turned out to be misplaced that evening. When my explanations finally wound down, I looked at her expectantly. Ann was colder than I had ever seen. In a few short sentences, she told me what she thought about me stumbling home with such a stupid scheme. It was probably significant that this was the first time she ever used the word "divorce" in a conversation involving our relationship. She stated, in no uncertain terms, if this incident made the newspaper, she would leave me. At the time of this pronouncement, I was still quite heavily under the influence of beer, and having difficulty understanding what I had done wrong. In fact, Ann seemed a little ungrateful for my efforts to provide wealth and financial stability for our family.

Fortunately, I still had enough sense to know I better get out of there. I went out to the living room feeling misunderstood, unappreciated, and alone. I couldn't even hug Julia, because I vaguely recalled Ann saying something about me being in no condition to hold her. In the living room, I sat on the couch in the dark pondering the unfairness of the world. At that moment, up came Tuna wagging his tail and putting his head between my knees. I scratched his ears and started talking to him. I explained about Ann and her unreasonable, misplaced anger. I could tell he was listening closely and clearly agreed with me. On many levels, I already felt bad for such a stupid stunt, not to mention my behavior when I got home, but Tuna was having none of it. I was blameless in his eyes. My state of mind was all he cared about. When I stopped petting him, he nudged my hand gently with his nose, urging me to continue. I let Tuna climb up on the couch and hugged and kissed him. He cuddled close and licked me. That evening, Tuna and I slept together once again. Tuna was on my side and always would be.

Over the next few days, it became clear Ann would need time to get over her disappointment in me. To say she was a little distant was an understatement. During this period of time Tuna was, by far, my best companion, confidant, and buddy. We both had one love – me. I instinctively turned to him while Ann was working off her mad. I knew he understood on some level my feelings of loneliness, guilt, and self-disgust. He had always been there in the past, and again he was right there, the only companion who would give me the attention I needed.

The morning after the game and all its aftermath I woke up late and hungover. I navigated through the morning routine with a glacially silent Ann. I was grateful to slip out the door to go to work. Arriving at the office, life was normal. I nodded good morning to staff and said hi to Joe. Neither of us brought up the goings-on of the previous night – it barely seemed real – a tacit agreement the night was best forgotten.

Around mid-morning, Joe had left the office to go to court for an appearance on a case he was handling. I had just finished meeting with some clients, when one of the secretaries called on the intercom to say there was a Mr. Charles O. Finley on the phone for me. I paused for a long moment before reaching for the phone, reluctantly thinking back to the drunken hilarity of the night before and what, in the bright light of day, was our preposterous idea of purchasing the Oakland Athletics. By the time I lifted the receiver, I had somehow convinced myself the call was most likely a hoax – it was probably coming from Jeff Cox at his probation office, or from Don McConnell over at Basalt Rock. Increasingly confident the call was as genuine as polyester, I decided to respond in kind, answering the phone with the assurance of a poker player holding four aces. With all the swagger I could muster, I boomed, "Hey Charlie, what's up? I take it you received our offer?"

The answer was not what I expected. It was not Jeff Cox or Don McConnell laughing at the other end of the line. I didn't recognize this person's voice, which sounded completely serious and to the point. "Are you for real?"

After a moment's hesitation, I said, "Of course we are."

Our telegram had indicated Joe was our spokesman, so the man asked for Joe to give him a call and gave me his Chicago number. It had an area code I had never used before. This, and the businesslike tone of the voice, made me think it could actually be Finley. On the other hand, I wondered, perhaps it was one of Cox's probation officers or McConnell's co-workers who were being put up to making the call? I still held out a hope the caller was a prankster, but I was losing confidence fast. I found myself calling the man "Mr. Finley"- no more "Charley" – and my heart was pounding fast.

Instead of ringing off, Mr. Finley suddenly asked me again, "Is this offer for real?"

I told him it was, but explained I was primarily an investor in the deal, and Joe would be the one to talk to. There was another pause – he still wasn't done.

"Why 15 million dollars?" It took a moment before my memory flooded back – that was the sum we put in the telegram after I had drunkenly argued against the number. The night before, our collective reason for making the offer 15 million dollars (over my strong objection) had been that it was "a nice round number." I couldn't give Mr. Charles O. Finley that for an answer, or he would know, in no uncertain terms, our offer was not genuine. Instead I told him we collectively believed the amount would be acceptable.

Finley, said, in a somewhat exasperated voice, "Well, of course it would be acceptable. I'm only asking $12 million!"

I didn't want the call to continue, but the cagey Mr. Finley was still testing the waters to see if our offer was genuine.

I was thinking to myself, "Mr. Finley, why don't you look at the time the telegram was sent?" He would have seen it was right around closing time for bars in California.

Finley pressed me on where I fit in. Desperately making it up as I went a long, I told him I was into the concessions and wanted to make sure we had good food to sell at the ball games. This is what happens when you start a conversation as fearless as an eagle and lose all of your confidence within seconds. I was just babbling. Suddenly the question popped into the back of my mind – I wondered if I might get sued by this man who had a reputation of being a hardnosed businessman who would not let anyone off the hook if he had any leverage. Sure, I was a lawyer, but I was suddenly so guilt ridden by our stupid telegram to a legitimate businessman, I figured there had to be a law against what we did. I wanted to blurt out the truth, but I was too afraid to admit we were just a bunch of drunken young frauds.

The phone conversation felt like it went on for perhaps an hour, but in fact could not have been longer than three minutes. Mr. Finley finally concluded by saying I seemed like a nice fellow and asked me to have Flax call him as soon as possible.

It would have been helpful if I'd had Tuna around to settle me down during the hour it took before Joe got back from court. With Tuna, I could have talked about the crazy thoughts I was having – thoughts like, should I leave in the dead of night before all of this hits the paper? In little old Napa, my practice would be ruined. Ann would now leave me for sure. What would Joe say to Finley? My imagination was exploding with wild thoughts.

Joe finally arrived back at the office around 11:30 and I immediately told him about the phone call. He could see I was upset. He was less so. In fact, he didn't even remember we had actually sent the telegram the night before until I reminded him. With a rising sense of panic, I finished my blow-by-blow report. Joe just sat behind his desk for a minute or two. Then he calmly suggested we call the number to see if it really was in Chicago and really Finley's office. I felt better already. Joe was thinking clearly. He was deliberate, and had no problem making the call himself (after all, he was the designated spokesman in the telegram).

After lunch, Joe made the call on speakerphone. We listened together as a female voice said, "Good afternoon, offices of Charles O. Finley." With that, Joe hung up. We both realized the morning caller had indeed been Charles O. Finley. After much discussion we finally decided the thing to do was absolutely nothing. If Mr. Finley called back, we would deal with it then. I knew I, for one, was never taking a call from him again. Joe agreed to take the call if it ever came. If Mr. Finley didn't call back, that would be the end of it. Finley would have figured out the offer was not for real, and we would be done with the situation as well.

He never called back.

As the days passed without a second call, I began to have a sense of cautious relief. This time no one had been hurt, but I realized I needed to be more careful when I was drinking with my friends and our celebrating started to get out of hand. My choice had not been a good one. It was not good for me to lose control of my conduct or judgment. Ironically, even though the four of us had been inebriated when we made our offer, we apparently recognized a sound business deal. In the end, it would have been a great investment if we had actually possessed the financial ability to make the purchase. The eventual new owner brought in the former Yankee Billy Martin to manage the A's and with that came "Billy Ball" and baseball success. Within a year of the change in ownership the franchise was valued at $20,000,000.

Oh well. What mattered was, Ann didn't leave me.

CHAPTER FORTY

Changes

We lived in the Cabernet Court home for about two years. During this time my law practice continued to grow. However, on October 24, 1978, my partner Lou Gasper died from his chronic illness. He was only thirty-three years old. This was devastating news for my family, for me personally, and for my other law partner Joe Flax. Tuna had known Lou, and though he didn't realize exactly what had happened, he sensed the sadness in me and did his best to console me. Tuna reflected my moods. If I was down, Tuna was always there to shadow me, cuddle, and give me a lick.

As we began to work through the personal tragedy of losing one of our closest friends, Joe and I realized we would also need to address his loss as a law partner. Overall, our small firm was prospering. When Lou died, I had been at it for almost four years, and Joe had been with us for two.

Joe had been a great hire and was fully and successfully integrated into the practice. Having also grown up in Napa, he had been able to contribute from the day he arrived. Though he had been a high school standout in sports, he was also smart and studious – back then he was just as likely to be found in the library as on the football field. A history buff with a thirst for knowledge, Joe had traveled extensively before he took the deputy city attorney job in Stockton. He later came over to the Public

Defender's office himself, so he had a lot of criminal trial experience by the time he joined us in Napa.

With Lou gone, Joe and I decided to recruit an associate lawyer to join our practice at an entry level. It happened Joe knew of a lawyer who had attended Hastings with Joe who was very bright and looking for a career move. Pat McGrath had been on the school's law review, which was a high honor reserved for exceptional students. I also knew Pat, but not as well as Joe did. Pat was working with our old boss Bob Chargin at the Public Defender's Office in Stockton, California, when we contacted him to see if he would consider a move to Napa.

Fortunately for the firm, Pat was agreeable to moving and accepting an entry-level position with our firm. As soon as he arrived, it became apparent Pat would be an excellent addition to the firm.

Around the time Pat arrived, Joe and I decided to bid on a contract with the County of Napa to represent indigents who had been charged with crimes. Although many people were surprised when the County announced our small firm was the successful bidder, there were some solid reasons for the award. Our three lawyers all had significant criminal defense experience. Joe spoke Spanish. And it certainly didn't do any harm that we had come in with the lowest bid to take on this group of indigent defendants.

Our rationale for taking on the contract was that it would ensure our firm a basic stream of steady income. We negotiated with the county to ensure we were also able to maintain a private practice, which allowed us to expand our civil work. During our first three years as a firm, we had been doing a fair amount of family law and probate law, as well as other general civil matters. The contract allowed us to continue to grow in this civil arena.

Just as we began to deliver the public defender services under the new contract, several fortuitous circumstances triggered a simultaneous surge in our civil practice. For starters, the civil practice was already expanding based on our successful efforts over the first three years. But equally important, it was around this time a local lawyer named Walter Zylinski passed away. His practice was transferred to Tony Intintoli, a lawyer who was renting office space in our firm's building. After a very short period of time, Tony was elected mayor of Vallejo, California, where he resided. Deciding the mayoral position was a full-time job, Tony turned over most of his caseload to us, including the wills he was storing – both those he had written and those he had acquired from Walt's practice. Just a few months later, John J. Quigley was elected to the office of Municipal Court Judge. John was a personal friend of mine, and when he was elected, he handed over his will files as well. These were both major scores for the firm because the law firm storing an original, signed will would often be asked to probate the estate when the will "matured."

These events provided me with an instant probate practice. Probating wills is a lucrative area of the law. And, once a lawyer has a probate practice, it opens the door to more immediate work, such as helping will clients avoid the expense of probate through options like revocable living trusts. It wasn't long before I found myself with an estate planning practice to go along with my probate practice.

The firm's practice was doing well in the areas of family law, probate, estate planning, and general civil law, which included personal injury cases. Add in the security of the county public defender contract, and our firm was now very secure, with good prospects for the future.

Back at home, my brief sortie into major league baseball had first been forgiven and then forgotten. Ann, Julia, Tuna, and I were comfortable in our home on Cabernet Court. My mom was babysitting Julia a lot, and Ann was working on acquiring her teaching credential. Tuna was the same old companion he had always been, and life was good.

1979 brought more of the same progress at the law firm. By this time, I had handled a couple of murder cases, which not only helped build my reputation as a criminal defense lawyer, but also involved an enormous number of paid hours. Joe was also handling high profile cases, including a particularly gruesome death penalty murder case. The civil practice was growing as well, and the probate section of our civil practice was giving us a good foundation for building future growth in the estate planning area.

CHAPTER FORTY-ONE

Another Addition to Our Family

In December 1979, Ann and I purchased a tri-level home located at 3768 Clara Drive in North Napa, about five blocks and one subdivision over from our home on Cabernet Court. The Clara Drive home was bigger, with four bedrooms and over 2,000 square feet of living space. It also had a huge backyard. The subdivision had been built on the site of an old walnut orchard, which explained why there were two very large, mature walnut trees in the backyard.

Ann, Julia, and I were delighted to move into this larger, nicer house. The four bedrooms seemed to be teasing us to have more children.

Tuna liked the house. He could roam around freely in the back and side yards. Inside, he had three levels to explore. When he was in a playful mood, Tuna would race around each level and then repeat the lap several more times at full speed.

We also moved in with a cat named Tiger. We had taken a several year break from cats after our previously described difficulties with the kittens, Bruno and Omar. But when we moved into the house on Mt. Veeder, we had "inherited" a cat from our seller. The cat was great and knew how to take care of himself. No one messed with Tiger. He was king of the neighbor cats. Tuna gave Tiger all the room he wanted, and Tiger did the same for Tuna. When we moved into Clara Drive, that was how the two of them handled it. They just stayed away from each other.

It wasn't difficult, because Tuna was primarily an inside dog, and Tiger was primarily an outside cat. But this living arrangement was about to change.

Ann and I had been talking about expanding our family, and so it was not surprising when we discovered Ann was expecting another child.

On November 14, 1980, we welcomed another beautiful child into the world. We named her Angela Elaine Guadagni. She weighed 8 pounds, 2 ounces, and was 20.5 inches long.

The impact of Angela's arrival on Tuna was not immediately apparent. Tuna seemed to understand another human being had been added to the family and that the little baby was welcome.

We all settled into life at our new home. I was busy with my growing law practice, and, in fact, busier than ever with the obligations under the county contract. Ann was continuing to work on her teaching credential and pulling the laboring oar on caring for our two-and-a-half-year-old and newborn. My mother proved to be of great assistance to us. She lived nearby and came over frequently to babysit and watch the girls. The girls could not have been luckier. They were better off for every day they were around my mom, who exuded love and kindness. Both girls adored her, as did Ann.

With so much attention on the girls, Tuna was less attended to, and found himself outside in the backyard more than he ever had been. At first, this did not appear to be much of a problem, because we noticed he seemed to be getting closer and closer to Tiger. They started hanging out and began to take long naps together.

It was now well into the year 1981, and I finally felt I was a member of a real family. One child was wonderful, but the addition of a second child completed our family. Granted, it was increasingly difficult for our family to get around. It seemed to take days to load up the car for an outing. Even going for a walk around the neighborhood took lots of set-up time. There was the baby carrier and the stroller to fold and unfold. There was the diaper bag. There were the extra blankets and sweaters. There were the water bottles. But all of this was so worth it. We were a real family. My heart was full.

Chapter Forty-two

The Lady and the Tramp Syndrome

The Lady and the Tramp, an old Walt Disney animated film, centers on a female cocker spaniel named Lady, who belongs to a refined, upper-middle-class family; and a male stray mutt called the Tramp. On Christmas morning in 1909, handsome Jim Dear gives his lovely wife Darling a cocker spaniel puppy named Lady. Lady enjoys a happy life with the couple. She is the center of attention, their baby. However, as time goes by, the couple has a baby and Lady stops being the center of their lives.

This became Tuna's plight. We started having him spend more time in the backyard so there would not be unsupervised contact between him and Julia or Angie. Where he once had free run of the house, he now found himself getting less attention, and would sometimes be isolated from his best friend. He must have noticed I was devoting much more attention to my children than to him. He remained dedicated and loyal to me, but it was no longer a two-way street.

I later decided I should have done more to prepare Tuna for our children's arrival. It would have been a challenge. Tuna was now about fourteen-plus years old in human time, massively older in dog time, and pretty set in his ways.

I'll never know whether a campaign of training and discipline would have been successful. Life with two very young children was hectic for all of us, and the demands on Ann as she worked toward her teaching credential and me as I grew my law practice seemed to occupy more time than physically existed. Instead of additional training, Tuna was getting less attention than ever.

Rather than developing Tuna to become a well-mannered house dog, we instead settled into a new order where he spent more time in the backyard, only coming in to join the rest of us when things were relatively calm and Ann or I could keep an eye on both Tuna and the kids.

Just when Ann and I were thinking Tuna's inside/outside status was going to work out, a scary incident occurred. I was in the family room with Julia, Angela, and Tuna. Ann was in the kitchen, which was separated by a wrought iron railing allowing a clear view of the family room. Tuna was standing near me as I played with the girls. In what seemed like a split second, little Angela put her hand toward Tuna's face. He uttered a growl I had only heard him make when he fought with other dogs. As he unleashed this shocking growl, he bared his pearly white teeth. He suddenly looked fearsome and dangerous. This menacing display scared Angela and she started to cry. I quickly thrust myself between Tuna and the girls and hustled him out to the backyard.

Later in the evening after we had gotten Angela and Julia to bed, Ann and I sat down and talked about what had happened and what to do. She had heard the growl, seen Tuna's snarling teeth, and watched me rush him into the back yard. We agreed the overriding priority was to protect the girls. While I felt myself wanting to protect Tuna, as well, I couldn't forget the feeling when it seemed he was about to take a bite out of Angela. Ann finally said she thought Tuna needed to become an outside dog for the safety of the girls. Sadly, I agreed – we weren't going to gamble on our daughters' well-being.

From that point forward, Tuna was an outside dog, even sleeping outside, which was a real step down for this formerly pampered inside pet. Heartsick over the choice we'd had to make, I asked my childhood friend Steve Ceriani to build Tuna a doghouse. Steve had been an industrial arts major in college and was a perfectionist. The doghouse had a real shingled roof and was spacious and comfortable. We installed it under an overhang of the house, to provide additional shelter from the elements.

Tuna began to adapt to this new life in the back yard. I made an extra effort to give him as much time and reassurance as I could squeeze in. The situation was not perfect, but we all made it work.

CHAPTER FORTY-THREE

Tuna's Twilight Years

This new living arrangement did have some beneficial advantages for Tuna. As he became primarily an outside dog, he began to grow very close to Tiger, our cat. I would often peer outside on a Saturday morning and spot Tuna and Tiger sleeping together on the deck. On cold days Tuna went into his doghouse. After a few weeks, I noticed Tiger following him inside. I loved this. Tuna and Tiger had become friends and were beginning to provide each other company.

When Ann and the girls were out of the house, I would let both Tuna and Tiger into the house to sit on the couch and watch football with me. It was great, although, to be honest they slept while I watched the game. It was so calming, I am sure I loved it more than they did. I had the sense they were my football buddies, just as if the guys had come over to watch the game with me. It dawned on me everybody in the household was female except Tuna, Tiger, and me. We guys had to stick together.

This living arrangement lasted for the rest of Tuna's life. We still had good times together, but he wasn't inside as much. I would spend time sitting with him and Tiger, who were now inseparable. Tiger was old by now, as was Tuna, so while they didn't really romp around or play together, they did lay around together. They were like two old guys in a rest home. I envisioned them talking about the good old days and embellishing their stories because no one was around to contradict them. I referred to the deck as Sunnyside Acres Rest Home for animals. This rest home had only two old residents, but they were special – Tuna and Tiger.

If Tuna resented his outdoor phase or felt I had let him down as his owner, he never showed it. Even in his twilight years, he moved his tail pretty fast when I came outside. He would come right over to me to greet me when I opened the sliding glass door from the family room to the deck outside. He didn't gallop and jump – it was more of a slow mosey, but over he came.

I still brought him dog biscuits, and once in a while I asked him to sit up, just to see if he could still do it. Tuna could still manage to sit up on command, though it was slower and more unsteady, and not for as long a time. In his youth, he had been able to sit for what I believed to be an outdoor record for sitting up, but those days were long gone. If he didn't get his dog biscuit in a few seconds, he would drop to a sitting stance and then try to sit up again without being asked. I tried to give him the biscuit before he had to sit down, so he would feel he had completed the trick successfully. This required me to give him the biscuit within seconds. That was fine with me, because Tuna was clearly trying harder than he ever had when his body was young and strong.

Life in his twilight years were not really bad years, but it is these years that have caused me more regret than any of his other years. I am sure I could have tended to him more. After all he had given me, the bargain was not equal.

CHAPTER FORTY-FOUR

Saying Goodbye

By 1984 Tuna seemed to have lost most of his equilibrium. His balance was very unsteady, and he stumbled a lot. He didn't seem to be in pain or hurting in any way, but it gradually became clear something was wrong.

I took Tuna to the vet for an examination and some tests. It was going to take a few days to get the results, so Tuna and I went home. When I put him into the backyard I spent an hour or so with him, watching his movement. He would do okay for a while, but then he would stumble again.

A day or two after the visit to the vet's office, I received a call from the doctor saying Tuna had uremic poisoning, which indeed affected his equilibrium. I asked how it could be treated. The vet replied there was nothing we could do for him. Old male dogs either get cancerous tumors or uremic poisoning, he explained. Tuna was very old, and this was not surprising to the vet. I asked if Tuna was in any pain because he didn't seem to be to me. My preliminary thinking was if Tuna wasn't in any pain, maybe he could go on this way indefinitely. I could just keep him as comfortable as possible in the backyard, and he could live out his days with Tiger.

The vet responded with a surprising analogy. He said the way Tuna felt was comparable to a human being with a constant, overbearing hangover. This was an unexpected description, but it gave me some insight into what Tuna was enduring. Having had the occasional hangover in my indiscreet younger years, I knew how miserable it was. With a sense of deep foreboding, I asked the vet what he recommended. He said Tuna was in constant misery. He recommended his suffering end as soon as possible.

I told the vet I would discuss it with Ann and call him back. I knew what our answer would be, but I just couldn't make the decision right then, not without digesting the news and talking to Ann. When I explained the situation to her, Ann was very sympathetic. She knew what Tuna meant to me, but she agreed the best thing to do was to end his suffering.

I called the vet and made the arrangements to bring Tuna into his office the next day. Naturally, when we arrived, Tuna appeared to be feeling great, almost like his younger self. He was not stumbling at all.

The vet assured me Tuna wouldn't suffer from the shot. He said I could be by his side if I wanted to. I had no hesitation – I owed it to Tuna to be there with him, as he had been by my side all of these years. Also, I wanted to see for myself that he went peacefully. I carried Tuna into the operating room and laid him down on the cold, sterile, gray steel table. The vet suggested I pet Tuna while he gave him the shot. He said it would be very quick. As I softly stroked Tuna's head, the vet administered the shot. Then he began to gently pat Tuna's side. It was just seconds later when the vet quietly said Tuna was gone. My friend had slipped away quickly and painlessly. I did not try to hide the tears streaming down my face.

As I look back at the seventeen and a half years of Tuna's and my life together, I think of good times and bad times, but most of all I think of the simple, everyday moments and what he meant to me. I think about routines: morning walks around the neighborhood before work. Watching movies and sporting events together on the couch as we cuddled. Playing together, including "big time wrestling" in the living room. Throwing his chew toy down the hall or around the backyard and watching him swiftly retrieve it and come back for another turn. The way he motored around my feet as I stirred his dinner bowl.

I understand no dog is perfect – which certainly included Tuna. You can't really leave a dog alone for extended periods of time, like you can with a cat. Dogs track mud – and worse – into your house. Dogs not well trained by their owners may jump inappropriately on your guests. Dogs get sick or injured and need medical treatment. Vet bills can be expensive – very expensive. Dogs can bite people and cause their owner to be sued. Dogs can get loose from their leash and run away, requiring you to bail them out at the local dog pound for a tidy sum. While it is true dogs love to play, they also can nag you to death about playing. Some dogs are a bottomless pit when it comes to playing catch. They never want to quit. This can get old.

But when you balance the good with the bad, I never found the question close. I never regretted having Tuna. He was my buddy. I loved him, and he loved me.

Over the intervening years, I've spent a lot of time pondering the specific things about my wonder dog Tuna that made me love him so much and why he was so important in my life.

I love Tuna was always happy to see me. And I mean always. Whether I left on a trip for a couple of weeks, or just went to the store for an hour, Tuna would greet me with tail wagging, jumping up and down with excitement. Even if I went outside just to get the mail, or took a quick shower, he was happy to see me when I reappeared. If I let him back in the house after he had been outside for a short time, he was excited to see me. He made me feel like a rock star, and his love was genuinely unconditional. Whether I'd had a bad day or good day, he was always there to greet me and cheer me up. He was a boost to my self-esteem. When someone thinks you are the greatest person on earth, it makes you feel pretty good about yourself.

I loved when Tuna wanted attention, he would come into the room with his chew-toy in his mouth, telling me it was time to play. This could always cheer me up, no matter how serious or upset I might have been the moment before.

When he wanted my attention at quieter moments, he would nudge my hand with his nose, practically lifting it up in the air, sending the unmistakable message he wanted me to pet him. He kept this nudging up until I petted him. If I stopped after a couple of pats on the head, the nudging commenced again. His relentless nudging always made me smile. He was such a great mood elevator. It was impossible to be down, when he was always so happy and entertaining.

I loved he was always in the mood to cuddle. He was simply the best couch cuddler ever. He dished out tons of affection, licking and kissing, until I couldn't take it anymore. He snuggled so forcefully and enthusiastically he would crowd me right off the couch or bed.

I loved seeing him in different situations. It would crack me up when he stuck his head out the window of the car, the wind blowing his coat straight back. He looked regal when he stuck his head out of the window and into the wind, so confident and proud.

I loved he was so protective of me, even though I pretended to be annoyed with him for barking at visitors who came over or growling at friends who showed affection by slapping me on the back or putting an arm around my shoulder. Tuna was my own personal bodyguard.

I loved watching TV with him. He would lie next to me on the sofa or the floor and just sleep. It was calming, peaceful, and relaxing. Tuna never, ever argued with me about what show we should watch on TV. He was always content to just be with me.

Tuna was a great listener. He provided the perfect audience for practicing my closing arguments. I delivered them aloud, with all the passion I felt. Tuna sat, or lay, in rapt attention (or peaceful sleep), and listened to my very logical argument as to why there was reasonable doubt regarding my client's guilt. He listened to me for hours about any subject. He was always there to listen.

I got more exercise because of Tuna. Tuna, being part Lab, needed exercise, and lots of it. By taking him for his walks and runs, I also exercised myself more than I ever would have of my own volition. In the interests of accuracy, it was really the other way around. Tuna took *me* for walks and gave *me* exercise.

For so many years, he was my only regular company, my only constant companion. Even after having a human family of my own, there were plenty of times when I would go on an errand, and Tuna was the only passenger keeping me company.

When I was a bachelor and cooking for myself, Tuna helped me clean up. If any scraps spilled on the floor, Tuna was "Johnny on the Spot," rushing over and inhaling them more efficiently than the finest Hoover vacuum cleaner.

Tuna never made me feel guilty. For example, I have always loved to take naps. Napping is so easy – just lie down, relax, and close your eyes. But I have learned napping does not impress other human beings. Tuna not only didn't object or criticize, but gladly napped right along with me. As an ancillary benefit, if the weather was cold, Tuna would keep me warm.

It would be difficult, indeed, not to like a companion who is affectionate, lively, happy, friendly, sensitive and forgiving. Tuna was all of these things.

It took me many years to realize Tuna had been one of my most influential role models. He demonstrated through his conduct how to forgive easily and forget quickly. He modeled the lesson of innocence – Tuna gave everything he had to me, and all he ever asked for in return was love and care. He was a great teacher of trust. Even when I made a mistake – if I yelled too loudly or waved my hand angrily or made him live in the backyard with a cat, Tuna still trusted me. I would just say, "I'm sorry," and give him a gentle head rub, and it made everything all better. He never lost his trust in me. Tuna taught me not to sweat the small stuff and to see what is really important. He taught me to be more aware of my emotions. When I became upset, it was obvious it disturbed Tuna. I learned to keep a check on my emotions, so as not to upset him.

My most powerful perspective on Tuna is also the most difficult to adequately express. Tuna understood my feelings and adopted them as his own. His emotions mirrored my emotions and he was a constant barometer of how I was faring. If I was feeling bad, he felt bad and tried to help. He understood when I was down and knew what to do, being right there with a wagging tail and a big wet kiss. He appreciated me for exactly the person I was. For a big chunk of my life, he knew me better than anybody else. For many years, Tuna was the only creature I completely trusted would never hurt me. And I was right. The only thing he ever did that hurt me was die.

Many years ago, fate and circumstances brought Tuna and me together, and my life has never been the same. Tuna may not have been overly smart or a super handsome dog, but he was to me and I loved him. I loved him because I took care of him every day. And he, in his way, took care of me. If you take care of someone, one day you will discover you love him and he has become a part of you… it's a part of your life that becomes empty when he is gone.

Although the title of this book implies it was intended to be about my dog, it is of course also about me. But my dog was with me during this period of my life and shared all of these times – good and bad. So, this book is really about me and about him. My life would have not been the same without him to enrich and comfort it. He was my only family for most of his life, and then was part of my family for the rest of his days. I hope he knew how much happiness he brought me.

There's a stanza in one of my favorite songs, *Mr. Bojangles*, by Jerry Jeff Walker, that always makes me think of Tuna:

> *He danced for those at minstrel shows and county fairs*
> *Throughout the South*
> *He spoke with tears of fifteen years*
> *How his dog & he traveled about*
> *His dog up and died, up and died,*
> *After twenty years he still grieved*

Every time I come home, I still expect to see my wonder dog at the door, wagging his tail, waiting for me. Tuna has been gone for more than thirty years now, and I still miss him even to this day.